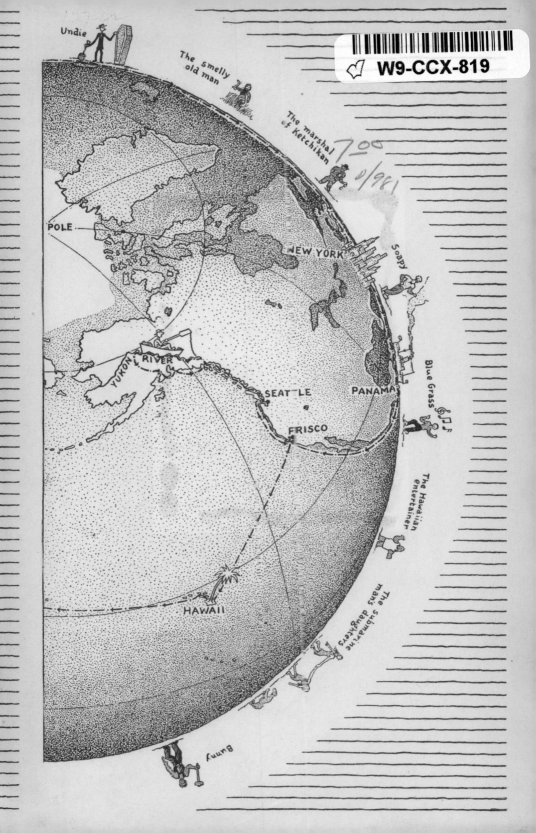

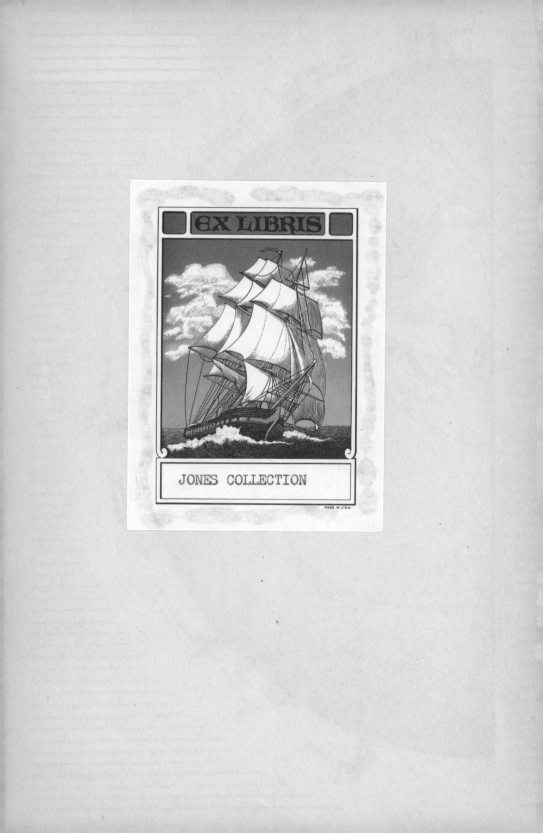

EX LIBRIS

JONES COLLECTION

MADE IN U.S.A.

DISCARD

Boarding the Japanese Freighter off the Korean Coast

MEN ON THE HORIZON

With Many Illustrations
by the Author

By GUY MURCHIE, Jr.

BOSTON AND NEW YORK
HOUGHTON MIFFLIN COMPANY
The Riverside Press Cambridge

The Riverside Press
CAMBRIDGE · MASSACHUSETTS
PRINTED IN THE U.S.A.

To My Beautiful
Young Mother
Who Loved the Sky and the Wind

FOREWORD

THIS is why I have written this Foreword:

I first became interested in Murchie; I liked his clean manhood and his ideals, none of which he seems to have lost in spite of his many experiences and hardships. When he showed me his manuscript, I began to read it because of my interest in the author, but, after the first page, I read it because of my interest in the book; and I must confess I lost hours of sleep before I finished it.

This Foreword does not signify approval or disapproval of his conclusions concerning the governments of the people he has come in contact with, but Murchie has given me information concerning the citizens of nations he has visited which was of absorbing interest. He seems to have a gift for observing human nature.

Murchie came in close contact with the people of many countries, and he saw that, however the governments may differ, the citizens themselves were not very different from us

RICHARD E. BYRD
Rear-Admiral U.S.N., Retired

CONTENTS

MEN ON THE HORIZON

CHAPTER ONE

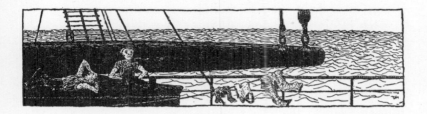

THE FOC'SLE

T HIS is an army transport ship. It is full of recruits, and officers with their wives, and fat old sergeants who wander about in twos and threes telling army stories. We are bound for the Canal Zone, and from there for 'Frisco and Honolulu.

I am rated as an A.B. seaman, and am writing this in the foc'sle, where I sleep along with a terrific assortment of gobs from different parts of the United States, Mexico, South America, Scandinavia, Italy, and Palestine.

They called me 'Slim' at first but now it's 'Big Boy,' because I have such a desperate time getting into my skimpy bunk. It is in a corner and about four inches from the floor, and to get into it, I have to climb through the overripe union suit of Pinhead which always hangs airing from his bunk, a scant foot and a half over mine.

I've finished this year an education supposed to prepare me for life, in a world of which I knew, definitely, almost nothing. By experience in my small segment of it, I've learned that it is a world of work, and of conflicting ideas.

About the rest of it I know only that it is made up of vast masses of men grouped in races and classes, unknown to each other, uninformed about each other, doubting and disliking each other — and yet, all of them made in the same image and of the same material, and all human.

This information, remote and theoretical, is not enough for me. I must prove to myself, through actual experience, the truth about these things. I must find out for myself whether it is not ignorance, and ignorance alone, that prevents friendship and understanding between these masses of human beings. I cannot commit myself to doubt or distrust of other men on hearsay. I want to come to some workable conclusions about this variegated world of men, and I can't do it until I have encountered it at first hand, and in the raw.

So, against innumerable and highly respectable reasons for staying at home, I've determined to go around and through the northern half of the globe where, I think, I shall meet with all the elements of man's immediate drama. The southern hemisphere may be the future — but the northern seems certainly to be the seething present of the world.

I intend to lay my course as close as I can to the life of the men within my changing horizons, irrespective of race, class, or condition — not so much to see, as to share, that life as deeply as I can, with my limitations of time and equipment.

I have started. It is June. The towers of New York have sunk behind us, and we've kicked the dirty harbor water from beneath our keel for the long, clean surge of the Atlantic. We are pointing southward toward Panama — the portal to the western seas and to the eastern world.

The first thing I had to do on this ship, and while she was still in dock, was to help lash the lifeboats in place and lace down their canvas covers. Then ——

'Hey, you, Slim,' shouted the bosun, with gimlet eye upon me, 'go get up steam on winch number two!'

He seemed to take for granted that I had been getting up steam on winches since birth, and although I had never met in person this bunch of handles, valves, and steam pipes, I sprang wildly to do his bidding.

By beginner's luck, I hit upon the correct valve. But there was still time to kick me ashore if the bosun found out how little I knew — so I assumed a superior air and toyed, casually, with winch number two.

When, to my great relief, we cast off, there was an interval of rest, and it was at this point that I met Soapy, a sailor with a mug like the front end of a freight locomotive.

'This,' says Soapy, 'is a hellova time ter be on a boat. Keriste! Just the woist time o' year. Think what we could be doin' this summer — if we was back in New Yoik!'

The men gathered around the foc'sle-head hatch to get acquainted with each other. There is Soapy, the Wop, Stuffy, Chup, Pinhead, and so on. Their opening remarks were uniformly pessimistic, their attitude disdainful. This is a social convention with sailors.

'God, that's a lousy stink-hole they give us to sleep in.'

'Vot vor zey sheep us to zat hot Panama ——'

'I'm thinkin' wot I'd be doin' if I was back wit' that little dame I met on Sout' Street las' night! Th' bes' goil I ever laid me hands on!'

'Who th' hell wants ter ship on this scow, anyhow ——'

I've been assigned to lookout duty, which to me seems quite a responsibility. My watch is from eight to twelve, day and night. By day, the lookout job is nominal, as the mate is always on the bridge and the world is plain to see, so my time is spent shining bright work and scrubbing paint.

But on night watch, I must report every light or ship sighted to Edwards, the mate, stating its direction in number of points off port or starboard bow; I must report 'lights burning bright' on our own ship — masthead, range, and both side lights — at every bell; and I must see that we keep on our proper course, reporting all deviation. Except when Pete, the Danish quartermaster, ventures over to my wing of the bridge, to tell me of his eventful ten years at sea, I stand alone on this lofty station and just gaze and gaze into the wind, searching for a speck of light on the hazy dividing line between sea and sky. This lookout duty is a lonely job.

But the foc'sle, with its layers of grimy tattooed humanity, is certainly not afflicted with loneliness. And it has inhabitants other than humans. Last night the bedbugs were bad, and I still itch from their bites. I suppose bugs are inevitable — these, at any rate, are inexorable in their devotion to me.

Soapy does most of the talking in the foc'sle, and whether anyone wants to sleep or not. He is about as hard-boiled as the Rock of Gibraltar, and looks it. There is a special set of wrinkles on his face, developed by scowling, and all of his face not occupied by wrinkles is covered with scars of various colors and sizes. Like many sailors, he doesn't know why he goes to sea — in fact, he spends most of his time in cursing the sea and the ship in most corrupt and biological language. And yet, here he is, as usual — and he'll probably keep on coming until his dying day.

The painter is something of a philosopher. This morning, reading the paper, he observed, 'Now here's a proist, leaves the choich ter go off wit' a goil. Then he shoots th' broad an' shoots himself —' pause — 'Now I wonder why them people does them kinder things ——'.

Before my watch last night, I found myself sitting beside the bosun on one of the foc'sle-head hatches. As I listened respectfully to this sandy-haired fellow with sharp blue eyes, he told me of his Scotch mother and his Irish father, and how he went off to sea at the age of sixteen.

'I sailed from England in 1912,' he said, 'an' I've seen plenty of the world since then — China, Australia, Cape Town, all around.

'Say, don't you think this is a fine ship? After you've been on a lot of different ships, you'll look back to this as one of the very best. It's few boats in the world has food like this one. If a fellow on this ship wants more pay, he can eat it.'

We began to talk about the other men in the deck gang.

'Say, yer know that feller Soapy?' he asked. 'Well, yer don't want to get in with *him*. I've seen his kind on every ship I ever been on, an' I know that them kind is no good — no good fer workin' or fer anythin' else. All night that feller smokes the weed — it's a kind of dope from Mexico — an' his eyes is all squinted up in th' mornin' an' he ain't worth half the food he eats.

'Bein' at sea gets 'most all of us after a while. I've never seen a man it didn't get. But if yer any good of a man yer can keep away from them dope-smokers.'

Practically all of the crew are foreigners — the Swede, the Wop, the Jugoslav, and others who are mixtures.

point which all on board have faith she will reach. I can see her unwavering form now, as it presses onward through this long night, while above, the wisps of cloud float backward past the stars and, on either side, the black waters hiss and disappear.

June 11. I saw the Southern Cross in the sky ahead of us last night — my first time.

I had to do errands for the captain this morning. After moving his safe, I had to get some things for him from the carpenter. The captain is a fussy old guy who growls, and shows the effects of sea life. Twenty per cent of the pictures in his cabin are of ships which he has served on, and the other eighty per cent are of young girls in a high state of nudity.

Later in the morning, I was assigned the job of polishing the whistle. It is a brass cylinder about four feet long located high up on the smokestack. I'm glad they didn't blow it while I was up there — it would certainly have been the end of me.

June 12. When I woke up this morning, I found that we had reached the Canal. It was my first sight of tropical country. As we entered the lagoon which leads to the three-step Gatun locks, we passed close to a shore covered with a vegetation of a color and composition such as I had never seen.

It is bright, dazzling green, and consists of low, closely crowded trees — of vine-like branches — which are interwoven with adjoining trees and with the underbrush below. The soil along the shore is of a reddish hue. These two — the green jungle and the red soil — being in sharp contrast to the rich blue of water and sky, make a most brilliant landscape. Everything seems strange and clear and dazzling under the blistering tropical sun.

As we mounted through the neat concrete locks, our bulk

lifted by the rising waters of each narrow tank, as we drifted stealthily on through deep cuts in the hills and across irregular lakes, I watched the flocks of parakeets flying across our path, and black buzzards which circled majestically at great heights. Below and beside us on the banks were occasional little square huts with tin roofs, about which sombreroed black families gazed boredly at our boisterous passengers.

Needless to say, as we approached the dock in Balboa, the sailors, and those soldiers who were allowed shore leave, were in a high state of excitement. We were to be in port only overnight, so they were prepared to raise hell without a moment's loss of time and as far as their money would permit. It was just as well for most of them that they had only five days' pay.

We put on our civilian clothes — it was so hot that few of us wore more than shirt, pants, and shoes — and came ashore. One of the chief sources of wealth to the natives of Panama immediately became evident, for there, lined up at the dock, were some hundred black chauffeurs with their open taxis. And their enterprise was justified. As fast as they could climb in, the soldiers and sailors piled into the luxurious cars and drove off toward Panama, the adjoining town to Balboa, a bigger place with better opportunities for debauchery.

I climbed up a steep hill near by, hoping to get a good view. It was a hot climb through the long tropical grass, but the sight from the summit was more than worth it.

Far to the northeast and to the southwest stretched the jungled mountains of the Isthmus, covered with a harsh green tangle, while to the southeast lay the calm Pacific, fringed along the coast with little blue islands, mysterious above the white strip of their beaches in the distant haze.

Less than a week ago I had sailed out of New York and

here — already — I was in a strange tropical land. It seemed to me that I was discovering an entirely unknown fact — something I had dreamed about, but of the actual existence of which I had never been fully convinced.

It soon was dark, so I started down and toward the gayly lighted town of Panama. There, when I arrived, I found debauchery galore. The natives were very dark-brown-skinned and very numerous. Practically everyone was busily engaged, somehow, in getting the sailors' and soldiers' money away from them. Some had taxis, some had lunch-counters and beer-bars, some ran dancehalls or sold hats and souvenirs, while almost all the women worked in their own way to great and deadly advantage.

In some places the houses of prostitution flanked both sides of the street, as many as thirty or forty in a bunch, one after another. They were really just booths, about ten by fifteen feet — with large doors that could be closed when in use — and a girl sitting outside.

Soapy, and other of my shipmates who are long acquainted with these places, all agree that nowhere on earth are the entertaining ladies dirtier than right here. And I think the ladies' casualness is sometimes quite irritating even to these hard sons of the Brooklyn water-front. I've heard Soapy complaining, in no tender language, about how, during a whole entertainment, his hostess had been preoccupied with a large bag of peanuts.

I had to be back for gangplank lookout duty at eight o'clock, and I spent the rest of the evening helping aboard the staggering drunken sailors and soldiers, as they returned to the ship. They needed help in more ways than one, and we took care of them as best we and the doctors could, and put them to bed. They ought to thank their stars that this is an army transport rather than just a tramp ship, where no one would care what happened to them.

June 13. This morning the poor fellows had to do regular work, although they were hardly able to stand on their feet. They exhibited every degree of what is poetically known as languor.

'Keriste,' said the painter to me in the foc'sle, 'my throat feels like a smokestack — I can't get up wit' th' rest o' the gang this mornin'.' Spitting dismally over the edge of his bunk, 'Will yer tell th' doc that I got yaller fever or somethin'?'

We took aboard some Marines to be dropped off in Nicaragua on our way north, and left the dock to the music of a brass band.

It seems absurd to go within seven degrees of the equator to get to Alaska — but it is to Alaska that I am going, and this is the shortest route by sea.

All I know about Alaska is that it is a young and raw and untamed country — the youngest in the northern hemisphere, geologically as well as in exploitation — and that its area, which is one fifth that of the United States, supports a population of less than one hundredth of the number of people in New York City.

I want to get an idea of this young and undeveloped country, before I go on to the old, old civilizations of the densely populated East.

June 15. It sure is hard to sleep in our foc'sle, with those bugs. Most of the old sailors use dope, and I don't entirely blame them. No human being could sleep soundly in that place without it. But the trouble with dope-users is that they try to make everybody else smoke it, too. They apparently feel better if their doping is supported by public opinion.

The soldiers and the crew have boxing and wrestling matches almost every evening, in a ring which is set up on

a tarpaulin on the after well-deck hatch. As someone suggested, I put in a challenge to wrestle anyone weighing over a hundred and ninety pounds, but, so far, I have had no acceptance — probably because there is no one of my weight on board who is not fat and soggy — like Ed, the fourth assistant engineer.

Ed is a great, tall bird with a saggy, sloppy build and a perpetual smile. He observed to me yesterday: 'Yessir — I've gained fifteen pounds last trip, an' I'm gonna gain fifteen pounds more this trip, an' then — when I get back to New York — I'm gonna see ma baby!'

We stopped off Corinto, Nicaragua, this morning while the Marines went ashore in a launch. The coast is very high and mountainous, and some of the higher peaks seem to have volcano craters. It is wild country.

Today when I reported the bearing of a certain island to the 'old man' — as captains are commonly called — he retorted, without looking up from his magazine — 'Well, let the bloomin' thing stay there!'

He appears to be sour all the time, but I am beginning to think it is just a manner he has acquired during many lonely years at sea.

June 18. Well, my wrestling challenge has been accepted. My opponent is a big, burly fellow from Texas, a soldier — and he isn't fat, either. He weighs about two hundred and five, is six feet, four inches tall, and looks as if he had spent most of his life roping steers.

This bout is to decide the wrestling championship of the ship, and the ship's paper says that it is 'the army versus the ship's crew,' which I represent. The fight comes off tomorrow evening, in the ring on the after well-deck hatch.

June 19. Every day I get more used to this life. Even the bedbugs don't bother me much now. It may be because I've become immune, or because they aren't hungry any more, or because they have given up hunting new places to bite. Or perhaps some have been killed off by the deadly fumes of dope smoked by my good friends Whitey the Swede, Soapy, and the Greek, who inhabit the next bunk tier.

I'm getting to know the sailors better all the time. When you get right down to it, they are a fine lot of men. Though they gamble a lot, they are for the most part absolutely honest about it, and take their losses philosophically, even when their entire pay for a week or two of hard work has gone because of a few untimely sevens on the dice. And most of them are loyal to their friends when the occasional scraps occur.

They have a pretty hard life according to the standards

of the average citizen, but for them it is the easiest way to live. They feel absolutely free, even to gamble away their last cent, for they can always eat and live on the ship, though they be denied a few days' high-pressure whoopee in port. And then there is always the next shore leave to look forward to, perhaps in some new and strange place — always the glamour of possible success at gambling, to further extend the range of their debauchery.

Most of them have no family or friends to worry about, as far as I can make out. Other than to their more or less temporary gob acquaintances, they seem to feel no ties. I guess the chief requisite for a sailor is to be lonely-proof.

This evening I was standing on the bow watching the day sink out of the sky into the western ocean. Gray-blue clouds drifted like ships against a background of pink and gold clouds at a tremendous distance, which in turn were profiled against a field of soft purple, infinitely remote. It gave such a sense of depth in the sky that the distant clouds seemed farther away than the stars. For a few minutes I had an inkling of the depths of space — of the appalling distances of the sky.

And then all changed to a dull gray as night came down — and I forgot about the stars and the sky and space, for at seven-fifteen my wrestling bout was to begin. I felt rather shocked at the nearness of it, and not being at all an expert wrestler, I felt utterly unprepared. But I knew I couldn't back out now, as it was already seven and there had been heavy betting all over the ship.

At first, it had seemed just a friendly little match with one of the soldier boys, but, as I began to realize how heavily my sailor friends were betting on me, to overhear discussions as to the comparative strength of my opponent and myself, to read predictions in the ship's paper, and to feel the curious eyes of the soldiers as I crossed the well-decks, the fight had grown in my mind until now I wondered why I had ever shouldered such a responsibility. I was still wondering, when it was suddenly seven o'clock.

So I got ready, by emptying my pockets and fixing my belt securely, and made my way aft to the well-deck where the ring was set up. The whole three companies of recruits were sitting waiting to witness the battle, with the officers and passengers crowding the rail of the saloon deck, and my sailor supporters cheering from the boat- and sun-decks.

Such conspicuous moments are awful to me, and it took all my nerve to walk in among the soldiers to the ring, where sat the heavy Texan — looking deplorably efficient and resolute.

The excitement steadied me somewhat, and I needed it — I had no real friends or adherents within a thousand miles, and here were three hundred bloodthirsty young soldiers jeering and yelling and crazy to see me licked. Even the ship's crew, which rooted for me now, as a matter of form, would probably sour on me if I began to lose their money for them. I felt anything but comfortable.

Temporarily my mind was occupied in taking off my shirt and shoes, and there was another period of sickening waiting while an officer announced our names and weights and introduced us. Then the referee appeared and stated the rules.

'Everything goes, boys,' he said, 'except a strangle-hold. It's the best two out of three falls, and the time limit is twenty minutes.'

More waiting while the time-keeper was summoned. I saw my Texan enemy across the ring from me, eyeing me and looking more than ever tough and powerful. I tried to look the same at him.

And then a whistle blew, our chairs were removed from the ring, and everybody but the referee got outside the ropes. The gong struck.

'Go to it, kid!' shouted somebody. A roar went up from all sides, cheers and encouragements to the Texan. We came together, and I felt terrific power against me — more than I had expected.

Nothing happened at first, and my enemy seemed to be fighting a defensive battle. He resisted my efforts, but didn't attack.

We kept separating and coming together again, and I felt rather worried that he was so calm, and that I couldn't do anything with him. Then I tried a Sonnenberg tackle — and the fight really began.

We hit the canvas tarpaulin — the only covering over the wooden hatch-cover — with a tremendous bang, and rolled, struggling frantically.

Everything went well at first, and I felt that I could get him, but soon I realized that I was weakening fast, and that I couldn't hold him where I wanted him. His strength was terrific and I felt horribly out of wind. We kept on grap-

pling and rolling around, and the minutes went by, and the
soldiers yelled directions at him, and I did less and less what
I wanted and struggled more and more defensively.

I felt more discouraged and tired all the time, and occasionally I heard the referee, who was a soldier, yelling
encouragement to the Texan. It was pretty horrible to feel
my strength fading that way, and with everyone yelling
against me and crazy to see me helpless on my back. I
prayed that the twenty minutes would go fast, but the end
never seemed to come. And then I heard, far off it seemed
— beyond the blinding lights of the ring — the shouts of
the excited soldiers:

'Get a scissors on him! Get a scissors on him!'

I felt that I didn't much care what happened, except that
it was sickening to think of being beaten and to fail all
those who had bet their money on me so confidently. The
next thing I knew, my opponent had a scissors hold around
my stomach and began to squeeze.

I thought I could stand it at first, but his legs were
enormously powerful, and soon the pain of it was terrific.
We were tangled up just outside the ropes at this point, and
I could hear a voice yelling: 'Get 'em in the ring! Drag
'em inside the ropes!' — and protests from the distant
galleries where my sailor friends were.

But nothing happened, and I was very weak and began
to cough up blood, and had to give up because the pressure
on my stomach hurt so.

Well, it was awful. I felt absolutely licked and all in,
though I managed to get on to my feet. And then, amid the
deafening cheers of the soldiers, the referee told us we had a
minute before the next round.

I didn't see how I could possibly go on. Everything was
swimming before my eyes, and I could feel somebody
vainly pouring water on my head. Already the taunts of
the sailors were in my ears. The gong struck again.

We were at it once more. I fought blindly and with little hope, praying that the twenty minutes would soon be up. I knew that the first round had been fourteen minutes, and that there were only about five minutes left.

We struck the ropes of the seemingly diminutive ring often as we lurched recklessly about — and then with a cruel force we struck the floor, I underneath. But soon we were rolling again, and tangled among the ropes.

Suddenly I realized that there was an extra lot of yelling, and that I was, for the moment, on top — a faint burst of hope — and then I saw that his shoulders were both touching the canvas as he lay on his back.

My round! But the referee says nothing, and we keep on rolling around, and I feel as desperate and weak as before.

Then, before I know it, my stomach is again enclosed in that crushing scissors — I know that it is almost over.

In a few seconds the referee has separated us, and the Texan is declared the winner, and given the prize — a small wad of money.

I shook hands with him, clutched my shoes and shirt which someone handed to me, and struggled through the crowd to the forward part of the ship.

It is futile to try to explain how you feel when you are licked. It was just utter disgust with myself and a need to get away from everybody. I felt that I couldn't possibly face the sailors after failing them so — and that I didn't have a friend in the world. I was sick, body and soul.

During the next two hours, I was alone on the bridge, and it was then that my strength began to pick up. The mate, Edwards, made me feel considerably better when he told me how the sailors had razzed the referee for not counting the time I had the Texas boy on his back, and for counting the scissors hold as a fall. That meant that my sailor friends were still back of me, anyhow.

He told me, also, that the boxing championship fight,

which came just after my bout, had been won by a young potato-peeler from the galley. The kid won by a knock-out in forty-five seconds. Which goes to show, I think, the condition of mind a fellow gets into after peeling potatoes for two weeks.

June 20. Feeling rather stiff and sore this morning, I spent my time off watch lying on a hatch-cover in the sun. The old painter, seated a few feet away, was explaining to the Jugoslav about the United States Government.

'Yes, py cheeminy,' he said, 'anybody born in the Yewnited States can be president. Yessir — anybody.'

'Good thod man yar be pyezidend?' asked the Jugoslav, pointing to a man who was sweeping off the well-deck tarpaulins.

'Well — er — no,' said the painter, 'not that feller.'

'Vy nod? Vazend he bown in der Onided Zdades?'

'Oh, yes — I guess so,' went on the old sailor, 'but that feller could never be president — 'e's sweepin' against th' wind.'

Other sailors began to gather around, and the conversation turned to a discussion of who knew the captain best.

'The old man asked me into his cabin fer a little drink this morn',' said Soapy, obviously lying, 'but I say, "Naw, don't t'ink I'll have anyt'ing this mornin', Cap."'

'Vell,' countered Whitey the Swede, 'da ol' man an' I, ve play chess lars' night,' hoping that someone might believe him.

Rarely do the sailors waste an opportunity to bluff high social prestige — not that they really value it, but because they think others do. And they spend considerable time also in describing what they would be doing if they knew certain of the female passengers who roam the saloon decks, and bluffing vivid accounts of past adventures with these same buxom females.

June 21. The coast of California was in sight when we awoke this morning — warm, bare, brown hills and cool, smooth beaches in the sunshine. At noon we were outside the Golden Gate, ready to pick up our pilot. The coast still looked bare and wild. One would never suspect that, behind those bleak mountains lay, scattered about the shores of a beautiful bay, one of the greatest cities of the world.

On board S.S. Admiral Peary, Pacific Steamship Company, freighter. Bound for Seattle from San Francisco.

June 27. This ship is much smaller than the transport, much more rickety, less efficient, and more informal. The crew is small — only seven sailors — a nice bunch, capable and hard-boiled. Aside from a couple of Hollanders, we have no foreigners on board.

I am sitting in the foc'sle, which is empty except for one bunk, where one of the Dutchmen is snoozing peacefully, making an intermittent buzzing noise, like a poorly oiled electric fan going at slow speed.

On the walls are various pictures of the absent sex. Especially prominent is one of a young trained nurse in a very thin and revealing costume. It is labeled, 'Good for what ails you.' And I think it would be good for most of us here.

When men have been alone in rough circumstances for any length of time, even the cheapest reminder of things feminine is very comforting.

We are two days out of port, pitching and rolling with most annoying persistence. This squat ship, with absurdly blunt bows, seems to remain stationary — writhing about with a slow, tireless energy through the heavy seas.

Just before we put out from 'Frisco, the bosun gave me the task of clamping the derrick-booms in place on the mast-head. This meant going aloft three times, up the rotten swaying shrouds. I felt exceedingly shaky on the way up the first time. I didn't dare look down, but kept on doing it in spite of myself, until I didn't care whether I fell or not, and my hands felt numb.

But I had to keep on climbing or I would lose my job. Soon the shroud cables, all of which converge to a single point on the mast, had become so close together that the ratlins weren't wide enough to put my feet through, and I had to climb up the almost single cable with my hands, until I could reach the bolts just below the cross-trees, and pull myself up.

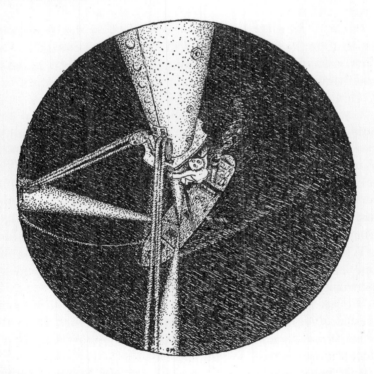

My head swam as I saw above me, on the naked mast, nothing to hold on to but these chance little bolt ends. Desperately I climbed, gripping to each precious bit of pro-

trusion with the last sinews of my soul — reaching to get up
to that feeble, skimpy disk, the 'cross-trees.' At last my
fingers are touching it. Everything is fearfully small and
rickety. The ship looks almost like a rowboat down below.
I pull myself out over a hundred feet of empty air, around
the forlorn rim above me, and stand at last on this eighteen-
inch refuge, hugging to the mast.

This is heavenly security for a moment, but the thought
of having to go down again freezes in my mind—and my
nerves are rigid as I reach out to clamp the booms and
hammer the wedges tight.

It was only after two similar ascents that I was able to
dilute that doomed feeling as I left the deck, because, no
matter what struggles for courage my mind made, my body
was utterly and horribly afraid.

This ship is steered with an electric device that is very
tricky. You have to concentrate every second while at the
helm. If you slip up for even a moment, the ship will slide
five or six points off her course, and then the mate comes
charging down from the 'roof' with a fiery harangue. I
know, because it happened to me this morning. The mate
doesn't like me much, because he sees that I'm green, and
last night, when I brought him up his coffee, it had some
grounds in the bottom of the cup.

There is one thing that you learn when you steer a ship at
night, and that is, that to be sleepy can become an actual
physical agony. You stand alone, and stare and stare — for
two long, silent hours — into the brightly lighted binnacle
which, although you must keep full attention upon it,
merely reiterates to your sleepy brain, with hypnotic monotony, the numbers of the course you must steer. You can't
divert yourself with other thoughts, because as soon as your
attention slips into them, away from the binnacle, you suddenly come to with a start and have to pull the spokes
frantically to get back where you belong, before the mate

notices that the Big Dipper is in the east instead of the north. Last night it was my wheel from two o'clock till four, and I spent the last hour in nothing less than physical torture.

Most of the crew are quiet old-timers, and are not very sociable except at cards and occasional inane talk in the foc'sle. As an example of their conversation, they spent close to two hours this afternoon discussing whether the bosun's shore hat — a light-colored Stetson — was the dukiest possible style to wear in port. Then, for another hour, they discussed shoes.

The best time of the day is just after my night watch, when Racetrack Harry, who used to ride at the Danbury Fair, Connecticut, makes toast with me in the galley, undisturbed by the big Negro cook who by day holds supreme power over that part of the ship.

Last night, in our midnight chat with the oilers, the conversation turned to the reason why men go to sea. Racetrack Harry, with his sly blue eyes twinkling, sipping away at a cup of thick black coffee, took a keen interest in the discussion, but couldn't decide whether you went to sea because you weren't married, or you weren't married because you went to sea. One of the oilers, a short, stubby fellow covered with all sorts of obscene tattooing, answered the question with a gruesome story of his own married life, and how it lasted two weeks. The moral of it was that you went to sea because you *were* married.

July 1. 1.00 A.M. I've finished my watch, and it is good to be through with that damned electric wheel.

We have just passed the mouth of the Columbia River, and the coast looks cold and rugged in the moonlight. The air is clear and cool and feels good to the lungs.

As I stand at the foc'sle-head rail, the stars seem near enough to touch, and it is thrilling to be riding, riding, rid-

ing, through the wind, above the black swirling waves which
boil backwards into the darkness. Black hills of forest beneath a silver-edged strip of clouds lie to the eastward, with
bits of ghostly fog dozing in the valleys, while a great,
veiled, salmon-pink moon slips up to a clear space to flood
the inky sea with light. The dim cabin lights, from behind
the complicated tangle of rigging and idle black spars, come
pressing toward me through the bulk of blackness, with the
faint warm hum of throbbing engines.

This is a wonderful feeling of security and progress and
peace. This, it must be, that keeps men at sea, but yet —
on a night like this — the sailors sit inside and worry their
lonely brains over a bench-top of dirty cards. They are
strange men indeed. I don't see why they go to sea.

July 2. We docked at Seattle early this morning, and I
received my discharge and eleven dollars pay, and went
ashore.

CHAPTER TWO

ALASKA

S.S. Admiral Rogers. We are now three days out from Seattle, already in Alaskan waters, and our ship is steaming northwest among the islands and inland channels of the Panhandle. We are bound for Skagway, from where I am going over the mountains into the interior. Every few hours we stop to unload at small cannery villages, and we of the crew do all the stevedoring.

Lying in my bookshelf bunk in the foc'sle, I have just finished nine hours of working cargo in the hold. Near me, old Pete, the winch-driver, is uttering obscene expressions of Dutch rage at the individual who has anonymously taken his last piece of soap. He is clad in a pair of the peculiarly unattractive long yellow union suits much affected by sailors. Although, now, he is too mad to speak to anyone, yesterday he was confidential with me.

'Say, big boy — you wanner look out fer that Paul,' he said. 'He's stationman down in th' hold, and between you an' me, he's crazy as a June bug. Nothin' real dangerous about him — but just don't get him goin'.'

I observed Paul with caution; he seemed extraordinarily meek. Today he spoke to me confidentially.

'Just take it from me, Slim,' he said, 'the winch-driver's a good guy if yer treat him right. But I'm gonner tell you sumpthin, Slim — that winch-driver's crazy. He's puffectly harmless, but he's nuts all right. So don't mind him.'

I came to the conclusion that they were both right.

July 9. As we advance along this broken coast, the cargo we unload is getting heavier and of greater bulk. Most of our empty salmon cans are gone, and now we handle machinery, cement, coal, and salt bags. In Juneau where there is a gold mine, we spent hours loading on ore in two-hundred-pound sacks. We dock about every forty miles. I am at work on the cargo more than half the time.

Yesterday, stopping two hours at a little cannery, it seemed hard to go below and leave the sunshine, the snowy mountains and untainted air, to sweat in an iron dungeon, stifling with the cargo dust of years, to lug heavy salt bags, which melt and sting the raw spots on the arms, or massive packing-boxes, raising putrid fumes with every jar.

But now and then, out of a porthole or for a moment on deck, I get a glimpse of the wild shores and the occasional isolated canneries, while, over it all — above the steaming folds of morning fog or the misty midday slopes of forest, above the deep blue arms of the sea — I see the mountains hurling themselves recklessly into the sky.

White Horse, Yukon Territory, July 13. 'Yer jes' the boy I been lookin' for,' said the old steamboat captain when I came to him at White Horse, hoping to sign on as a deckhand on the next boat for Dawson. 'I can't put yer on a boat down-river directly, but yer'll be fireman on this freighter we're buildin' here when she pushes off next week — pervidin' yer do your job good in th' meantime. Come on, now — here's yer paint-brush. We're gon'ta give her upper decks a coat.'

That is how I got my present job of putting finishing touches on the Yukon Navigation Company's new freighter, which will add one more to the little fleet of three stern-wheelers which ply up and down this great, rushing Yukon River. I arrived here at White Horse last night, and this job will give me four dollars a day.

Up through these ragged coastal mountains there runs a narrow-gauge railroad, from the rotting shacks and wharves on the beach at Skagway up over the ranges to the Yukon Valley and this little town of White Horse.

It was along this route — the 'Trail of '98' — that the prospectors filed by on their long pull to the Klondike in the wild days of the gold rush. On the single track of the railroad which now follows the line of their desperate plodding, I have been working a couple of days at laying new ties and pounding spikes — to earn my way into the interior and White Horse, this bleak hamlet of about three hundred people, the junction between the railroad and the river traffic.

All along the river's edge, hauled up on the bank, beside the houses of logs and mud, lie the worn-out hulls of old scows and steamboats — left-overs from the rush days. From this ragged graveyard of a wild past, I intend to go northward, down the river into the heart of Alaska, according to present prospects, as a Yukon fireman — throwing wood into a boiler furnace and helping to 'wood up' at intervals along the river where Indian woodcutters work.

In the meantime, I am doing everything on this freighter from adjusting the boiler mechanism to painting the thirty-foot smokestack, by far the biggest thing on the boat. Today when I was hoisted up in a bosun's chair for the latter activity, I was disconcerted by the strong wind which was shaking the stack and tackle so unrestrainedly that it blew the paint out of my can down upon the old captain. He was holding on to my hoisting line with one Billy, an Indian boy assistant.

For a while I was in doubt as to whether the old man and the boy would keep hanging on to my supporting rope when subjected to a shower of buff-colored paint. But men of the North appear to be used to unfavorable conditions.

'Never mind the paint, boy,' the captain shouted up to me, 'it's good for me. Jes' remember this here's a steamboat — not a sailing vessel — an' slap the stuff on good!'

I did so — for hours in that wild wind — while the creaking stack and swaying tackle reminded me that my two hundred pounds of well-being depended, at the moment, upon four pulleys, two blocks, seven rope sections, three hooks, and various connecting links; not to speak of the integrity of the bosun's chair, the strength of the captain, the unselfishness of the Indian attendant, and exceptions to the law of probability. It was a perfect day.

With a fellow named Leskosek, after supper, I took a short hike to the top of the bluffs, where they have a small two-seater biplane stationed at the new aviation field overlooking White Horse. The air was as warm as California, as we looked down upon the clustered cabins of the town, but the small sturdily built log houses, the sledges in the backyards with sledge-dogs lying about, and the enormous woodpiles, all bespoke of the long Arctic winter which waits behind this summer warmth to grip the land in merciless cold.

The mosquitoes were pursuing us so we descended to town again, where Leskosek, somewhat to my astonishment, suggested that we get up a dance.

'There hasn't been any excitement around here,' he said, 'for weeks — and something's got to be done about it. In Alberta, where I came from, there are about five women to every man, but it's just the other way around here — no girls at all. But I know where a couple of pretty good ones live — they ain't so bad-lookin' either — and they like a good time. Let's go.'

The girls were at home. They seemed rather lacking in lure to me, but he, being used to unfavorable conditions, thought they were superb. This in spite of the fact that they were, in reality, only a sallow, skinny bartender's daughter with hair like dried spinach, and a sickly, flat-breasted waitress with goldfish eyes and a burlap skirt.

With a rickety phonograph wheezing out some tunes of 1906, a few guys in dusty clothes pump-handling around with the two horrible ladies, and no conversation for the simple reason that no one had anything to say, it was a most unappetizing party.

July 14. After another day's work in the boatyard, myself

and my overalls having become almost completely covered with buff-colored paint, I decided, as the whistle blew, to go down-river immediately. I repaired, at speed, to a boiler-maker friend of mine who knew a photographer who had a boat for sale.

It was a small flat rowboat, twelve feet long, with square bow and stern.

'Yust der t'ing,' said the boiler-maker, 'for goin' down der river.'

He was a huge, fat fellow with one ear — the other just wasn't there ——

'Yer wanna be careful in the rapids, though,' he continued; 'it's wery few that escapes if they gets dumped over in this river. Wery fast river and wery cold river — but you'll get along all right, I guess. You'll have a long row gettin' 'crost der lake down dere — it's forty mile long — but after dat you get a strong current ter help ——'

Having achieved a boat, I procured some grub for the journey — beans, raisins, bacon, and hardtack — and got a fishline, mosquito net, and map. I had a last large meal of moose steak and soup, loaded everything onto my tiny craft, and was about to depart, when Leskosek, who had come down to see me off, asked me if I had a blanket. As I had none, he offered to give me an extra one of his, and, although it was full of holes and rather smelly, I accepted it with a gratitude that was to increase through each cold night. He wished me luck — and I pushed out into the stream.

In two minutes the current had carried me three hundred yards down the river, around a bend and out of sight. The little town of log cabins, the boatyard with its rotting scows — its plethora of buff-colored paint — the river-bank, the boiler-maker, the photographer, and Leskosek, had all disappeared into memory. There was no sign of habitation within my horizon. Nothing but the vast spruce forests stretching from the top of high clay river-banks back into the mountains. All about me the rippling, swirling river, making a soft swishing sound like a steaming kettle. The next town that I shall see is Dawson — four hundred and eighty miles through the mountain ranges to the north.

Soon it would be the brief twilight night of this country and cold. As the sun sank ahead of me — about eleven P.M. — I got my equipment arranged, put on my extra shirts, and rolled up in my blanket in the bottom of the boat for a good sleep.

I drifted quietly along past the shadows of spruce trees, under steep yellow cliffs of clay, winding among the hills from which rose a cold mist — my little boat drifting always onward, toward the sun's dull glow behind the tumbled mountains to the north.

July 15. I awoke sometime in the very early morning at the southern end of Lake La Barge. Ahead, as far as I could see, it extended like a mirror of deep blue, spreading its narrow arms in among the spruce-clad mountains. Picturesque all right — but a tremendous obstacle to me, all alone in a little boat in dead water at the upper end. There seemed nothing to do but row, so I headed north, and started off at a steady easy stroke, calculated to last a long time. But the outlook was not pleasant.

Four miles in a shell with seven other men to help you is bad enough, but forty miles in a rowboat all alone seems like something worth writing home about. However, after I had been going for an hour or so, and the shore seemed to be in exactly the same position as it had for the last forty minutes, I noticed a slight ripple on the previously smooth surface — a following breeze! Perhaps I could sail!

I hastily made for shore, cut two strong driftwood poles for masts, and rigged up a sail with a piece of canvas with which I had kept my blanket dry. Having no hammer or nails, I managed, by the liberal use of twine, to lash my two masts erect, one on the starboard and one on the port side of the bow, with the sail stretched taut in between.

It worked beautifully, and to my great joy the breeze strengthened, coming still from the south. I took my place in the stern, steering with an oar, and soon was skimming across the huge expanse of water at the rate of four or five miles an hour, in the warm sunshine. The bubbles slipped by on either side, and the waves slapped against my square prow. I fed myself raisins with my free hand. Jehovah was with me.

Once the wind got so strong that the waves became a danger to my small craft, and began to slop over the side with alarming frequency. I bailed with my cooking-pot and made over toward the nearest shore. It wouldn't do to swamp in that icy water so far from land. But in time the wind lessened, and, as the sun finally swung below the northern horizon, I had crossed the lake and reached the river at its farther end. I felt happy to relax my steering arm, and go ashore to cook a few beans before starting once more on my downstream drift.

July 17. This is a great life — to be totally alone, drifting, drifting through this endless wilderness, never knowing quite where you are, and always in doubt as to what to expect around the next bend, perhaps a lake, perhaps an Indian camp, perhaps a woodchopper's shack, or a swift rapid to be navigated.

My map is not drawn in sufficient detail to locate accurately my position except occasionally, when I come to an unusual landmark. Sometimes I have to pole my way out of the numerous sloughs and blind lagoons which are a waiting trap for any drifting body; sometimes I slip quietly up to a flock of feeding duck or geese, or I fish for the abundant grayling which splash playfully after water-bugs in the twilight.

The river winds aimlessly, cutting great arcs through the soft clay lands which support the forest. This country is obviously in the early stages of erosion, full of bare jagged peaks and rushing streams and swift-flowing rivers; a country which is just beginning to feel the power of wind and rain and snow, swirling sand and sliding pebbles, and all the tireless, persistent wearing-down and leveling-off processes; a country which is young in the geological sense as well as from the point of view of human settlement.

On all sides I can see the excited streams rushing downward, each with its store of sand and pebbles as a continual offering to the mighty cargo of the river, and I hear incessantly the rumble and sizzle of this burden of rock, pebbles, and voluminous sediment as it sweeps along the bottom beneath me. The high clay banks constantly release showers of earth and stones and boulders — bits of the mountain's bulk — which avalanche to the water's edge. Day by day this hungry stream eats its way into the forest. There is a never-ending file of uprooted trees and torn branches floating down with the current, to pile up on a flat somewhere miles below and become seasoned driftwood for Indian camp-fires.

Everywhere, always, a continual rushing, rushing, rushing — down with the Yukon current to the sea. It never ends. In places the stream widens to drift lazily through a broad level valley, among little islands, or beside intricate lagoons; sometimes it winds in a series of tremendous loops through hills of clay, and again it is constricted to rocky cañons, and forced to increased speed until it assumes the form of rapids. All around loom rugged mountains, sometimes bare, again heavily wooded.

The forest — that mysterious army of birch and spruce — extends almost beyond belief, climbing to the summits, fringing the banks of rivers and lakes, reaching beyond the ranges for thousands upon thousands of miles in every direction, west to the sea, north to the Arctic ice, to the vast central plains in the east, and far south to the arid deserts of California. It is a horde of dark-green, delicately

pointed spires, each struggling to hold its head above its neighbors and into the pure winds. Along the clifftops and above the river-banks I can see the great trees, and hear their faint, deep whisper.

The vitality of this country is enormous. Life is crowding in the rivers and woods — salmon so multitudinous they can scarcely force their way up the shallower streams, grayling in every lagoon, ducks and geese flying low with the noise of a squadron of airplanes. Out from the cliffs, eagles — preying upon fish, snipe, gophers, and this morning I saw one kill a duckling. A big splash, loud squawking by the fleeing mother duck and terrorized brood, and the great hoary eagle rose into the sky clutching the unfortunate one in his talons.

Myriads of cliff swallows inhabit little holes beneath the overhanging banks; there are noisy gulls and kingfishers, and dainty sandpipers skip up and down the flats.

In my boat is a representative delegation of Yukon bug-dom, quivering moths, and crawling things which have escaped the jaws of fish and the darting swallows. With so much and varied companionship, I can scarcely feel lonely, although I am paid as little attention as are the rocks and the clouds and the sky.

Everything is busy, rushing back and forth for food, dodging the enemy, building a home, raising a family; each individual is deeply involved in its own little struggle, so intent that it takes no notice of anything outside. All the time I pick up small squirming insects that come swirling down on the flood and need to be dried out in the sunshine before making a fresh start in the strife.

This morning I rescued a bumble bee, feebly twitching his drenched furry limbs, and rather hopelessly done in. After straightening out his crumpled wings and legs, I laid him out on my canvas in the sun. In two hours he was dry and well. He crawled up and down, exploring his new habitat, periodically stopping to comb his tangled coat with his little hind feet. Soon he was trying to fly, making short hops up and down the bottom of the boat, until I had to corral him in mosquito netting along with one or two other convalescing comrades, to be freed when I went ashore for supper.

It is never really dark. When night comes down upon this endless wilderness there falls a grayish, purple veil over everything, with the trees standing black-green, and a low pink glow always to be seen in the north. It grows colder, and I have to put on all my clothes.

I make sure that my small craft is in order, well bailed out, and as near the center of the current as possible. Then I wrap myself in my well-worn blanket, lie down among the spruce boughs which serve as a mattress, and soon am dead to the world. Through the eerie night of Arctic summer, I sleep soundly, waking only when the boat strikes a protruding heap of driftwood, or a graveled bar, and is whirled back into the torrent.

At dawn it is very cold. Up here the sun doesn't come up vertically like a balloon, but rises like an airplane on a long slant along the horizon. It is still too early to feel its warmth, and the clammy night's dew lies thick on my blanket and on objects about me. Cold mist hangs along the river's edge and marshy deltas, and I feel stiff and hungry.

Mustering all my dormant energy, I reach for the oars and pull shoreward. With chattering teeth I scramble out and kindle a fire of dried spruce poles to thaw my joints. As I watch a pot of beans stewing among its embers, and smell the frying bacon, I appreciate the addition of fire to man's group of domestic servants.

After breakfast I drift on again, wondering where the night has brought me, and try to locate myself on my map, calculating time by the sun, figuring my average speed of four or five miles an hour, and guessing as to which of the multiple bends of the river I am on.

I doze awhile. In this two thousand-foot altitude the sun has heated the air so quickly that I can take off my last and innermost shirt and marvel, as I feel the warmth on my shoulders, how — only two hours ago — I could have been shivering in one flannel and two cotton shirts, a wool vest, and an oilskin slicker, woolen trousers, overalls, heavy boots, and my smelly blanket.

Then, perhaps, I will hear the roar of rapids. I hastily cover my chattels with canvas in preparation for the spray, and stand by the oars. It is over in a minute; a sudden boiling sea, hard holding on the oars to keep the boat from being swirled out of control, a flash of chilling spray — then calm again, drifting on and on. The rapids never amount to much of anything. The only reason they give a thrill is because my boat doesn't amount to much of anything either.

On I go, always rather lonely, rarely seeing anyone, and yet constantly busy — keeping in the swiftest current, trying to beat floating trees which race along beside me, studying the map, caring for the despairing bugs, arranging my paraphernalia.

They say that the caribou herds cross the Yukon in this district in their hundred thousands, during the early days of August, swarming so compactly that steamboats have stopped to avoid running them down. It being the middle of July, I have seen only one young caribou, which galloped fearlessly toward me down the beach of an islet. All brown, with the general aspect of a thin little horned pony, he stood still, not thirty yards away, and gazed until I landed downstream of him and started up the beach. Then — with a terrific clatter of hoofs he was off, scampering over the gravel with a noise like a couple of ice-wagon horses charging down a cobblestone alley. Strange little creature, galloping about all alone that way!

Last night I reached the hamlet of Selkirk, two or three cabins grouped about a trading-post store, and ghostly in the half light of midnight. Long before I got there, the presence of the town was heralded by that never-forgettable sound — the unearthly night cry of the sledge-dogs. Arriving, I beached my boat and entered the store to find an old man reading by candlelight at a table. I got one or two cans of provisions from him, a spoon and a can-opener, reloaded my camera in the rare darkness of his cellar, and returned to my boat to shove off under the suspicious gaze of three Indian children who had turned out to witness an unusual nocturnal event.

Another day, the fifth now, I drifted among numerous islets and lagoons, past bare hilltops, passing in the morning a steamboat struggling up-river, to be waved at by thrilled tourists. At sundown, around a bend, I came upon the once-famous town of Dawson, a tawdry accumulation of frame houses, and my immediate destination.

Dawson. July 19. After landing beside the cable ferry, I walked slowly along the main street before an array of restaurants and heavily advertised 'hotels,' with gaudy fronts of fake magnificence, but constructed in the hinder parts of logs, tin, and scrap materials.

The first human I saw was a friendly-looking old man in a straw hat, sitting in front of a grocery store and obviously very much under the influence of liquor.

'Shay there, young feller,' he addressed me in a fluid whisper, 'have a chair. Stranger around here, eh?... Oh, so you're from the outside?'

'I'm just an old sourdough,' he answered to my questions as to his occupation. 'Came here in ninety-et wit' the rest o' the boys. Been here ever since. Sometimes I think I wanter go back — but it takes a lot o' money ter get outer this country. An' I don' han'le much of th' stuff nowadays. Not like th' old times in these parts — no, sirree.'

He lapsed into memories of the turgid youth of himself and Dawson.

According to him, the real gold-diggers of the early days were the dancehall girls, who flocked into the new settlements close in the wake of the male stampeders.

'Why, Keriste, man,' he said, his opaque eyes brimming with reminiscent bleariness, 'them dames got every dollar we ever took outen the creeks. But, hell, in them days we didn't give a damn for money anyhow. Why, I know that, t' show yer how we flung the stuff around, I gave up the creeks myself, an' took a job sweeping out the dancehall floors. Every night you could see the boys spillin' the dust when they paid fer their drinks an' the girls, an' sure, I jes' panned the dirt I swept offen th' floors, and got ten times as much gold as them poor suckers got outen th' sluices.

'The smallest coin we knowed was two bits — an', by Gar, it still is. Why, when I fust come up in ninety-et, one day I give a dime to one er them girls fer somethin' er other, an' she jes throwed it inter th' stove. "Aw, that's no good," she says, "we don't use them things in this country," an' that girl was talkin' true. We didn't use 'em then — an' we don't use 'em now, by Gar.'

This ancient and cock-eyed sourdough went on to describe the life and wild adventures of those high old times, with stories far too wild and far too high to repeat. Dawson then had more than eight times its present population. People lived in tents and shacks and in the scows that had brought them down-river, but no one had time to sleep, for saloons, gambling-houses, and dancehalls were running and packed the full twenty-four hours.

I asked this dilapidated relic where all the girls came from and how they got here.

'Oh, they came from all over the Pacific Coast,' he replied — 'from Seattle, Victoria, Vancouver, an' all around.

They came by the hundreds, on the ships with men, workin'
as waitresses an' such, an' then over the mount'ns an' down
the river wit' the crowd. They always came in bunches —
an' they would always be sayin', "When yer go down back
home, don't tell mother where I am, will yer. She thinks
I'm workin' in Vancouver. Whatever yer do, don't tell her
I'm here!"'

He paused to sigh hoarsely before continuing, punctuat-
ing his remarks with languid spitting of tobacco juice.

'Aw, but man, them days is long gone. The Mounted
Police, yer know, chased 'em all out. Hell, yer have ter be
acquainted ter go out with 'em now.'

Sadly he turned his maudlin attention to the relatively
drab details of present conditions; people in Dawson, he
said, had become very particular about appearances.

'Them pants o' yourn now,' he said, 'don't look none too
good. I got a pair that's got more style by a darn sight, an'
if you'll come around ter my shack I'll give 'em ter yer.
What about a little drink afore we drift?'

I took the pants.

Then on through the town again, among its many deserted houses and cabins, with marshy rutted streets flanked
by sidewalks of rotting planks. Some of the windows, because of the scarcity of glass at the time of their construction, are made of rows of empty beer bottles chinked with
homemade plaster.

The whole atmosphere and life of Dawson is permeated
with the past. All the older people remember the days of
the great stampede, and the influence of this memory has
signally affected more recent settlers. The dancehall girls
have disappeared, and gambling at the rate of one thousand
dollars a pass is extinct, but that frontier valuation of gay-
ety above comfort, and even above safety, still exists.
Drink still flows in considerable volume, gambling in a
moderate form is far from absent, while men continue to

live in cramped log huts, dining on stale crackers and stews of suspicious odor and composition.

I ate my dinner at a species of Arctic hash-house, where the standard of feminine charm among the waitresses was lower than anywhere on the Yukon, which is pretty low. I went early to bed, already for the job in the mines which, through the activities of my sourdough souse, I had arranged to start in the morning.

July 20. At six-thirty there was a great roar in the street. 'Brains,' as the boss of the mines is called, had started his car. With his vast hat shading a corncob pipe, which protruded from his shaggy mustache, he bounced along over the ruts to the 'hotel' where I had spent the night. Grasping my bag of belongings, I climbed aboard his car, which had a lantern hanging out from either end, and an old window frame, with six panes of glass, for a windshield.

Br-r-r-r-r-r rattle, rattle, chug — boom — rattle — off we went to the mines.

Some ten miles up the Klondike River Valley we stopped beneath a huge wooden flume, a sort of aqueduct exhaust of the hydraulic placer mines, where I was to work.

This is the heart of the very country where the Klondike gold-seekers extracted twenty million dollars' worth of gold in the single season of 1898. All the gold has been taken from the creek beds and wherever there was water to pan or sluice it. It must now be sought with dredges in the valleys and with high-pressure hosing systems on the heights. In the latter, since water is essential in the washing-out of the gold, the problem of getting gold is principally the problem of getting water.

Extensive piping systems stretch through the valley for forty miles, to feed the great hydraulic hose nozzles which hurl tons of water a minute upon the mountain-sides. The débris of rock and sand washed away under this impact is

funneled into a narrow wooden sluice. My job — to repair
parts of this flume which had worn away — gave me a good
opportunity to see its corrugated lining, coated on the bottom with quicksilver, and designed to catch the elusive gold
dust away from the enveloping sediment.

I worked all day, doing various jobs along the ditches,
surrounded by other overalled miners. Many of my companions were old men, over sixty or seventy years of age,
working side by side with young half-breed Indians, Swedes,
Russians, and other laborers such as can be seen anywhere
in the United States. To see the tottering old fellows struggling ineffectually with their shovels, and for high wages,
showed me what a scarcity of labor there is up here. They
are getting from four to eight dollars a day, plus board and
lodging, worth about three dollars, for work which in the
States would hardly pay them enough for food. Fine for
them; but tough on the industry which employs them.

The next day I decided that I would give up my job on
the flume and investigate other gold-getting methods. To
get to one of the monster dredges, I walked for miles, struggling up the valley through swamp land and quick mud
which all but kept me for good. The thermometer stood at
ninety-eight, and it is no joke to cross the Klondike Valley
in that heat.

The dredges are almost two hundred feet in length; great
four-story structures which dig their way back and forth, up
and down the marshy valley, sifting the gold dust out of
their diggings as they go, and discarding the barren residue
upon the vast heap of tailings in the rear. A digestive system on a grand scale and probably much like that of a
dinosaur — but without his sanitary responsibilities.

I made my way back toward Dawson through a sudden
thunderstorm which broke overhead, letting loose the heavy
cargo of the clouds. The noise was like a strong wind tear-
ing through a forest. Marshes became lakes, and brooks,

rivers. My clothes hung on me like so many bags of water.

When I reached the road, a lightness appeared in the inky heavens and soon the storm ceased, leaving a mysterious stillness in the air, and, on the earth, a sound of water as it sought the muddy channels to lower ground. On I trudged in the new fresh air, making spongy noises with each step and a splash with each movement of my saturated attire.

Arriving in town, I saw standing by a doorway a thin, elderly man dressed in a black suit with a black string tie.

'Hi, there!' he said, as I went by, 'have yer been out in the rain?'

'I'll give you three guesses,' I replied, and stopped with a swish.

A toothless smile oozed over his face.

'Well,' he said, 'come on in and get dry anyhow, while I'm thinkin' it over.'

I accepted his invitation and entered — and that is how I came to meet 'Undie' Andrews.

We had supper together in his little kitchen in the rear of the store, and partook of delicious Mulligan stew, while my clothes were drying out over the stove. Such is Northern hospitality.

Undie told me his story. He was born in Australia, and came to Dawson in 1910, where he has been ever since. He was in the midst of an explanation of why he couldn't get away when in came a robust old woman wrapped in a shawl. Undismayed by the presence of a stranger, most of whose clothes were hanging up to dry, she went up to Undie and said in a queer, hushed voice, 'Is it all right, Mr. Andrews, for me to see Mrs. Bundy? — er — do you mind?'

Undie's manner changed instantly. Most lugubriously he

nodded, and led the woman through a doorway into another room which I had not seen. In a few moments they returned, Undie still very solemn, and the woman pale and quivering as if she had undergone some terrible shock. I was very curious to see this Mrs. Bundy, who seemed to make such an impression on people, and, after the visitor had gone, I asked Undie about her.

'Well, it's a long story,' he replied, resuming his former ease of manner. 'It's all part of what I was tellin' yer.' And he continued his interesting tale — until finally it developed that he was an undertaker. Yes, and, as we ate our stew, the corpse of Mrs. Bundy, who had died that morning, was lying in state on an ancient square piano in the next room.

'She drank herself to death,' he revealed. 'A good woman in her way, but she — well, she was kinda wild at times.'

When Undie had finished eating and had put away his false teeth — which he kept on the window-sill between meals — he showed me around his place. In addition to being an undertaker and storekeeper, Undie is a boat-builder, grave-digger, trapper, cook, and dog-breeder. Of course this wide range of occupation is prevalent throughout the frontier country, but Undie's case is an exceptional one. The versatility, resourcefulness, and broad understanding which his diversified activities have given him are nothing short of phenomenal. He can do anything from cooking apple tarts to trimming a coffin.

He exhibited to me his undertaking equipment and flesh-preserving fluids, explaining them with unconcealed pride. His 'dead wagon,' a rickety homemade bier, a ride in which makes doubly certain that the corpse is dead, stood in his back yard.

Having sufficiently impressed me with his more solemn activities, he went on to explain the difficulties and problems

of an Arctic storekeeper. 'Yer can't succeed in this country,' he said, 'unless yer cut yer overhead right down to the
very minimum. Yer see, electric power, an' heat, an' food,
an' all yer equipment costs so bloomin' much here. If yer
buy wood ter keep yer stove goin', ye're jest on the road to
failure, that's all. It's jest too damned extravagant. If
ye're goin' to succeed in this damn country, yer got to cut
yer own wood.

'Some o' the other fellers in town here hain't larnt that
yet, so I'm still goin' while they're gettin' run outa business,
an'll soon prob'ly be out thar in the mines diggin' their
arms off ter make a livin'.'

In the spring Undie builds long, narrow, flat-bottomed
skiffs, with outboard motors in them, to sell to anyone who
wants to go up-river when the ice breaks up at the end of
April.

All summer he keeps store for long hours, especially when
steamboats are in, in order to catch the tourist trade. His
prices are not what is known as reasonable. He also spends
a good part of summer training his dogs, fine young Mala-
mutes with perhaps a trace of Husky. They are the ideal
breed for this country, and can live on fish tails and haul the
sledge thirty miles a day, for weeks on end. Their fur is
thicker and finer than on any animal I have ever seen. Even
their toes are well furred, which is very important as a protection against sharp ice fragments.

In the fall Undie digs his graves for the winter. He has
to thaw the ground with a succession of fires as he goes
down, but it is better than to hack through eight feet of
snow and ice, which he would have to do if he waited until
winter.

When the snow comes, he starts his trapping. Every day
he goes over the trap line to collect the day's catch: mink,
marten, beaver, ermine, muskrat, wolverine, bear, lynx, or
wolf. Undie says it is one of the most remunerative of his

jobs, in spite of the short hours of light — from ten-thirty in the morning till half-past one in the afternoon — and the bitter cold and the driving blizzards.

During the long winter the people here have a great deal of leisure. They get in the wood while daylight lasts, and look at their traps, but for the rest of the time they have nothing to do but sit, or go to the movies. The movie-house, in winter, is always packed to the doors.

Apparently those who can survive the long hardship of cold, darkness, and isolation become philosophical in a typical Alaskan fashion, and have quite a merry time.

In summing up Undie's occupations, I think it is clear that the one in which his heart is most firmly ensconced is his undertaking.

'There was a lot o' business last winter,' he says. 'A lot of Indians died off an' they like fancy burials. There was big profits. I got twenty-five dollars for caskets that I made in one day an' cost only four dollars to make. Yeh, an' trimmin's an' fancy carvin' is all extra — I sure made a lot o' money.'

Then, pausing to take a deep breath, a wistful light flows into his eyes, and he remarks as an afterthought: 'I don't think it will be so good this winter, though. There ain't many old Indians left. But I did hear o' one bein' drowned the other day' — sigh — 'I hope they find his body.'

Undie is also a justice of the peace, and sometimes, when there are murders along the lonely river, Undie, as coroner, gives important testimony, coöperating with the Royal Canadian Mounted Police. The Mounted Police — formerly the 'Royal North-West' — are very active in this British territory, keeping track of all who pass through and helping travelers in difficulties. There is always one of them strutting about town, in his dazzling scarlet uniform, purple pants with yellow stripes, polished puttees, dangling sword, and brass buttons. If there were any girls here worthy of the name, these vivid boys would have a big advantage.

July 22. Today, feeling I'd seen enough of Dawson, I gathered my stuff together, up in Undie's attic where I had been sleeping on an old rug, said good-bye to this hospitable heart, and started once more down the river.

In spite of the loneliness, it is good to be on my way again, among the familiar bubbles and wandering currents. The water is getting muddier all the time.

I tried to fish in water so full of silt that the fish cannot see the fly, and I achieved only a deeper realization of the difficult life of a Yukon salmon. He is driven by a reproductive urge — more a matter of domestic duty than of any apparent diversion for himself — to swim up this river, the mud of which must blind him to the scenery or, in fact, to anything more than an inch from his nose, and in which he has to buck a four-mile-an-hour current for two thousand miles. I don't see why, for such a drab objective, he should make such an effort. Fish, in some aspects, are very unselfish.

Every time I take a drink of the Yukon River I sympathize more deeply with the salmon, for, as the mud thickens, I have to drink more and more of it to quench the same amount of thirst.

Drifting on at the same steady speed, I speculate as to where I shall be two days hence. My provisions will last only as far as a town called Circle, on the Yukon Flats, where the river widens out several miles among innumerable islands, and near to the Arctic Circle from which it derives its name.

The town, however, may be hard to find. Many of these posts, which, on the map, look as important as New York, turn out to be nothing but a couple of shacks hiding under a bush away off on a mountain-side.

Twice last night I was awakened by the sound of falling gravel — caribou running along the flats. Again, at dawn, as the mists were moving mysteriously among the hills, slowly rising with the new warmth, suddenly came a great splashing from up the river. A huge bull moose was at his morning bath. Slashing around, tossing his massive head in wild glee, the commotion he made was terrific. With excited snorts, he kicked and bucked, sending water flying in every direction and making a noise that could be heard for miles. It was a wild sight — that great creature, so free and so thrilled with himself. Finally he dove into deep water and headed across the stream.

In the heat of noon — to add still another event to this most eventful day — sitting on the bank, about a hundred yards distant, appeared a large brown bear. He was a lazy-looking beast and lolled about, licking himself and trying to scratch his back on a log; but his scent and hearing were very acute, for, when I landed and tried to creep close to him, he ambled away, never allowing me to get any nearer.

Back in the boat again, drifting — drifting northward through the endless wilderness. I pass occasional fishwheels along the banks now, slowly turning with the current, to scoop up their portion of the struggling salmon hordes.

Near two of these wheels I came upon their owner's farm. The racks of drying red salmon, under canvas awnings, looked like so many red socks on a clothesline. Dogs were all about, making a wild racket — a pen for the puppies — a vegetable garden — a woodpile — and everything rosy.

The man and his wife came out of the cabin to quiet the dogs. 'Takin' life easy, ain't you!' he shouted to me as I drifted by.

'Sure, and how about yourself?'

'Well, I catch just about enough to live on. How are they up-river?'

But there ended our conversation, for the dogs set up such a baying that all other sound was lost.

As the sun went down about half-past eleven, in a flood of strong red beyond a strangely darkly blue forest, I was treated to another acquaintance — a timber wolf — running along the bank, stopping to sniff the air suspiciously every few steps, always restless, watchful.

July 25. I went to sleep last night — almost a thousand miles from my start at White Horse — in broad daylight, for there is no darkness in this Arctic Circle country. My calculations would bring me to Circle about half-past twelve, and I dared only a series of brief snoozes, keeping a sharp lookout at each interim. At last, sticking up out of the low hills, I saw a tower — a steel wireless tower. Circle!

But it was still miles away. There was time enough for a final short snooze.

Suddenly I was awake. It seemed as if I had slept not more than fifteen minutes — but the tower was nowhere to be seen! This was serious, for, if I missed Circle, I would have to go all the long five hundred miles around to Tanana, in order to get to Fairbanks.

I hustled to shore and climbed a tree, peering anxiously around for my tower. What a relief! There it was, not a mile away. I was directly opposite the town, but on the wrong side of a large island that intervened. I must go upstream to get around it.

The next hour was not pleasant. The current gave me still another taste of the troubles of a Yukon salmon. Keeping as far as possible out of the swifter channel, I rowed hard and steadily against the tide, gaining inch by inch, and close to the steep jungled bank from which descended armies of fierce mosquitoes, taking cruel advantage of the fact that my hands were full. Wherever my head net touched the skin, there was a platoon of the scoundrels all ready with set beaks.

At last I rounded the point at the head of the island, and came into view of my destination. But trouble is still with me. I must drag my loaded craft across two mud flats where sea-gulls circle squawking overhead, laughing piti- lessly as I sink deep in the mire. Finally, however, I arrive and beach beside a weirdly creaking fishwheel. It is dawn. This collection of log cabins, called Circle, is still asleep — except for the unearthly squeaking of the wheel. Even the dogs are quiet.

Having pulled up my boat, I walked through the little village, among its cabins with sod roofs. The grass, which grew longer on the roofs than on the ground, gave one the impression that the town needed a haircut. I climbed the huge wireless mast to view the surrounding country — but there was nothing to be seen except a great deal of Alaska, and thousands of cliff swallows which sat on the guy cables, twittering in the morning sunshine.

When I descended, I made the acquaintance of a little old man with a long beard, who was hunting in the weeds of his potato garden for pieces of a stove which he said he had left there.

'Mornin', young feller,' he began hoarsely, 'just come down-river? Wal...' and he soon became very communica- tive. I couldn't stay near him because he smelt so badly, but he was very kindly and, as he showed me around his workshop and told me his story, we were friends in no time.

'Yeh, my boy,' he said, 'I'm a mechanic by trade. I was a locomotive enguneer in Floruda once. Yeh, 'n' I've been all over South America as a hobo mechanic.'

After an hour's recital of his seventy years of adventure, each year of which was wilder than the preceding one, my unsavory friend came across with a real project — a plan for the future — a proposition which bade fair to make us both millionaires in three years. His eyes fairly burst out of their withered sockets as he poured forth his great plan.

'M' boy,' he began, 'you are a strong-lookin' young feller. You are goin' ter be my partner. This is th' idea. I'll put yer up here fer th' winter, an' in the spring we're goin' ter set out fer Miami, Floruda. We're goin' in my tractor. Yeh, an' I got wonderful equipment — th' most up-ter-date outfit thet's ter be got in th' world. We're goin' ter tow three wagons with our stuff in 'em. Come on here, let me show yer.'

He was old and fat and tottery — and horribly fragrant.

Out behind the shack, sure enough, was his equipment, the tractor, the three wagons, and everything. With ravenous enthusiasm he showed me each minute detail. On one wagon was a wood-sawing machine with which we could prepare our fuel, as well as earn a great deal of money selling cordwood along the way. The second wagon was a machine shop, in which all the tools and repairing equipment could be kept, and the third was a house, with double walls to keep it warm in winter, and a stove, and all sorts of luxury. How the old fellow got hold of all this stuff, the Lord only knows.

'Yeh, my boy,' he went on, his little eyes glittering as he stuffed into his mouth another wad of Copenhagen snuff, 'an' if we get stuck in the snow in them yar mountains, it don't make no difference. We'll just spend the rest o' the winter there. We got double-thick walls an' everythin', an' we can trap plenty of stuff to eat.

'An' when it thaws out we can go on ——' and he continued to describe our progress to the Alaskan coast and, after shipping to Seattle, how we would travel eastward to Idaho and Wyoming, working our way as hobo mechanics, woodchoppers, and all sorts of things. Then, at last, after 'two or three yar, I reckon,' how we would finally pull into Miami with our well-equipped train.

As he drawled on, and continued to be as smelly as ever, I made up my mind then and there that, if I accepted the proposition, I should drive the tractor myself and keep him to leeward on the last wagon — and head for the first 'Mum' dispensary I could find.

By now the town was up and having breakfast, so I lost no time in selling my boat, and making preparations for a three or four days' hike over the mountains to Fairbanks, a hundred and seventy-five miles on what was cheerfully alluded to as 'the new road.' I arranged to have my sack of stuff sent on the stage, a rickety automobile which navigates this rugged route once a week all summer. Into my knapsack went only the barest necessities: a map, four cans of beans and spaghetti, mosquito netting, sweater, and raincoat — my plan was to travel light and fast. I didn't take my blanket because I had decided to sleep in the daytime when the sun was shining hottest and keep warm at night by hiking.

How all this would have worked out, I never had a chance to discover, for once more I became the recipient of a superb phase of Northern hospitality. No sooner had I started on the new road to Fairbanks than along came a car and in it a small family, and I was offered a ride. They were migrating from Circle to Valdez for the winter, and they said that there was plenty of room for one more. So I climbed in among the bundles, tools, and oddments on their back seat.

Papa drove most of the time, but Uncle John took his turn at the throttle occasionally. Whenever we had a blow-out or got stuck in quicksand, the whole family pitched in to help. Papa was very wise to carry among his tools three shovels, two large jacks, a crowbar, heavy rope, and seven spare tires. Without all of them, we would never have arrived in Fairbanks.

If this is a new road, I should hate to see it when it gets old. There are several tractors and some men working on it; but the ruts, two and three feet deep, are almost continuous; and once, when we had our third blow-out, we had to go two miles to find ground hard enough to support a jack.

The greatest weakness of our equipment was the lack of defense against mosquitoes. By millions they pounced on us as we plied our tools, and raked us to the bone like a pack of vultures. The mosquitoes here are quite a different tribe

from the ordinary variety. Instead of buzzing daintily
about to choose a good landing-place, and making a cautious approach, as is the practice at home, these brutes
form in a solid phalanx and, growling formidably, charge
upon you at top speed. With their eyes shut and their
beaks fixed, like bayonets, they drive into your flesh in
overwhelming numbers.

You slap them desperately, leaving the imprint of your
hand in their dead bodies where you strike. But it makes
no impression on the others. They are wild savages, and
continue the onslaught more frantically than ever. It is
said that sometimes dogs are killed by them and men driven
insane. I can easily believe it.

We drove through beautiful mountains, naked land
spotted with snow, and where bleached caribou antlers lay
about, and eagles soared over the valleys. Sometimes we
passed forests of stunted spruce and birch, and patches of
purple fireweed.

For lunch we stopped at a cabin belonging to a road
worker named Si. He had electric lights, with power from
a tiny trickling stream near by, its volume so small that his
wife said she could tell by watching the bulbs in the kitchen
how big a drink of water Si was taking outside.

Rattling into Fairbanks at sundown — in the middle of
the chronological night — we went to sleep in the Pioneer
Hotel, in an inexpensive room above a lobby where two
tables full of Russians, Chinese, and Irishmen were playing
blackjack. Behind the counter sat a pretty girl with yellow
curls and roving blue eyes. She was quite gaudy, and when
she smiled you could see a diamond set in one of her front
teeth. She must be a great help to the hotel business. They
call her 'Diamond Tooth Ann,' and the old miners are wild
about her.

Many of the houses here are built of logs, and there are
gardens everywhere, although beneath the top two feet of

soil lies the eternal ice. The shortness of the season is made up for by the long hours of sunshine.

I've decided I must somehow go down to the coast, because soon the fall stampede of people leaving the country will make it very hard for me to get a place on a ship. To my great joy, I've learned that a freight train with 'many empties' is leaving early tomorrow morning for Seward, and the sea.

After selling my surplus baggage I've made careful arrangements for departure. In my equipment is food to last three days and an emergency beer bottle full of water. Though very optimistic about this adventure, I realize I may have some trouble getting aboard the train unobserved, with my bulging laundry bag, of Czecho-Slovakian design in bright red, blue, and green.

July 27. Early this morning I left my stuffy little room for the freight yard. The rooms are always rather stuffy here because the windows won't open: too many mosquitoes in summer and too cold in winter. When I got to the yard I concealed my sack behind a bush, and wandered about seeking information. After half an hour I had made friends with the car inspector and, on seeing an empty gondola coal car which I thought would be going south, I asked him if it was to be part of the morning freight.

'Sure,' he replied. 'Thet battleship's goin' all right. I'll see ter thet, but don't you hang aroun' here or you'll be caught sure. The boss is right over thar in the roundhouse.'

I dumped my sack into the gondola and, taking the inspector's advice, retired into the brush to await further developments. The mosquitoes howled like wolves. I put on my head net and smeared it with mosquito oil, and waited and watched. After a time one of the engines began to puff about, making up a train. It jockeyed around for two hours picking up a car here and a couple more there until, finally, it hooked on to my gondola and put it next to the tender.

To get aboard undetected did not look easy, but I had to attempt it immediately, as the train might start at any minute with all my earthly possessions hidden within the high walls of gondola number 28. I wondered if I had any chance — the engineer was looking out of his cab within thirty feet of my car and there were several brakemen farther toward the rear of the train.

I walked along beside the track as the train approached, and managed to meet it on a curve and on the outside, which position limited their view of me to a minimum. I swung aboard and soon lay beside my bag at the bottom of the car. Everything had worked well so far.

All I could see was the sky and the bare coal-crusted walls of my rattling conveyance. We stopped and reversed our direction, and I could feel and hear more cars being added to the train. This alternate going ahead and backing up and hitching and unhitching continued for about an hour, while I lay and waited and hoped we would get under way.

After a while I heard many voices and the sound of baggage trucks on the freight platform — and then a voice, 'All right!' followed by two short blasts on the engine whistle. We were starting.

Chuff!——Chuff!—Chuff! We jerked, moved, slowly gathered speed, and were off for the south. When we were well out of town I ventured a look over the edge of my surging craft. There were about thirty cars, ending with a red caboose. I was glad it was so far off — the less chance of being seen — although I surely would be found if anyone tried to get to the engine along the train.

Mosquitoes swarmed upon me in large forces. I killed hundreds, but never could eliminate them, as every time we stopped — which was often — reinforcements appeared.

As time went on, I began to feel more daring, and moved

two cars aft where there was a coal car with a flat bottom — better for sleeping than my chute-bottomed gondola. Rattle... rattle... on we went, and all was well until we stopped at a water-tank in the midst of a vast tundra near the Tanana River. I heard somebody climbing up the side of my car. My heart thumped audibly. Then the head and shoulders of a brakeman rose into view — a weather-beaten man with a kindly boyish face. He saw me almost immediately and his blue eyes widened at the sight of me and my gay laundry bag.

'Hello, there,' I said, smiling hopefully.

He grinned. 'Hey, why don't yer come back to one o' the box cars? They're much more comfortable an' yer won't need to worry about the rain.'

What a pleasant surprise — I had expected to be kicked off the train. But Northern hospitality extends even to railroad men, thank God.

'Where're yer goin'?' he asked.

'I'm tryin' to get to Seward,' I answered. 'Are the box cars going there?'

We talked for a couple of minutes while the engine took on water, and soon I knew that I had at least one friend on the train. In the course of our conversation, I learned that 'prob'bly nobody'll say nuthin' to yer s'long's yer keep out o' the way — s'far as Curry, anyhow. Only yer wanna keep low in stations so's the officials don't see yer.'

I relaxed considerably at these words, for they meant the probable success of this venture.

When we started again, no longer feeling any great need to keep out of sight, I began to explore. Aft, over a dozen or so empty flats and coal cars, there were two water-tank cars. I would have plenty to drink, and wouldn't have to live on the contents of my beer bottle. Farther on were more flats, carrying lumber, various sorts of pipe, and wire. One looked inviting — it contained a hand-car, tools, and planks — so taking my blanket out of my bag, I lay down and went to sleep, rattling steadily southward across the flat tundra country with here and there rising a grove of stunted spruce.

When I woke up we were still in the marshy, mushy, mossy tundra, which breeds mosquitoes by the billion. They were bad, even on the moving, wind-swept train.

July 28. I am now riding in a box car and no longer alone. With me is a fellow who has been prospecting in the mountains. He is bound for Anchorage, one hundred and fifteen miles this side of Seward, and says that, as he has to travel often in the course of his prospecting, he finds this the most economical way of making a journey.

This part of the country, he says, is chiefly a coal-producing area, all locally consumed, and has a little placer gold. We rumble slowly up into the mountains, past where the highest peak in North America rises into a curtain of thick clouds.

Sometimes, out of our sliding door, we can see caribou grazing on the bare mountain-sides. My friend says there are also large herds of mountain sheep roaming about this high tundra country. In Curry, a coaling station, where we stopped for the night near a small brook, we saw trout actually so big that they could hardly find room to swim.

While my companion was arranging his fishline, I stealthily crept out of our refuge. All day I had felt the presence of that chill ghost of the sky, Mount McKinley, although it had been hidden from us by the fog. Now, hoping to get a glimpse of it, I started to climb a near-by mountain. I soon found that the going was hard. The grass, eight feet high, was alive with mosquitoes. It was full of dead branches and great logs, and weeds which looked like wild rhubarb, ten feet high, and all sorts of things to stumble over and get tangled up in.

Finally, after hours — the top. But the clouds still hid McKinley. And the mosquitoes roared, and mosquito oil and sweat blinded my eyes, so I came down in a hurry — tripping over logs, sliding, rolling, tumbling through the giant swamp grass.

Gaining at last my box-car refuge, I found my fishless partner resting quietly. He didn't have, he said, 'th' right kind of flies fer them foxy bastards.'

Food here at Curry costs a dollar and a half a meal at the cheapest, and three dollars a night for a lodging-house room. So we stay in our car and live on the remainder of my Swedish bread and raisins. I don't know why my companion has no food with him; with his experience of freight-car travel he should be better supplied.

Morning. With a great jerk and rattling roar, we were off — already the sun was shining through the window crack, and my partner was describing the nice breakfast which he wished he was having. Very conversational this empty morning, he asked me about my trip down the Yukon, and seemed to think me very hardy. But he couldn't understand why I had no squaw along in the little boat, comparing me unfavorably to his father.

'When Pa was up here prospectin',' he said, 'he was drunk th' whole time. Yeh, he was drunk for six years. An' he had four squaws, Pa did. I never have more'n one m'self — but, Keriste, I'm not rich like Pa was.'

It developed that my partner wanted me to go prospecting with him in the mountains north of Anchorage. It seemed to him perfectly absurd that I should return to the 'outside' while there was still gold in the mountains. He had the true Alaskan spirit.

The train continued slowly, stopping frequently for scrap iron which was loaded upon flat cars for Seward. We wondered what so much iron was for, anyhow.

Finally, crossing seven switches in a row we came to a stop in Anchorage, informally emerged through our window, and shortly afterwards were partaking of a hearty repast in the Main Street Restaurant. It seemed like being out of jail.

In the evening, I went to a movie accompanied by practically the whole town — coal miners, fishermen, cannery workers, restaurant keepers, Indians, women, and children. Some of them look pretty hard up by day, but they certainly seem to enjoy themselves after supper.

I talked to a shabby old man who was sweeping out the theater. He was lazily swishing his old broom back and forth, and appeared one of the very humblest of the humble. But, in the course of conversation, he remarked that he had just sold a hundred and fifty shares of Du Pont stock in order to invest more heavily in aviation. This was staggering, from such a lowly bum, but it is characteristic of Alaska. Wealth and adventure are things to play with — the old gold-digging spirit.

Slowly I wandered down Main Street, past the lighted restaurants and bakeries, each with its serving girl at the counter surrounded by three or four hungry swains. Girls are at a premium here, and even when, to the impartial eye, they are of somewhat meager seductiveness, they seem to lead very active, and probably interesting, lives.

I purchased a few groceries and returned to the car, where I feel more at home all the time. Once you get used to it, there's nothing in the world more comfortable to sleep on than a good wooden floor.

It was the middle of the following night when we arrived, in pitch blackness and fog, at Seward. This was the first full-fledged night I had seen in a month. We were on a long, lighted dock where many men were at work. A freight steamer lay alongside: I could hear the rumble of her winches, for she was loading scrap iron.

All day and all night the men work at this task, in twelve-hour shifts, some on the dock and others in the hold. I have arranged to begin work among them tomorrow at one A.M. They need men to finish the job by next week, and I must earn my living while I wait for a ship.

August 1. In the morning, I proposed to myself to use this day of grace in climbing one of the neighboring snowy mountains, to get a good look at the surrounding coastline.

Up a gushing brook to the wind-worn upper shoulders I followed, to where the air was so clean and clear and the snow so white that I seemed living in a new world and breathing a new element. Sometimes the loose rocks and shale made the going hard, but to reach that intense white-ness just above and ahead was so exciting that it made struggle negligible. I gained the crest by way of a thousand-foot chute of smooth snow set almost like a wall straight into the sky against the side of the mountain.

Seward, from my heights, looked a pitiable collection of huts, cramped, as it was, on a small flat far beneath the contempt of the peaks, at the head of a narrow fjord.

When I stood, ankle deep in snow, at the top, it seemed as if I had never been in that other world below, of stuffy freight cars and cheap restaurants, but had always known and been known by these wild companions, the immutable pinnacles around me. I had a momentary idea of how it must feel to actually *be* a mountain-top; a sense of complete detachment and independence, in which condition of elation I started to explore the ice-clothed precipices on the other side. But a human and uneasy feeling at the pit of my stomach brought me to the realization of my enormous isolation on these frozen heights, and that the sun was swinging low.

When I returned to the head of the pass, and looked down, it seemed steeper and much more slippery than when I had come up. If I lost my footing on that icy glissade, I should be swirled down over it for a thousand feet to the rocks at the bottom. I no longer had the sensation of immune detachment, and it is well that I lost it, for that almost hysterical feeling, I think, is probably responsible for the deaths of many lone mountaineers.

I had to go down backwards, feeling my toes into the holes I had made on my way up, because the snow had frozen, with the advancing cold of twilight, into a solid icy slide. It was no joke.

August 3. Yesterday, when I started work as a longshoreman again, they told us we could stay on the job at ninety cents an hour as long as we liked. So I liked — and worked from one o'clock in the morning until five the following afternoon, earning almost fourteen dollars — a good day's wages.

We are unloading sections of dredging machinery from a coastwise freighter, hurrying to get this precious cargo off to Fairbanks as soon as possible. I am in the hold under hatch number 3, starboard side, working with a Swede and an Indian.

This job is not very hard, because the pieces we handle are so large that the winch does almost all the work. Great naked pieces of steel machinery — girders, plates, boilers, and derrick arms — in riveted sections sometimes eighty feet long, must be dragged out from the corners of the hold, and slung up through the hatchway.

All the Swede, the Indian, and I do is attach shackles and slings to these pieces where they lie in the darkness, then, when the hook is made fast, we shout to the winch-driver far above. The cable tightens; with crowbars and wedges we guide the huge mass to the light under the opening; the

'Where yer been all this time wit' thet water-can?'

winch-driver holds it poised, while we turn its bulk so as to clear the hatch — and then it is whisked up and up out of darkness, to vanish into the tiny spot of sky.

You have to keep your eyes open when these great hunks of steel are whirling about on the end of a thin fallible cable, writhing in their unmanageable strength. But as soon as the load is once clear of the hatch, we have time for a brief nap while it is being loaded onto a flat car on the dock. Our whole life in the hold centers around the hook. The hook is our only connection with the outside world. When the hook goes up, we are left marooned in a dungeon. When the hook comes down, we must spring to life, to get the load on as quickly as possible. When we need water, it comes down on the hook. Everything we do — everything we either give or receive — depends on the hook.

During the night the work is rather slow and uneventful, but after breakfast, along around nine o'clock, the winch-driver begins to really 'get hot.' He swishes playfully about with his hook and, before lifting away a load, he jerks it up and down once or twice to tighten the slings — incidentally nearly breaking his cable and threatening all our lives.

Once the cable actually did break. It happened just as a gigantic steel section, seventy-five feet long and weighing many tons, had cleared the hatchway, so that fortunately the load did not fall back on us. But a passing Filipino steward tried to dodge it as it crashed upon the deck, and fell forty feet down the adjoining hatch upon the steel cargo. One of his arms was mangled to almost nothing, poor fellow.

August 6. We are at work on a large Japanese ship now, loading scrap iron, and it is another ticklish job. A huge magnet at the end of a cable is dipped into a flat car full of nuts, bolts, springs, wheels, axles, grubhoe-heads, old tools, and all the worn-out multitudinous odds and ends of a mechanistic era.

It rises and swings to a position above the hatchway, the current is switched off, and the magnet releases its clustered store of ironmongery, which falls through the opening, and, with a deafening explosion, strikes the cargo surface to be hurled like shrapnel in every direction. Down in the hold you feel as if you were under shell-fire — sparks fly, dense clouds of dust rise up, and, to all appearances, a high-explosive bomb has gone off.

As the magnet swings overhead, we all scramble to the farthest corners and hide behind posts, but no place is perfectly safe. This morning, during an unusually ferocious period of shelling, a twenty-five-pound anvil struck the wall a foot or two from my head. It is none too comfortable down here at such times.

Every few minutes the barrage is called off so that we can throw the stuff back into the wings of the hold. Our mixed gang crawls out of its various places of retirement and boisterously falls to work. Everyone has a different idea as to what and which should be done, and what all this junk is for, anyhow. There being no bosun around, we voice our opinions vehemently. A little Swede, when confronted with the task of dragging back some tangled sheet iron explains in disgust: 'Olie Yeesus, each o' dese plates could make two tin Lizzies. Vy do dey ship 'em to der Yaps for battleships ven Henry Ford vould make pleasure crafts outen 'em?'

It is always rank with dust in the hold and we have to spit frequently. Some of the men must have developed special salivary glands, for I have timed them, and find that they get in three good spits a minute regularly, during a whole eight-hour shift.

One of my confrères is a burly Scotch-Irishman, closely resembling Premier Ramsay MacDonald except for an undue bleariness of the eye. His possessive instinct being highly developed, he is sorely tempted by some of the useful bits of our cargo. I think he would make off with the whole

shipload if given a chance, for even as it is, at every meal-
time, he smuggles out all his pockets can hold. Yesterday
his acquisitive tendency got him into trouble. As he
climbed out of the hatch, bearing an extra heavy load of
flatirons and axe-heads secreted under his coat, he assumed
a nonchalant air calculated to deceive the mate, who was
regarding his humpy outline suspiciously from the sun-
deck. Unfortunately, as he sauntered casually toward the
gangplank with his gaze high in the heavens, his foot became entangled in a coil of loose rope and he went sprawling.
BOOM! rang out his trophies as they struck the iron deck,
with an impact audible from stem to stern.

The poor man tried to get up, but the load of his illicit
acquisitions was too much, and he could only grunt and
strain. With the veins standing out on his neck, he was
anchored fast, till we had to unpack him and set him on his
feet, amid the jeers of the gang.

August 7. At last a ship bound for Seattle is in, and perhaps with good luck I can get a job on her. Jobs are very
scarce and in huge demand. I have already inquired extensively into each of the three departments — deck, steward,
and engine-room — without success; also there is not even
passage to be bought, either first-class or steerage, nor on
any of the next four boats south. If someone does not quit
soon and give me a place, I shall have to take desperate
measures.

Hundreds of Filipino cannery workers are returning to
the States for the winter. They form part of Alaska's large
migratory population which, like me, is now trying to go
south — with the sun.

Aboard S.S. Yukon — August 9. There was no way out
of it. I had to stow away on this ship — or winter in
Alaska. A waiter in the steerage said that he would provide

me with food, so I bundled up my belongings in preparation to go aboard. I waited until low tide, when the deck was on a level with the wharf, and under the cover of darkness, I sneaked onto the fore well-deck and down a companionway — as far as I know, unobserved.

I soon found, way down in the hold, a secluded space in the overflow cargo, which is stacked near the steerage quarters. This, my lair, is up on top of the salmon cases, just under the hot steam pipes along the ceiling. I think I am pretty safe and I know I am very warm. I am below water level so that there is no fresh air nor light — but to be aboard at all is enough to keep me contented under any conditions.

The situation is more hazardous from the fact that I went to every officer on the ship with my story of being unable to get passage, and they all know me by sight.

I have one piece of chocolate to eat from time to time, but otherwise remain unnourished. This has been my lot for the last thirty-eight hours, ever since we sailed. The steward knows me well, so I can't risk approaching the steerage dining-room region, and have been unable to notify my waiter friend as to my whereabouts.

Until we get across the Gulf to Juneau, I must take no chances. Once there, I shall feel much safer, because at Juneau, if I get kicked off the ship, I can still go south on a fish boat, or one of the small steamers which are comparatively plentiful along that part of the coast.

August 12. The night before last, I got my first real food. I was looking around in one of the forward holds when I found two bear cubs which were being shipped in crates among the rest of the cargo. There was a large supply of raw meat there for them, but they were already stuffed, and it made a regal feast for me, much to their grunted disapproval.

Returning to my place, near the crowded steerage bunk tiers, I continued my solitary retreat. I could hear the noisy chattering of the two hundred Oriental steerage passengers — Filipinos, Japs, and Chinese. They were gambling in small congested groups, along the dirty floor of the bunk aisles, jabbering incessantly and having a merry time. Above me a large rat scurried down the steam pipes, kicking off the heavy dust as he went. I know him well, and often encounter him as he scuttles by on his extensive beat. Time goes slowly, and it seems we shall never get to the end of our string of cannery stops and reach the Gulf.

Last night, however, I had an hour's diversion, which helped tremendously. I crawled out and attended the 'Firemen's Ball' with a fireman friend named Sullivan. He was thoroughly primed and kept telling me that he was a Norwegian fisherman from India.

We clambered up to the firemen's mess, where there was a wild party staged by Sullivan's cock-eyed confrères of the boiler-room. Sullivan had a huge bottle of whiskey in his hip pocket, and swayed to and fro, reciting to his unheeding companions the astounding adventures of one 'Cast-Iron Fred.' At each reel Sullivan's hip came in contact with the table behind him, and smashed still another section off the bottle in his pocket. Eventually he became aware of this tragedy in his pants, and called upon us to drink the remaining whiskey before it should be lost. This we did, and I was also making good use of opportunity to satisfy my howling appetite and to fill my pockets with provisions for the future.

Sullivan's recital about Cast-Iron Fred was characteristic of most sailormen's stories. Whether Cast-Iron Fred actually existed, or whether he was Sullivan's invention, it is impossible to say, but Sullivan gave his tale all the vividness of actual fact. And considering the recklessness and hardihood of this type of man, it might well have been true.

Cast-Iron Fred had been fishing with two companions near a peninsula called Rock Point, when his boat capsized in a storm, forcing the three to swim for their lives.

After a half-hour in the raging sea, two of the men had practically succumbed. Cast-Iron Fred, however, still as strong as ever, towed them several miles to shore, swimming with his legs and a man on each arm. When he reached the beach, his two burdens were completely unconscious and he was somewhat weary himself, so he sat down beside them on the sand for a rest. They failed to come to, and he decided to take them to a doctor, who lived in the nearest town, some twenty-four miles away over the mountains.

Cast-Iron Fred was in the habit of eating canned heat as a delicacy on his bread, and happened to have four tins of it in his pockets. He needed a stimulant, and so, Sullivan explained, instead of reserving his canned heat for its usual supplementary rôle in his menu, he ate the whole four tins at a sitting. He then set out, a man on each shoulder — headed for the hills. On and on he trudged, all night, now and then shifting his load, but without rest. He reached his destination at dawn.

Having saved two lives, he then took sick himself. Possibly he had gone too strong on the canned heat so soon after swimming. Sullivan described his dying day. It was horrible. His face got green and blue, and his blood vessels burst one after another. It was too gruesome to relate here.

While such a tale as this sounds fantastic, knowing these men, their enormous vitality and their reckless expenditure of it, it seems possible to me that Sullivan's story was absolutely true. Cast-Iron Fred's unthinking sacrifice of his life for his friends is another element of the tale which seems entirely characteristic.

August 13. This morning I feel safer. I have made numerous friends and soon we shall be in the Gulf. Even the Filipinos and Japs are friendly with me, and emit cheerful gibberish for my benefit. I am saving three big hash sandwiches which I got at the party, to eat in time of dire need — if my rat friend doesn't steal them first.

The rats are extremely large, and fast, and bold. They are the most extraordinarily agile creatures I have ever seen. One of their most skillful maneuvers is in running along a steam pipe when they come to another pipe resting across the top of it at right angles and against the ceiling. As there is no room, in this case, to jump over the crossing pipe, friend rat must go under this obstruction, swinging out sideways, down underneath it, and then up and back to his slippery course again — all with but four tiny clawed feet to grip the smooth round surface. This feat is performed like lightning, and with a grace and nonchalance that has been my only real thrill in this long cramped week of waiting.

August 14. At last I need worry no longer. We are in the Gulf. We left Cordova late last night and, my cubby-hole having been absorbed by additional cargo, and the danger of being forced to winter in Alaska over, I decided to risk confiding in one of the stewards, hoping to get food from him.

He is a kindly and completely sympathetic fellow, fixed me up a bunk, and sold me a ticket for five dollars which he says will get me by all right. He went so far as to invite me to visit him at his home in the States, and I find he loves to talk about classic literature, despising all modern authors.

Protected by my ticket, I can now go out upon the open foc'sle-head. The wind, as we plough eastward across the Gulf, feels delicious beyond expression after the cramped murk of the hold. It rushes through you, binding the windward side of your clothes to you with a fierce adhesion, and tugging desperately to rip them loose to leeward.

Then back to my narrow canvas bunk at the bottom of a lively tier of Chinamen. Four or five pairs of bare, brown, Oriental legs dangle from the bunks above, and many slit-eyed, high-cheek-boned faces bend over a game of blackjack beside me as I write.

August 15. Times have changed. My situation is very different from what it was yesterday. This morning the mate, who was naturally suspicious of me, asked for my ticket, and, upon examining it, pronounced it 'no good.' It was careless of me to have neglected making certain that my ticket was O.K.

I was taken before the captain, a salty, grizzled old scoundrel, to be arraigned and sentenced for my crime.

'Well, what're you here for?' he bellowed, trying to look as terrible as possible.

'I'm a stowaway, sir,' I answered.

'A stowaway! Hah! And where did you get this fake ticket yer tried to pass off on us?'

'A feller sold it to me,' I said.

At this the blood showed red in his leathery face. He was getting mad.

'Come on!' he roared. 'Who sold it to yer?'

I hesitated. My steward friend would be in dire trouble if I weren't careful. He had tried to help me, and perhaps had made a mistake about the validity of the ticket. At any cost I must remain true to our collusion, however illegal it had been.

I tried to explain this to the glaring skipper — but it was like spraying gasoline on a forest fire. His rage grew almost unmanageable. Holding it barely under control by an effort, he settled slowly back in his chair, glanced briefly at the mate and chief purser, who were looking on, and then, turning to me, grinned from ear to ear. There was no love in that face, however. It was a cold dental smile — about as friendly as the scooper on a steam shovel.

'So yer are standin' in wit' th' rest o' th' bums, eh?' he muttered, in a voice tense with suppressed wrath, 'an' yer don't give a damn about us, eh?' He paused, and his rage seemed to grow till he could control it no longer.

Whirling toward the mate he said viciously: 'Put him in irons, and lock him up in the brig! Give him water, but I'll fire any man caught givin' him anything to eat!' — and, to me, 'Yas, yer goddamned ——! I'll find out from yer yet who gave yer the ticket. Yer ——!'

Well, it's a grim outlook for a while. It was best to submit peaceably to the handcuffs, so here I am. This is the ship's storeroom, but acts as the brig on occasions, as I see by writing on the wall. One inscription reads, 'H.S.S. kept prisoner here on bread and water — May 18th, 1928 — caught two hours out of Seattle.'

Apparently the captain intends to keep me here until we reach Seattle, which will be about four days. He hopes to starve me into squealing on the steward. The nights will be hard, because I am shackled to a short cable leash, the other end of which is fastened to a steel stanchion, and they don't give me a blanket or anything to keep me warm. I don't mind the iron floor, but the cold is weakening, and it is drafty. A little open hatch in the ceiling lets in a chilling wind all night. All this seems rather unnecessary.

I am much comforted to hear the swish of the waves outside our hull as we continue to plough southward. At least I am leaving Alaska. The storeroom door is locked and it is very dull here, but I can keep occupied, as my handcuffs are far enough apart to let me write in this little notebook.

There is much to learn in this room full of piles of rope, tools, various sorts of soap, and ship necessities. On the labels of the packages I can read engaging descriptions of the compositions and uses of lye, lime, and other products.

August 16. Things are much more comfortable. I was rather cramped during the night, but solved the problem of keeping warm by wrapping up in a piece of sail which I found behind some nail kegs, luckily just within reach. The sailors and my friends, in spite of strict orders to the contrary, come and talk with me through the door cracks and through the little hatch. I don't like to ask them for food, and haven't, but several have brought me candy and raisins, so I am having a good time.

The mate came in just after we left Wrangell last night, and let me out for a drink before leading me back to be shackled to my post for the night. It was hard to sleep because of the tight handcuffs, which cut my wrists, but I had rope for a pillow and, with my sail blanket, did quite nicely.

In the morning, the mate appeared again.

'How do you feel now?' he said.

'All right, sir,' I answered truthfully.

He was looking more sympathetic than he did yesterday and, as he unlocked my handcuffs for my morning drink, he said: 'It's too bad you have to stay this way. I don't believe in this sort of stuff, myself, but I have to obey the old man's orders.'

One of the ship's officers, a little later, crawled down through the narrow hatch into my prison — I can't say who he was, as it might lose him his job — with a napkin full of buns and sausages from the galley.

'Here,' he said, in a low voice, 'take this, and don't let anyone know you've had it. And if, by any chance, the old man hears of it, for God's sake don't let him know who gave it to you — or I'll lose my job.'

'Thanks very much, sir,' I said, and he oozed quietly out through the hatch.

The food tasted good and made me feel better, especially as I now knew that I have friends on the ship who are even risking their jobs to help me out.

Later. Yesterday I was quite hungry; but today the presents of sandwiches, candy, apples, oranges, cookies, eggs, meats, and other goods are coming in through the hatch so fast that I have a big supply stocked secretly under various piles of rope. Each donor thinks that he is my sole benefactor, and faithfully contributes his little offering after each meal, entreating me not to tell a soul. I don't, and consequently my food supply is continuously augmented and

more people take pity on me every day. I don't know where I shall put all the food.

The Orientals are not as generous as the whites, but have, nevertheless, contributed an orange and two apples to date. Most of them sneak up to the little hatchway opening, and gaze morbidly at me in silence. I am getting more publicity all the time, in fact too much, as it is very unpleasant to be stared at all day as if I were in a zoo — especially as I cannot avoid their scrutiny. This experience gives me a much better understanding of the feelings of circus animals.

August 17. My friends are getting very bold now — even the Chinese take pictures of me through the hatch, and ask all sorts of questions. Apparently there are rumors around that I have murdered a woman back in Seward and done various other horrible deeds of one sort or another. A friend called Gus went so far as to offer a blow-torch cutter from the engine-room, to cut the cable between my handcuffs and the stanchion.

Gus courageously climbed down the ladder from the hatch into the room here, with a platter full of lettuce, meat, and jam sandwiches — a regular feast — while a Russian friend stood watch at the top. I stowed it all under my rope piles, and Gus was about to leave when the Russian gave the danger signal — so he had to stay down. Then we heard a footstep at the door and a key turning in the lock. The mate! Gus scrambled desperately up the ladder while I tucked the platter out of sight. By that time the mate had entered, and, seeing and hearing Gus as his feet disappeared through the hatch, immediately gave chase. Up the ladder he went, after the culprit — but fortunately Gus got away all right. Gus always was pretty spry.

I am afraid that this incident will not help my relations with the mate. Anyway, starvation is very remote at present. The captain will be much disappointed when he sees me in such robust health when I emerge at Seattle. I wish I knew what he means to do with me.

Finally, after a hearty feed of chicken, cold lamb, salmon croquettes, lettuce, buns and jam, with dessert of apples, oranges, and chocolate cake, I rolled up in my sail for the night. I dreamed of a sandy island somewhere in the South Seas. The beach was coral, the air was balmy, the ladies were broad-minded.

I woke, to find myself in irons in a ship's brig. We were at Ketchikan. In a few minutes the mate came in and unlocked my cuffs. I thought it was for my usual morning drink — but no.

'Follow me,' said the mate.

He led me to the gangplank, and told me I was to be taken ashore. At the foot of the plank, on the wharf, I saw the marshal of Ketchikan and his lieutenant, waiting to meet me. All about were the mountains — spruce forests, bleak cliffs, and the ragged town upon a blue strait.

I didn't like the idea of going to jail in this little town, but realized that it could not be for long, and went peaceably to the marshal's office, where I was put behind the bars in a small, three-cell jail out in the marshal's back yard.

Here, after a few hours' waiting, my Russian jailer gave me a breakfast of hot cakes and syrup, while the marshal, a fat, goggle-eyed party, investigated my baggage and read this notebook. At ten o'clock my case was taken up. It was all very informal. They could prove nothing on me except that I had stowed away, and seemed satisfied that I was neither a pauper nor an habitual criminal. Things got brighter. I paid my fare all the way down from Seward, to put things right with the steamship company — which I had offered to do all along — and they turned me loose.

I stuck around awhile to talk with the marshal, and he

conducted me about the town and introduced me to various fish men with whom I might get passage to Seattle.

Ketchikan — which name struck me as being peculiarly appropriate, both to its circumstances and to my own — is a fish and cannery town — salmon, halibut, and herring. Everybody talks fish. Owners talk of the various species of salmon — kings, pinks, reds, and sock-eyes. Workers talk of salmon — sock-eyes, reds, pinks, and kings. Men who are not working sit around on the fish wharves, talk fish — pinks, sock-eyes, kings, and reds — and clean their fingernails with scaling knives.

I got a room for the night and a much-needed bath — also a date with a deputy clerk girl whom I had met at the marshal's office. But I couldn't keep it, as a little freight and passenger steamer, loaded with salt herring, was sailing at once for Seattle. In the morning sunshine, we chugged out of the dock, limping along on three propeller blades, the fourth having been broken off on a log on the way north. I watched the fish wharves gradually fade into the distance, with the men still sitting — still talking fish — of kings, pinks, reds, and sock-eyes — and cleaning their fingernails with scaling knives.

CHAPTER THREE

HAWAII

Aboard S.S. Manulani, docked at Crockett, California. Between me and Asia there is now but one obstacle — the Pacific Ocean. Midway across its monotony lies Hawaii, peopled by field laborers from every corner of the globe and by every race of the Orient that works — black, brown, and yellow.

Such a collection of different races must afford contrasts that I could find in no other place. It seems well worth while to stop off a week or two in Hawaii, to see how Chinese and Swedes, Filipinos and New-Englanders get along together.

So Honolulu is my next port of call.

When I came aboard last Saturday at the northern end of San Francisco Bay, where this ship was unloading sugar from Hawaii, the first thing I did — as all sailors do — was to find out what kind of a fellow the bosun was. I learned that he is an Italian, that the skipper is Irish, the chief mate German, the second mate Norwegian, the steward Jewish, the carpenter Scotch, and most of the crew Hawaiian. This polyglot outfit get along together in more perfect harmony than on any ship I've seen.

The Hawaiian boys hang on to the revolving windlass as if it were an amusement-park wheel, and dance about, and play beautiful chords on their guitars. Everybody seems in good spirits and very expressive. I saw two Swede sailors kissing each other a fond good-bye on the dock yesterday.

Next to me sleeps a young fellow from Kentucky on his first voyage, and whom we call Blue Grass. He knows nothing about the sea except what he has culled from romantic books, and he is possessed of a certain wistfulness which disarms everyone.

This morning the mate told him to get a broom and sweep off the bridge. He looked a little surprised at the order, and I wondered why he started down the gangplank.

Our dock happened to be beside the huge suspension bridge which spans the Carquinez Straits at this point. Part of Blue Grass's code is to do his duty without asking any questions — no matter how difficult or unreasonable it may appear. Behold Blue Grass — hundreds of feet above our heads on the great steel structure, dutifully working away amid the traffic — sweeping off the bridge!

On Friday we steamed out of the Golden Gate. We had anchored out in the bay to load on some dynamite. Upon weighing anchor, Kane, a Hawaiian boy, and I were sent to the chain locker to stow the great links of anchor chain as they rumbled in from above. It is a gruesome job.

You climb down a hole, just big enough to squeeze through, into a tiny iron box, and stand on the loose chain, struggling to keep your fingers from being knocked off or your legs mangled, as the massive weight descends steadily upon you from the ceiling. You fight and sweat to pack it in the hollow places, and relentlessly the floor rises up beneath you till you have to stoop over and work with the ceiling pressing upon your shoulders. By this time you are exhausted, and wonder how soon you will be swallowed up under this thundering stream of iron. Then, at last, it ceases. You get a little breath, climb thankfully up to the light again, and return to the deck, gouging the rust dust out of your ears.

There are few jobs on shipboard that do not quickly get us filthy, and were it not for the simplicity of taking showers, our skins would never feel the air. But sailors keep themselves surprisingly clean at sea. Washing clothes is made easy by the abundance of buckets, soap, and steaming water in the washroom.

In our cargo we have several hundred chickens which are stacked in crates on deck — and officially presided over by Blue Grass. A fresh egg is a great delicacy to the salty palates of sailors, who, day after day, are fed on insipid stew and uninteresting chunks of meat. We envy Blue Grass, who, privileged with the job of feeding the hens, is in a most advantageous position in regard to eggs.

Bowed with responsibility about hens though he be, Blue Grass is still full of romance about the sea. Whenever he is on deck, he stays on the starboard side and gazes wistfully at the blue vastness before him.

'I much prefer this side of th' ocean,' he says. 'It don't seem nearly so good over on th' other side.'

The old man is trying to learn the principles of calculus, and seeks assistance from everyone from the chief engineer to Blue Grass, who contributes the most interesting solutions to his problems. Blue Grass, who never got beyond algebra in school and doesn't know that this is calculus, has a grand time figuring.

The skipper, a thin, wiry man, has a nervous step, and whistles 'Lilac Time' as he ambles about on the bridge. The third mate, being very lazy, always walks downhill, waiting at each turn for the ship's roll to tilt the bridge to a favorable angle.

Sometimes, on lookout duty, I hear the skipper conversing with Jantzen, the German chief mate. They discuss all sorts of problems and, no matter how little each knows of the particular subject under discussion, they always come to some profound scientific conclusion. The other day they gave a solid hour to the question of how Arabs earn a living. At first, it seemed that the Arabs maintained themselves by stealing from one another, but finally, after lengthy debate, they decided that the Arabs were farmers, and lived on 'herbs and vegetables' grown on 'the fertile Arabian prairies.'

It is getting so hot now that you nearly burn your pants off sitting on the iron hatch. Blue Grass seems to be strangely affected by it, becoming more romantic every day. As we spend the long hot hours hammering rust, he pauses every now and then to burst out with some sententious remark about 'Water, water ev'rywhere an' not a drop ter drink'; or, 'There'll be no moanin' on ther bar when I put out ter sea.'

September 19. I had the four to six wheel this morning, and as the sun rose, toward five-thirty, there before us lay the beautiful island of Oahu.

Japanese, Portuguese, Chinese, ease, and disease, with modern American improvements and tropical surroundings, make up the city of Honolulu.

It is a relaxed and crowded city set among green volcanic hills and translucent waters — a city where everyone seems sufficiently prosperous without undue effort; where electric lights break the warm seduction of tropic nights, and trolley cars clang through every shining hour.

The population is made up of sample groups, large and small, of every race upon earth that dares to set forth upon the sea. The tourist element is largely composed of men who are following the bait of a visionary grass-skirted and lenient brown temptress, and of women who wish to investigate or exploit the well-known laxity of a tropic clime.

It being Sunday, we sailors had the day off, and a gang of us set out toward Diamond Head and the famous long running surf. Waikiki Beach, crowded with tourists and predatory commercialism, seemed rather disappointing and tawdry, except for the surf. The breakers are said to keep their form for a greater distance than anywhere else in the world — about a quarter of a mile — and rows of brown figures could be seen riding shoreward on the crests. It is an art, surfboard riding, and requires, I soon found, long experience and much exasperating failure before your technique enables you to get any thrill from it. Few except natives are at all accomplished in the sport.

You swim out to where the huge combers are formed and are charging in upon you. You jump upon your heavy ten-foot surfboard, trying to work up enough speed not to be left behind as the frothy mountain strikes and bears you toward the beach. You must keep your balance so that the board is continuously coasting down the forward slope of a breaker. Although, to the eye, it appeared simple, I tried all day and never rode more than thirty yards. Nevertheless, even from that, I got a measure of satisfaction, as the other boys, thoroughly disgusted, had given up long before, and returned to the beach to gaze deliriously upon its colorful padding of prostrate society girls.

At sunset we dressed and trolleyed back to town for the evening. It was the last I saw of the crew of the *Manulani*. She sailed the next day, and I repaired with my bulging luggage to an Oriental rooming flat.

September 20. This domicile is run by a deep-voiced Hawaiian of middle age, assisted by a couple of wrinkled Chinamen who talk with their hands, and smile eerily in the presence of strangers. There are also several small black-eyed Hawaiian entertainers, females whose company, I understand, involves an extra expense of three dollars. On inspection, I decided to remain unentertained, but, not wishing to hurt anyone's feelings, I evaded the issue by explaining that, to my capricious taste, these girls were too little. Having disposed of this problem, I went 'proprietously' to sleep.

Sometime in the middle of the night, I was awakened by a stealthy someone entering my room. I thought at first it was a thief, and was acutely aware of the disadvantages, in any possible altercation, of my being so extremely lightly clothed. It was no thief, however, but a Hawaiian entertainer, dark-skinned and very, very, very fat. My obliging

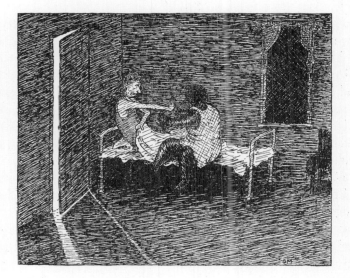

host, wishing to please, had scoured the neighborhood for hours for an entertainer who was not 'too little.' This lady, hopefully provided according to specifications, and who closely resembled a stout baboon, was about five feet tall and must have weighed well over two hundred pounds.

She was pertinacious in her intention to entertain, but without unduly hurting her already lacerated feelings, I finally
persuaded her to retire, on the ground that I was too sleepy
to receive callers.

Since then I have dwelt uneventfully in this crude abode,
though not without hearing much of interest through the
thin partitions.

By day I explore this balmy isle. Traversing Nuuano
Pali, a pass in the mountains, I reach the northern coast and
wander among the native banana plantations and see the
brown surf fishermen who harpoon squid, a small species of
octopus, for food. Though reticent until you get to know
them, they are very friendly. They seem to take pride in
avoiding as far as possible the ways of civilized progress,
and play and sing much of the time, seeking food only when
there is none left in the hut.

'Aloha, Aloha,' one greets me, asking in childish glee if I
will come and have a little dried fish or some poi, a native
food made by mashing the doughy taro root. They all speak
some English, but their simple life is still virgin to the education rapidly spreading outward from Honolulu. They
never wear shoes, and keep on the same scant clothes all the
time, in the water and out.

'Maikai maanei — plenty nice here,' the Kanaka says,
and tells me of the comforts of never having to worry about
hunger, and how delightful it is to make mele — music —
all day, or sleep on his soft grass floor. Prying further into
his life, I hear that once the men who were the best poi-
pounders got the most beautiful girls, but that now 'you
mus' go halekula — school — mus' got money.' 'Ev'thing
go fish,' he says — 'Everything has gone to the dogs.'
'Wahine no come — The girls don't come across,' he adds
sadly.

Hawaiians such as these are the last vestiges of a lost
Paradise. Most of the native population is of an Oriental

mixture, educated along modern lines, and living much as does the Oriental element in California.

Sugar is by far the most important industry in these islands, and its cultivation requires a squatting position for the worker. Orientals squat much more successfully than Nordic races, and the labor problem here has been to induce races with squatting proclivities to come to Hawaii.

A century or so ago, Chinese were imported as field workers. Then came Japanese and a sprinkling of Portuguese and Russians, as the industry grew following the reciprocity treaty of 1876, when the United States extended tariff aid in exchange for the Pearl Harbor naval base. But after 1898, when the islands were annexed as a Territory of the United States and received the full benefits of a protective sugar tariff, the industry assumed such proportions that a tremendous labor problem arose, especially after the immigration restriction on Orientals. Labor was sought all over the world; they tried everybody from Swedes to Cubans; but a solution was reached only with the comparatively recent importation of Filipinos, who are now squatting all over the place. All this explains the weird mix-up of races in these islands.

Filipinos seem more turbulent than either Japs or Chinese. You should see one of them drive a trolley car. A trolley is usually an unemotional conveyance, but Filipinos put a lot of expression into their driving. Sometimes when you hear a trolley coming down one of these hills, you can tell from the noise that the dusky driver suspects his wife of perfidy.

My exploring continues day by day. On my way up a mountain, I pass a gigantic drooling banyan tree, under which native women weave mats of lahola leaves, and soon I am enveloped in the mist which lies along the heights. The windward sides of the mountains are dense with heavy jungle, massed with fern and vines. The leeward slopes are often arid desert, yielding only sparse grass. The reason of this is that the clouds, borne on the trade winds eternally from the northeast, drop all their moisture in rain upon the northern side of the mountain barrier, and leave the southern slopes unwatered.

Climate here is therefore distinctly local. I know of an aged lady who has moved, upon doctor's advice, to a new house, hoping to benefit by a change of climate. Her new home is scarcely half a mile from the old. The rainfall on Hawaii varies locally from fifteen to two hundred and seventy-seven inches a year.

Yesterday, while walking along the road near Koko Head, I was picked up by two Hawaiian boys who gave me a ride in their flivver. In this easy-going country hiking is apparently unheard of, and they couldn't believe that I had come on foot from Honolulu. They were going fishing, so I went along too. We wound our way on and on through a sort of desert, greatly resembling the more arid parts of Arizona, where there was nothing but red dust and gray, bony algaroba trees, until we finally reached the sea.

From the cliffs, we threw our weighted lines far out into the thundering surf and hauled in all sorts of gaudily painted creatures. My companions, who, I think, were not pure Hawaiian, but part Portuguese and Chinese, seemed well educated, and they volunteered much information about Honolulu. They were workers in the great Dole Pineapple Cannery, and today being the legal holiday when the inter-island rowing regatta takes place, they had time off in which to go fishing.

September 24. I have made great social progress lately, and now reside in a hospitable household far removed, both physically and spiritually, from my former ignominious abode. I dine with Honolulu's best and, between meals, continue my private explorations.

Today I visited the fish market, which purveys every-thing fishy from goldfish to octopi — its customers all the races of the East. I saw a Chinese fish dealer trying to sell a large eel to an old Japanese lady who didn't want it. He kept poking it at her, with his eyes bulging and emitting a stream of Chinese fish-sales-talk. She had good Japanese sales-resistance, and backed away, but he pursued her for some distance, holding the slimy carcass into her face and explaining passionately the good points of the eel.

My host's cook is a Japanese woman, and tells me much of how to prepare tropical fruits, from roasted breadfruit to papaia in rum. She is stocky and nervous and, like most of the ignorant population, very superstitious.

There have been many violent earthquakes on Hawaii Island in the last day or two, and a few slight shocks here, and it all has a very portentous significance for her. The Hawaiians are greatly excited about it and hope for a violent eruption. Far from fearing a flow of lava, they regard it as an omen of good will from Pele, the fire goddess, who is the outstanding power in the Hawaiian religion. Apparently no native Hawaiian has ever been harmed by a volcano, except in 1790, when an entire division of an army, march-ing against Kamehameha the Great, was wiped out by a sudden eruption; but that incident is justified, as Pele was defending the future king, Kamehameha, the Napoleon of the Pacific.

The Hawaiians are thoroughly used to volcanic dis-turbances, and have good reason to be. This whole coun-try has been piled up by volcanoes, until now the heights of Mauna Kea rise fourteen thousand feet above sea-level, and over thirty-two thousand feet above the ocean floor, which profound abyss completely surrounds the islands.

September 27. There are girls here of all shades from pale yel-low to chocolate. Some of them are really lovely, but their lure in many instances is materially deadened by the fact that a tot or two is trotting along behind, and, with some, there is an attendant flabbiness which is a very poor stimulus to romance. The competition for the good ones is far too keen for a man of my sartorial squalor, and the ones not so good — are not so good.

The climax of my recent social ascent has been reached. Yesterday I had tea with the Governor of the Islands, from whom I learned much concerning Hawaiian political machinery, which is similar to that of Alaska, these two being the only Territories of the United States.

The Governor showed me around his house, which is something of a museum. In one room is the bed of Queen Liliuokalani, the last monarch of the Hawaiian dynasty. This piece of furniture is built of the strongest koa wood, and covers about six square yards of floor space. Judging from this and from her violent political record, Queen Lil must have been quite a girl.

September 29. Football seems to be the most popular sport among the brown boys, with the possible exception of swimming. It is played from the moment they can walk, and barefoot — which bothers them not at all. They punt and drop-kick as well as any boys with shoes.

Yesterday morning I watched a game played by a bunch of Chinese, Japanese, Portuguese, Filipino, Irish, and whatnot kids, ranging from the ages of four to ten, and of all sizes. The individual star of the game was a Chink kid by the name of T. Fat. He would call out the signals, 'Fort-i-eight, nine-ti-t'ree, a hundert-'n-six, banana!'

Then the ball would be snapped, and, catching it and poking it under his arm, off he would go around the end as fast as his little legs could flutter. When his Portuguese and Irish interference had been left behind, he would resort to a wild straight-arm accompanied by a savage glare from little black eyes and a formidable showing of teeth. Down the field he would dodge his way — like a chipmunk on a wall.

This continued all morning, and when the game ended, our hero was whisked ignobly home to dinner by his pig-tailed big sister, K. Fat, aged eight.

By good luck, I have become *persona grata* with a Japanese family in Kaimuki. The first I saw of them was a tiny black-haired baby sitting under a giant monkeypod tree, sucking his fist, and an old brown horse grazing in the long grass a few feet away. There was no one else in sight — just the horse and the baby, each completely absorbed in his own gustatory endeavors. After I had made friends with them both, which I did shortly, along came the mamma, a sturdy Japanese lady with bare brown feet, all muddy from weeding in her vegetable garden.

She smiled, and we all sat down under the tree — the baby, the Japanese lady, and I, with the horse — to talk things over. Later, I met papa — a man of political ambitions. He sometimes delivers fiery stump speeches to large brown crowds in the city park, propounding the favorite code of 'Down with the big industries! Give the common people a hand in managing the sugar plantations! Down with the rich business men who do none of the work, but reap all the rewards!'

October 3. This town is a hell of a place to get a job on a

ship, especially going west to the Orient. The foreign
ships have Oriental crews entirely, and the American ships
are completely filled up by the time they get here.   Evidently my only chance is that one of the sailors off a west-
bound ship may get pickled on shore and fail to get back
aboard on time, and that I can get his place. Of course this
is unlikely — not the pickled part, but that I could get his
place. There are hundreds of sailors on the beach here,
hounding every mate in the port for a job.

Last Thursday, by good luck, I met a fellow who knew
the chief mate on the Dollar Liner, *President Madison*, and
finally we got the chief to promise me a job should any of
the crew fail to turn up.

As I waited drearily on the dock, hoping hour after hour
to hear of somebody's quitting the ship, I watched dejectedly the first-class passengers trooping to and from
their floating palace. Occasionally I conversed with loiter-
ers like myself who were, also, probably waiting for their
break. One was a curly-haired fellow of about thirty-five,
dressed in a blue shirt and black pants.

'Tryin' to get a ship out of this place?' he asked, with a
cultivated accent.

'Yes,' I replied, 'and you?'

'The same,' he said. 'I'm aimin' for Asia, and it's slow
goin'. I've plenty of money to buy my passage, but I like to
save money when I can. This ocean's such a long way
across, it's worth waitin' a few weeks to get a job, instead of
payin' a hundred and fifty bucks for a ticket.'

Hank, as he called himself, seemed to think that the
quickest and surest way to get to the Orient from Honolulu
was to ship back to 'Frisco and to sign on for the Orient in
that port, where the crews are originally made up.

'There's very seldom any vacancies for the East out
here,' he said, and advised me to return to 'Frisco at the
first opportunity. He seemed a well-meaning fellow, and I

thanked him for his advice, but, for myself, decided to remain in Honolulu till I could go East direct.

When it came time for the Madison to sail, as Fate would have it, every man jack was on board. I had been under terrific temptation to give a little party on shore for the sailors, and get them sufficiently fried so that one of them, at least, could not walk up the gangplank. But such a course would be most unsportsmanlike.

I shall have to wait for a break. Anyhow, I know the brother of the second mate on the next week's Dollar steamer. To anyone on the beach in Hawaii, this offers a glittering possibility.

I met a barber the other day who advised me, as a solution to my problem, to state that I was shipping for the whole voyage — Kobe, Singapore, Suez, New York — and then desert the ship wherever I wanted to get off. This idea seemed to me the depth of nautical perfidy, and, besides, I didn't like the haircut he gave me. He got his job, he told me, by saying, although he knew nothing of the tonsorial art, that he had been a skilled barber for years.

October 7. I have just returned from a most horrible experience, which I was extremely lucky to get out of at all. It has taught me a lesson — you should never go mountain-climbing with submarine men's daughters.

Today I set out for a peaceful walk with two girls who are daughters of a submarine commander. Suddenly they said they wanted to go up a mountain. Unwittingly, and to my undying regret, I took them to the base of a steep ridge and started to lead them upwards.

All went well for the first thirty seconds, and then they began to give out. To make matters worse, they had with them their dog, Dan, who, being extremely old, did nothing to aid our progress. In fact, I was forced to boost his woolly frame up many a rocky knoll.

The girls were even worse. I gave them fight talks every few feet, telling them how much nicer it was higher up, and what a wonderful view they would have at the top, but to

no avail. They persisted in flopping every time I let go of their arms. The higher we went, the more hopeless the situation became. Finally, one of the daughters refused to go another inch, and flopped into a pink heap on a little ledge of rock. I continued with the other daughter, leaving the tottering hound and his gasping mistress to be picked up on the way down. Resolutely, I pushed and dragged the surviving daughter on and up, till finally we could see the top, a few feet above us. Notwithstanding the fact that we were only eight hundred feet above sea-level, she gave, at this juncture, vivid symptoms of exhaustion and collapsed in her thirty-seventh swoon, complaining in mortal terror that she couldn't breathe because of the rarity of the atmosphere.

I dragged and dragged, and after another hour got her to the top. She then positively refused to go down again. She wouldn't budge, and I certainly would not carry her down through all that jungle, single-handed. It was getting dark, and here I was, on a mountain-top with two passed-out submarine man's daughters lying in heaps and a considerable distance apart. What should I do? Personally, I think few men living have faced such a problem.

Finally, I persuaded the highest-up daughter to be led down the other side of the mountain, where I was fortunate to find a fairly smooth path; and at length I got her down to a town where there was a trolley line. She said she could get home all right from there, so I rushed back over the mountain to rescue the other daughter and the hound before it was pitch-dark. By seven o'clock I got the dog and the daughter from the ledge and safely home — but the other daughter, whom I had left to come home by herself in a trolley, had not appeared.

The submarine father began to get panicky at this point, so I set out once more on a search. I went over the whole blooming mountain again, to be sure she had not changed her mind and tried to come home that way — you never can tell about submarine men's daughters. Not a trace; so I ransacked most of the suburbs of Honolulu for her — all in pitch-darkness and in vain. I got back just before midnight, to find the submarine family in a state of uproar over possible perils to the absent daughter. As they approached the verge of summoning the militia, in comes the daughter, somewhat bedraggled and looking utterly irresponsible. I never was more delighted to see a dame in my life. I vowed then and there never again to go near a mountain with a submarine man's daughter.

October 10, *still in Honolulu.* This job situation is getting serious. I am certainly on the beach. I have missed my chance again. It was a close call — I was aboard and in my work clothes with my stuff all stowed in the foc'sle, but the reveling sailors appeared, and I had to go ashore just as the gangplank came up. Nothing could be more exasperating.

Hank, of the cultivated accent, was there on the dock at the time.

'Yes,' he said, 'I'm sure the only sensible thing to do is to ship back to 'Frisco. There's a boat goin' tomorrow mornin'. I think I'll go on her. What d'you say?'

Talking further with this smooth-shaven loiterer, I learned that he is an aviator, human fly, and professional dare-devil. He gave proof of his statements by producing hair-raising photographs of himself in action. He further admitted that he has five wives in various parts of the world — whom he always tries to keep from knowing about one another — and that he is at present on his way to the Orient in order to escape from a concubine who wants to do him in.

Again I am in a rooming-house, a different one, which is presided over by a gaunt, bushy-haired white woman, who drinks beer all day and, whispering to herself, scuffs down the hall with jangling keys to open the mop closet. She is stone deaf and can talk only in a faint murmur which, together with the effects of drinking, renders her almost totally inane. Between swigs of beer, she gnaws constantly at a handful of lettuce, and as constantly entertains favored lodgers in her room. She is obviously the ruin of something — of just what, the Lord only knows.

Going along the street last night, I heard, from a vine-covered bungalow, a group of Hawaiians singing some of their old, old songs. In these islands of many pleasures, nothing has been such a joy to me as the native music.

The deep and mellow voices are accompanied by the steely twanging of the Hawaiian guitars. Each chord is a somnolent harmony, with a vital insistence in it — a call, that must be answered in the chord following. You anticipate this answer, agonized by the realization that nothing in the world but one particular chord can satisfy your starving ears. It comes. You feel the utter hopelessness of trying to appease your hunger for it during its fleeting contact with your senses, and even in its answering harmony is another asking that must be answered again. At last comes the tonal fulfillment of all these insistent askings, and you feel that you cannot hear it enough — you can't absorb all there is of answer in its harmony. Even hard-boiled sailors on the loose are reduced from noisy jeering to humble silence under the spell of this music, that works like a strong opiate, at the same time arousing and obliterating — utterly primitive, and completely sad.

October 17. Yesterday I had a job on the *President Jackson*, but today I haven't any job on the *President Jackson*. As soon as they found out that I would go only as far as the Orient, they gave it to another fellow. Very discouraging — I shall have to concentrate on freight steamers. Freighters are far less exacting in making up a crew.

To my surprise, Hank was still there on the dock.

'I've just missed that last boat for 'Frisco,' he said, 'but I'm all set for one the day after tomorrow. Yes, that's the only thing for us to do. We'll be waitin' till Christmas if we stay here.'

October 19. Since my latest failure to make a ship, on Thursday, I have been staying at the Seamen's Institute with other unemployed sailors. It is a dreary place. The men hang around all day, playing cards in the common room, or lie on the grass plot out in front and beg nickels and dimes off passers-by to keep fed or, if possible, boozed.

I can lie on my bed and put each foot and hand on a different one of the four walls of my cage-like room. The partitions are made of chicken-wire except for a strip of beaver-board at a height above the floor most conducive to modesty. Sleeping is difficult because of proximity to other caged inmates and the inevitable sounds and smells.

The man next to me is a burly cook with long red hair which hangs before his face in a carroty streamer as he leans over to prune his feet, just beyond my feeble chicken-wire barricade. Every night at about ten he starts, and chokes steadily until morning. With an explosive sound ending in a convulsive gulp, he clears his throat and then gags desperately for several minutes, when, after a brief respite, he repeats the process. I feel quite concerned about him — the lining of his throat must be in a hideous condition — and yet he seems not in the least ruffled by his experiences, and in fact maintains an attitude of the most phenomenal serenity and endurance.

Fortunately for me, I am a high-powered sleeper. It takes more than an average ability in that line to become or to remain unconscious, with a red-haired cook choking apparently to death only three or four feet away and with nothing between save chicken-wire. As sailors, we are all inured to snoring, which rolls like a great chorus from every foc'sle on the seven seas. But here, in this nautical refuge, where every known type of marine nasality reverberates through the dark halls of chicken-wire, accompanied by an overtone of esophical spasms from my culinary neighbor — it is almost too much.

On the street today I encountered Hank again.

'Oh, hello, so you're still here?' I said.

'Oh, yes — but I shall be goin' on the next boat for 'Frisco. I've decided that there's nothin' in waitin' here, and I've just come from Pier 13, seein' about a freighter that sails tomorrow. Perhaps you can get a place on her if you hustle — how about it?'

CHAPTER FOUR

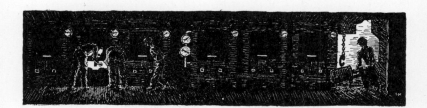

THE ENGINE-ROOM

Aboard Dollar Liner — Japan bound — October 28. At sea again! My chance came at last, yesterday, when this scow docked at six A.M. It is known as the worst ship in the fleet, and there were seven vacancies, three on deck, four below.

I signed on in the 'black gang' as a wiper, it being an unskilled job in which they care little where you quit. The two wiper vacancies were caused by the first assistant engineer, who sent the boys diving in the bilge for his pet monkey wrench. They dived — and deserted. The oiler who quit was lovesick and wanted to get back to 'Frisco. A fireman had to be taken ashore because Bunny, the junior engineer, accidentally broke four of his ribs with a sledgehammer. This engine-room seems full of human interest.

Oddly enough, the wounded fireman's place has been taken by Hank, who is now in the boiler-room watching the steam gauges — and probably wondering, as he paces up and down, whether his five wives are still in the dark as to his whereabouts.

Heat and sweat and oil. That's all we see, feel, hear,

smell, and taste in the engine-room. Everything, even the railing, is too hot to touch. Gloves are a necessity, and our pockets are stuffed with dozens of rags to supplement the gloves in handling hot machinery. We glisten all over from oil and sweat; we drip and trickle all day long, and drink water constantly — four of us emptying a two-quart pitcher every fifteen minutes. Even so, our mouths are so dry we can't spit. The water pours through us like a brook, and our sweat is almost as pure as the water. The heat is so terrific that we must stand one minute under the ventilator to about every three minutes of work.

All today we wipers worked in the boiler-room, blowing tubes, taking turns in holding the steam blower against the hot-air pipe ends till all the soot was gone. The boiler-room is a narrow passageway between eighteen boilers — the hottest place on earth. Before my eight hours were up, I was sick from the fierce heat, the smell of oil, and a belly full of water. Gulping such floods is not good for anyone, but it is ecstasy to feel it trickle down your gullet, and we all do it anyhow.

October 31. In an engine-room force — the black gang — there is more individual responsibility than among men employed on deck. There is the independence of mechanics rather than the subservience of gang workers. We have a certain amount of polishing up gadgets and so on, but none of the squeegeeing and rust-chipping of the 'top side.'

Down in this dark, hot jungle of machinery we must tend every minute the enormous arms of steel, bathed in oil, that surge in and out of blackness. We serve the leaping piston rods through their untiring labor; the propeller shafts of three hundred feet of steel, eight feet around; the journals, bearings, cross-heads, crank-pins, guides, and joints. Night and day — day and night — in and out — up and down, we tend this ordered violence with sweat and toil and oil.

The propeller shafts — the core of the ship's movement — turn in their journals without variance of a thousandth of an inch — a glistening mass of power so smooth that you can inadvertently lean against it, so terrible in its strength that it can drive a ship of twenty thousand tons across the Pacific Ocean at fifteen knots an hour.

The firemen must always be on watch to keep the fires and oil pumps right, and the steam at 230°; the water tenders can never let up their vigilance in watching the gauges. The oilers must be ever on the job to keep the bearings lubricated; and we wipers must help with all manner of undertakings, and do odd jobs for the engineers.

I like being a wiper because I do so many different things and learn more than if I were specializing. You must be alert down below. The massive lengths of steel are gesticulating on every side of the narrow passageways, the floor is hot and slippery with oil. I have to stoop almost everywhere, and where I can stand upright it is most uncomfortable, as the heat rises, and the higher you are, the hotter. Nothing is large enough for me around here — doors, ladders, and passageways are built for shrimps like Freezer, the refrigerator engineer.

Bunny, the junior engineer, is another victim of size. Half Hawaiian, half Indian, he is built like a cave man and weighs about two hundred and forty pounds. His extreme absent-mindedness makes him a thoroughly dangerous associate in this engine-room region of ruthless forces. Yesterday he wrecked Red, the Jewish wiper with a mouth like a tapir, who was holding a bar wrench which Bunny was turning by great strokes from a sledgehammer. In an absent-minded moment Bunny hit Red instead of the wrench, and when that unfortunate had been removed to the sick bay, I warily took his place.

'Say, big boy,' says Bunny, between terrific swats at the wrench I was steadying, 'you're just the right size for a cop' — whang!

'How about yourself?' I reply, my eye on the swinging sledge that had ruined two of my predecessors.

'Aw, Kerize, I'm not big enuv,' he goes on, wielding the sledge with strength like a steamhammer. 'But say' — whang! — 'you ought ter be a cop in Los Angeles. Ever been there? It's a great town if yer got a job' — whang! — 'but no good if ye're broke. Too many jugs. When they get enuv guys workin' they put the rest in the jug. Kerize — what a town' — whang!

I was still alive and uninjured when we got the dynamo plate loose, and he then asked me if I would help him find something that he had been working on the day before, and had absent-mindedly mislaid. It was a piston head — a cylinder of steel four feet long and weighing two hundred pounds — and he said he simply couldn't remember where he had left it.

In our black gang also is Fatty, the oiler, an Irish socialist who tells me how to get by with the shaft-alley station. Being the coolest place in the engine-room, the job of wiping in the shaft alley is a wiper's idea of heaven.

'Ya wanna get th' shaft-alley station and keep it,' advises Fatty. ''Tis th' only good job in th' whole stinkin' place. 'Tis a job ya can do in fife minutes — but take yer time — take yer time. Shure, take th' whole eight hours to it ivery day, an' yer'll keep th' job. 'Tis easy, shure, to get by, wit' brains.'

But I would rather work with Bunny, in spite of the incidental risk of being crippled for life; his knowledge of mechanics is extraordinary — he is a cave man with first assistant engineer's papers and an active mind that works with the exact logic of his machinery.

His character is a constant interest to me. About food, women, and other human necessities his psychology is that of his Indian and Kanaka forebears — these things must be obtained by measures fair or foul. This is just as logical to Bunny as that too much steam pressure will burst a boiler.

But about things beyond his experience — beyond the engine-room and the simple needs of man — he has no sense of relative values, and his keen and restless brain wanders away from this well-understood job before him into an abyss of speculation. No wonder he is absent-minded.

Yesterday we collaborated on a job of plumbing, which is difficult work for Bunny — he's a bit too vague to be a successful plumber. Undaunted when he bores a hole askew, he says, 'Aw, Kerize, look what I done. But, hell, it don't make no difference — I don't hafta bore straight 'cause I can bend pipe with m' hands' — which is true.

Yet, during the moments when his mind is on his work, he will file and fit cylinder rings with the most amazing skill and precision — until, as always, he turns, in disconnected musings, to the troubles of his lonely, unsatisfied soul.

It is in books that poor Bunny seeks things outside his own sordid experience, explanations of the life that he sees around him and that he neither shares nor understands. Last evening, up on hatch number four, he was reading a book called 'Silken Sin,' and suddenly threw it on the deck. 'Kerize,' he said, 'that book's too ord'nary fer me — I know all that stuff already. It don't tell me nothin' I wanter know.' Then his attention drifted upward to the saloon deck where the passengers were having their evening dance. His deep-set black eyes changed as he beheld the young female forms whirling to the bleating saxophones. 'Cheesus — I could do with some of them,' he said.

November 1. We have an Eskimo fireman in the boiler-room. His name is Pooph. It seems a strange place for an Eskimo, but, as a matter of fact, he stands the heat better than anyone. Pooph informs me that, contrary to the common belief, Eskimos live in quite a high temperature and are used to a stuffy atmosphere. According to him, they spend almost all of their lives indoors. He says that the thermometer in a well-run igloo seldom stands below 80° and is generally about 90°. A fire is always going, and the family, usually fat, and wearing caribou underclothes, fills up most of the igloo. Eskimos also are used to grease and oil, so Pooph gets along finely in the engine-room — he even chuckles with little grunts as he trudges sweating up and down.

After we finish work we have our daily grease-removing session in the firemen's can. At lunch we wipe only around our mouths, but at five o'clock we try to clean the whole of our faces and as much of our arms and bodies as we have soap or strength for. It takes hours, even with the aid of coal-oil, and we never completely cease to be greasy. Everything is greasy where we live, the walls, the bunks, our clothes, our blankets, our food — even the air we breathe.

The only relief is at night after work, when we can sit on deck and feel the cool winds of the mid-Pacific. The waves have steadily increased in size since we left port, and now assume proportions such as I have rarely seen. They zoom past us in great frothy ridges some two hundred feet apart, over which our hulk levels and dives in compliant solemnity, surrounded by a border of foam, rebellious that we should interrupt its wild spree with the northeast trade.

These are more than mere waves. They are part of the ocean's body, and seem the surface gestures of some spirit in the black depths reaching for miles below us — its power moving in their compacted ranges as they sweep over this desert of water.

November 2. In this little world that is a ship, the Chinese mess boys are at the bottom of the social ladder. The sailors make the poor creatures' lives even more miserable than they already are, worrying them like a pack of hounds, and sending them on all sorts of fool errands, just for the satisfaction of giving an order and seeing them cringe and quail. Spoons are thrown — curses yelled by these firemen covered with grease except around their mouths, and howling for more food.

'For God's sake, Charlie, snap out of it wit' that pie! Hand it over or I'll kick yer in yer bloomin' Chinee tail!' The ultimate brotherhood of man is hardly helped along by our meals.

And yet I talked this evening with a bunch of the older sailors about the oppression of the working classes, as I have on other ships, for it is a favorite subject. Most of the younger men are making a temporary expedient of the seafaring life. They have hopes and ambitions to advance themselves — to become engineers, aviators, or business

At Sea — Off the Coast of Japan

men. But among the old salts who find that they are still
in the foc'sle after years of sailoring, there is great dis-
content.

They have very primitive and radical ideas. To 'capitalism' — an utterly vague term to most of them — they
generally attribute their failures, disappointments, and de-
ficiencies. They are convinced that 'capitalism' is responsible for all the present-day ills, and that things were better
in the past. Progress, with its context of higher prices, pro-
hibition, laws restricting personal freedom, unemployment,
and world wars, compares unfavorably with the 'good old
days.'

'Sure,' says Fatty the oiler, whose eyes always bulge
under the strain of mental effort, 'sure, capitulism is th'
roun of us all.'

He is the staunchest socialist in the entire force of engine-
room radicals.

''Tis true. Once I had near fife hundert dollars wot I got
in business wit' a feller from Pago Pago. But hell! Cana-
paltism! 'Tis why I am only a stinkin' oiler tiday. Thim
rich loafin' canipalists is gyppin' all the hard-wirkin' guys
in th' wirrld — th' wirkin' men wot keeps th' country goin'
while thim loafers sits on their fat tails. Cheesus! I wisht
it was still th' good old days whin an honist man had a
chanst. Sure,' he continues, 'canibulism's what caused th'
war, yer know. Iverybody says so — iverybody wot wirks.
Whin I was in France that's wot they all said. Th' rich
loafin' canibalists lended money to th' allies an' thin they
made all us wirkin' men fight so's they wouldn't lose it.
Cannibalism!' Then, virulently, as his eyes bulge even larger,
'Muther o' Cheesus! I'd like ter git me hands on 'em.'

It seems tragic that so many of these men are discouraged, and filled with rebellion and complaint. They have
given up trying to coöperate with employers or to better
themselves, and have fallen to a life of animal gratification,

tormented by unfulfilled ambitions which they feel have been balked by a vague thing they call 'capitalism.' It becomes a sort of delusion of persecution.

Perhaps if public schools taught the principles of economics in place of the date of the Spanish Armada or the names of the African rivers, these men would be less unhappy in their point of view.

November 6. It is hard to write on this ship. The only available place is here in the messroom, where a lot of the old-timers are always talking. They pester me with questions as to why I am writing — why do I want to get off at Kobe, and don't I think it's a shame that steak costs so much these days?

Meanwhile, I struggle to record that, being considered more powerful than the other men, I was yesterday given the job of lifting the steam-pump pistons out of their cylinders, and carting them back and forth up the three flights of engine-room ladders to be reconditioned in the machine shop. To carry a hundred-and-seventy-five-pound piston in that heat, and with the steps oily and slippery, was a ticklish business. If I had lost my grip, it would have fallen down about eighty feet to the engine-room floor.

At night we sleep on deck on the hatch-covers, as no one could rest in our quarters, which are directly over the engine-room and as hot as a foundry. Sometimes, during the night, we hit a squall. We wake up to find ourselves marooned on a little tarpaulin island and the decks awash, as great obsidian mountains of water jar the ship, and plunge, and sweep sizzling around us. We can't sleep then — we can only look on in awe, and feel the overwhelming power of the sea.

CHAPTER FIVE

JAPAN

November 7. Last night was stormy — high waves, wind, and black rain. But this morning, as the fog thinned, we could see to port a rugged, mountainous coast — the first land for twelve days. Japan! Soon ships appeared near us; passenger ships, freight steamers, battleships, and lateen-rigged fishing-boats. We were in Kobe Harbor.

I had to work below till two o'clock, overhauling the main crank-pins, then got my pay of twenty-four yen, said good-bye to my oily friends, and went ashore.

At first, everything appeared just as in any port in the United States — except for the sampans with square-ribbed sails. At the foot of the wharf, I climbed into a rickshaw.

My sack of possessions, added to my weight, almost lifted the wrinkled little rickshaw man off the ground, but away we trotted, silently and swiftly through the streets. It was still foggy and, although the rows of sooty office buildings and automobiles which occasionally glided past us seemed familiar enough, I became aware of an intangible alien presence in the atmosphere. Then pretty soon the Orient began to define itself.

As we penetrated deeper into the misty city, things grew smaller and smaller and Japanesier. There was an end to the brick warehouses and banks, and we passed only frail little shops of teapots and strange vegetables. The streets grew narrower. The people were tiny — little men with brown shaved heads, doll-like women in delicate silks scuffing along in their wooden sandals and carrying babies on their backs, and children in black uniforms playing on the sidewalks. There were no more automobiles — the streets were too narrow for them. Instead, we were surrounded by hundreds of bicycles, pushcarts, wheelbarrows, and other hand conveyances — all moving rapidly, rattling and zipping hither and thither in complete confusion. Some held tremendous cargoes of vegetables, or lumber, or clinging human forms.

We came to some railroad tracks where, down the line a way, were several Japanese freight cars on a siding. They were each about fifteen feet long, and two men were pushing one up the track toward us. On we went among the swarming crowds and clattering sandals and whizzing wheels, till we came to a certain alley, where we stopped. It was a Japanese hotel.

I alighted with my bag, and walked through the garden to the door, as the rickshaw man trotted off into the traffic. There was an old bald-headed Jap there, and, as I mounted the steps, six little Japanese ladies appeared, with their high black hair and dainty silk. I took off my shoes at the threshold, according to the Japanese custom, but the Japanese ladies couldn't find anything to fit me among all their slipper supply. There was much laughter and tittering as I entered barefoot and followed the old man upstairs to my room.

This was a very small enclosure, quite empty except for a little square table about ten inches high, and a screen standing in a corner. The room was oddly beautiful, because of its simplicity, the irregular mural design and the position of the screen. But what on earth to do with my lamentable six-feet-five of person I couldn't imagine.

It seemed queer to be in such a bare room — with no chair, bed, or anything to sit on but the floor, and I was considering the situation when in trooped the six little Japanese ladies. They had a teapot, teacup, and various other things with them, including a huge glazed pot full of ashes which it took three of them to carry. They set this down on a cushion, then gave me another cushion, and proceeded to pour out some green tea. So I sat down on the floor, and while I was quaffing tea, they continued to shuffle about with short steps, arranging more cushions and crockery and muttering mirthfully in Japanese. I offered them some tea too, but they only tittered the more.

What was it all about? I had not the slightest clue as to the purpose of the pot of ashes, and didn't know whether to use it as a spittoon, as an ash tray, or whether it was some sort of toilet arrangement. I later knew it as a hibachi or fire-pot, with which the Japanese warm their houses in winter.

The girls looked to me like rosy little babies about four years old, and, as I couldn't understand their language, or make out what they were up to, I anxiously waited to see what would happen. Presently they produced some soap and a scrub brush, and took me into a tiny place which seemed to be a sort of bathroom. I thought that they now would leave, but no — the six of them insisted on taking off my clothes and giving me a thorough bath, during which they scrubbed my back with their little brush and chattered gleefully the while. It all was, apparently, a Japanese custom, so I submitted, although slightly disconcerted at first.

The cleaning done, they rinsed me by pouring warm water over me in insignificant pitcherfuls, and I got dressed again and returned to my room. It was now time for dinner. I sat down on my cushion in hopeful anticipation as a large tray appeared, laden with manifold pots and containers. This was promising, but when the tray came near enough to smell, the repast seemed less and less inviting.

There was something decidedly unhealthy in the odors that came from those mysterious little covered pots, but I uncovered them one by one and looked in, and in some cases even tasted the contents. A bowl of rice was quite good and so was a small saucer of fish — but the rest of the dishes were too horrible for words. They consisted, I found, of various dark-colored liquids of unappetizing smell, in which floated minute specimens of nasty-tasting Oriental vegetable which looked like bits of toadstool and decaying artichoke. I stuck to rice and fish, though the latter, being full of bones, presented something of a problem to my two slippery chopsticks.

Having conquered the fish, and washed my mouth out with the 'gobboon' brought for that purpose, I decided to do some exploring. Recovering my shoes at the doorstep, I returned to the crowded street and headed toward the forested hills to the west, barely outlined in the fading daylight.

The passers-by and loitering shopkeepers stared at me as if hypnotized, and burst into boisterous chattering and laughter after I had passed. They seemed never to have anticipated the possibility that any human creature could be so much larger than they, and the grotesqueness of it apparently erased their last veneer of reserve. Even the busy silk merchants rushed into the street to see what the commotion was about — and stared and stared with the rest.

At the upper extremity of a muddy lane I came to a forest. It was dark there, and high above the jumbled gray tile roofs, among which threads of colored light, from street lanterns, wound among the houses. It was cold, and great knotty pine trees stirred in the chill air — such a contrast from the excessive minuteness and delicateness of the city, from paper-covered latticework, silk flags, lanterns, screens, teapots, and baby's wooden sandals. Being in a substantial world again was restful — a world where you could move about and wave your arms without knocking over crockery or partitions.

An hour later I was back in the town. Above, the sky was black as ink; on either side, the narrow bustling lanes of dangling paper lanterns and little shops of countless teapots, and persimmons, apples, and tangerines, the soft colored lights from passing loaded carts, and gliding shadows of bicycle cargoes — all flowing past me, beautiful, delicate, and fantastic as a dream.

Along the wide and brightly illuminated theater street, sauntering crowds wandered and gazed and bargained at little fruitstands, and then scuffed onward again. Some of the many signs and placards were written in English — 'Blue Funnel Bar,' and 'Yebisu Beer — $\frac{1}{2}$ Yen,' for the benefit of foreign sailors. All foreigners not elegantly dressed are assumed to have a sailor's reactions.

Every few steps I am confronted by smooth-domed old Japs in brown haori coats, who bow appealingly before me with the words, 'Want p'itty girl? P'itty young girl — short time?' — pointing toward some alley or other where the harem presumably is kept. 'Come in — see p'itty girl? No costee see all same.'

Finally I come to an exceptionally mysterious-looking alley. As I turn to go down it, the aged promoter at its entrance seems to lose all self-control in his excitement. 'P'itty girl, p'itty girl,' he murmurs with popping eyes and a senile smile. Then, trotting eagerly ahead of me in a springy jog, he turns frequently to grin and lure me forward with pantomime suggestive of the 'p'itty girls' I am to behold.

At last appears a screened doorway, over which is written 'Boston Bar.' The usual old fat mamma sits on the steps, beaming at the lucrative prospects. I go in. It is a small low-ceilinged room with a bar counter at the far end. Several men are standing in front of this, and to my surprise, one of them is Bunny. Red, the convalescent tapir-mouthed wiper, and Hank, the fugitive aviator, are there also, and considerably cock-eyed.

After cordial greetings, I sat down and immediately one of the little 'p'itty girls,' in her wide obi sash, trotted over to me from where she had been talking to a sailor, and hopped into my lap, clinging to me with all her strength. She was only about four feet high, but extraordinarily aggressive and talked very appealingly in pidgin English and Japanese. I had a hell of a time negotiating her, until Bunny and I got about ten feet apart and tossed her back and forth between us till she was absolutely all in.

We then set her down on the bar, and she gave us no further trouble. 'Fer Kerize' sake, be good now,' says Bunny to her limp remains, 'or we'll hafta give yer some punishment.'

I wandered off with the gang, who seemed intent on visiting the very filthiest and lowest dives that their several bleary memories could conjure back to mind. One after another, we invaded these retreats of itinerant debauchery.

These narrow alleys of Kobe are certainly a region of hundred per cent licentiousness. But these sailors have, in their casual animalism, a sort of youthful, skylarking attitude which minimizes their degradation. And, anyhow, a man cannot degrade an ideal which he has never possessed.

Finally, in the most secluded retreat of all, Hank, the stunt man, proposed, if financially assisted, an extension of his exhibitionary powers in a realm into which the publishers do not wish me to accompany him.

It was nearly dawn when I headed for home again, walking past the shops, past a few of the old men, still murmuring, 'P'itty girl? Short time?' past the long rows of display stands to the little alley and upstairs to my room. I found my bed arranged. It was a five-foot piece of padding spread upon the matted floor, with a blanket, six inches thick, which reached only to my knees. The pillow also was rather strange, being almost square, filled with compressed tea leaves, and as hard as a sandbag.

November 8. In the morning — after a horrible breakfast — I took the train for Kyoto, on my way north through this long, narrow, crooked, mountainous island of Hondo, the mainland of Japan. As the little train pulled out of the crowded station, I looked out of the window and wondered at the incongruities about me. On the one hand there were narrow, muddy streets full of tiny pushcarts, flanked by delicate cardboard houses with gardens and paper latticework, and little shops selling knick-knacks and pottery — while, on the other hand, all around were great towers to hold up the network of high-tension electric lines, and here and there a gigantic transformer — as complicated a piece of construction as I've ever seen.

There seemed to be all stages of industrial evolution going on at the same time. Here the Osaka silk mill with all its ultra-modern machinery; there, next door, in a paper shack, a little old man working away, moulding crude bowls for his family table, shaping them with his fingers, and baking them in his little hibachi.

According to Western standards, the Japanese, though hard-working, seem a very inefficient people. Most of their industrial effectiveness comes from foreign influence — American automobiles, cement and brick buildings, electric locomotives, and factory machinery — while all the things of exquisite and fragile beauty, the paper houses and minute gardens, the porcelain and silks and lanterns and little shops — are what has remained essentially Japanese.

I have never before seen such crowded living conditions with so little ugliness. Almost nothing Japanese is ugly. Everything is minutely delicate, irregular, and full of color. Even the advertisements in the latticelike Japanese script, and painted on screens or flags or lanterns, seem to blend into their surroundings and are never harsh and grating as in America.

No two houses are alike, although they are all made in the same general style and of the same materials. You seldom see a perfectly even row of windows; ornaments are never placed in the exact center of a table nor the table in the exact center of the room. All gardens, all designs, even all architecture, is completely and refreshingly irregular — just as is Nature itself.

This explains — this Japanese love of irregularity — why the old man making rice bowls for the family table will never consent to give up his painstaking labor. It would be distasteful to him and to his family to eat out of stereotyped, machine-made bowls. When the Japanese cease to feel this way, there will be an end to the native Japanese art.

We were now among the paddy-fields — patches of vary-ing color, down the long valleys, some flooded with water, some with thick growths of rice, and others where straw was piled on racks to dry. But today the rain was coming down in a steady drizzle upon the men, women, and children, clad in bulky ponchos of rice straw and wide hats, stooping, hoeing, and carrying the great bundles to the racks. They seemed very cheerful about having to spend all day knee-deep in mud, and I could see whole squatting families chat-tering with animation, making a social occasion of this wallowing labor. Perhaps their smiles mean that there is a clean little house of sliding screens in a garden with ever-green trees, where, at the end of the day, they come home to warm themselves 'round the hibachi.

Every square inch of the valleys is crammed with rice and vegetables, and the hills are terraced upward to add still more to the area of cultivation. Above are the cliffs, and great pine forests and mountain lakes — a rough contrast, in their natural ruggedness, to the flimsiness of the man-made houses and gardens of the valleys.

November 10. This is Kyoto, which for ages was the capital of old Japan. I spent last night in a Japanese hotel, made almost entirely of sliding lattice partitions, and this morning I started off toward a Shinto temple which I could see rising above the gray tiled roofs to the westward.

As usual, my height caused a commotion among the crowds, and many people followed me, gazing as if they couldn't believe their eyes. One old shopkeeper turned over a whole table of teapots and crockery in his reckless haste to see me, and didn't stop to consider his loss till he had pursued me for several blocks.

It was like being Gulliver among the Lilliputians. Most of the houses were so low that I could look right over the roofs, and few of the many people who filled the narrow streets were over five feet tall. The largest vehicles were little two-wheeled carts, and the shops were but cubbyholes filled with microscopic knick-knacks.

At length I reached the shrine gardens, full of shrubs and flowers, with little convex bridges here and there, and the tall temples with wide roofs, delicately carved, and hundreds of years old. Mellow and red and gold, and set in the soft gray-green of rock and tree, these temples were built by men who loved the thing they made, and spent themselves and time in an ecstasy of detail and of color.

Through a great Shinto torii arch, I passed into the busy traffic of the streets again, among shops where workmen were carving bamboo, making copper pottery, hammering bronze, cloisonné and damascene ware; selling silk kimonos, handkerchiefs, brocades, haori coats, obis; making lacquer, fans, lanterns, umbrellas; carving 'geta' shoes; weaving mats, baskets, and screens. Some of the workers would ask me to come in, and so I did, bending low to get my head under the roof, and there I would see such delicate creations of little carvings and hammerings and mouldings and paintings and weavings as cannot be surpassed.

Yesterday in a tramcar, I paid seven sen for fare, as I had seen someone else do so, and had no other way to find out what was due. Today on the same car line I paid but one sen — which seemed equally satisfactory to the conductor. Later on, a third conductor, who got off the car and pointed out my way to me, refused to take any fare at all. There is far more politeness than business efficiency on a Japanese tramcar.

On the way back to my hotel, I saw an example of high-powered Japanese solicitation. It was Tojo, the proprietor's son, trying to persuade a Japanese couple to take rooms in our hotel. He walked backward before them, bowing very low and pointing invitingly to this humble assemblage of bamboo screens. The more they tried to evade him, the lower he bowed, and the more enthusiastic his gestures. Finally they acquiesced — whether from pity or exhaustion I couldn't tell. Bowing in Japan is the real thing. The head is sometimes bowed down below the knees as an indication of respect between friends.

Babies rule Japan. Babies get the best of everything, they go everywhere, they see the world, and they ride. The women — and old men and children — fasten the babies on their backs with their obis or with straps, and take them along wherever they go, to the market, to the movies, to funerals, to the baths. The babies solemnly listen in on all the conversations, observe with unprejudiced eye all that goes on, and keep their opinions to themselves. The baby-carriers, on the other hand, seem to regard their burdens as merely a part of their clothing — which is interesting and educative, though highly dangerous, for the baby.

I have seen a little girl about ten years old, with a tiny infant strapped inside her kimono to her shoulders, playing in the street with other children and apparently completely oblivious of the baby's existence — running about, chasing a ball, and dodging traffic, without a care in the world.

The babies maintain a very observant and philosophical attitude as they ride around. Occasionally, however, they are careless and slip too far down on their mother's back, which is very bad. A baby should never let this occur, as he soon pays the penalty — very frequently I have seen it happen. The baby slips down. The mother, then, in order to get her load back in place, puts her head down between her knees and gives a sudden and violent jerk upward with her hind quarters. She literally bucks the baby into position again, but nearly snaps its neck off in the process, which is very disconcerting to the baby, but never seems to remedy its total lack of coöperation with the mother.

Only once have I seen any coöperation. It was in a crowded tramcar, and the baby was holding his mother up by keeping a firm grip on the hanging straps, while she, below, conversed unmindfully with a companion. This was an unusual baby.

On the train to Yokohama. Right opposite me here, in this cheap, scrupulously clean, and comfortably upholstered car, is traveling a Japanese family. They are enjoying the ride. The pa sits in a compartment separate from the rest, as is customary, leaving ma to look after the brood. The little boy spends his time with his nose to the window-pane, while his two sisters take turns trooping back and forth in the aisle with the baby on their backs, just like ma. Now and then they mop the baby's face and blow its nose with little paper handkerchiefs which they keep handy in a big supply pile.

Bright-looking and intelligent, with clean black hair and little shiny black eyes, they seem very healthy and full of pep as they eat lunch together out of small bowls with chopsticks, and have fun feeding tidbits to the baby from time to time. At first they regarded me as quite a curiosity, but after an hour or so of considerable reserve, they became convinced of my harmlessness and are now very friendly. They climb all over ma, but pay not the slightest attention to pa, which seems to be a custom of the country. A man must appear aloof from his wife in public, and consequently to ignore her attendant brood. Any show of feeling between men and women is considered a sign of weakness, and kissing in public is unheard of in Japan. A man is severely criticized if he makes any demonstrations of affection for his wife outside of his own home.

This is but one manifestation of a great code of non-expression — which we Occidentals find very difficult to understand, and which we almost invariably misinterpret. Here, in Japan, the social system is based upon the subordination of the individual to the interests of the family. Individual fulfillment must never come at the expense of the unity of the family, or of the great family, the nation, with the Emperor at its head. The family, not the individual, is the social unit — the nation is an aggregation of these units. At the head of each unit, as at the head of the nation, is the patriarch — the chief. To him, and to his will, is bound, by the inexorable traditions of filial piety, every individual man, woman, and child. Thus it has been for thousands of years, and thus it is today.

No one can understand the Orient who does not understand this basic idea and its endless effect upon human behavior. For thirty centuries it has ruled the minds and hearts of these people of the East until it has all but eliminated the individual as a unit, as we of the West understand an individual.

It is behind the impassive, almost expressionless, face of the Orient. It is behind every social custom, every national trait, every characteristic mode of thought or speech or action of these people.

As I meditated upon these things, and watched my Japanese companions, and traveled northward toward Yokohama, I came to the conclusion that the gap between East and West lies mainly in the limitations of mutual understanding. Like the hungry youngster across the aisle, I too have guzzled my bowl of rice in three mouthfuls so as not to miss out on seconds; the reactions of that fellow down the car, gazing longingly at a sleek bit of Japanese femininity, are no enigma to me.

But we are disguised from each other by the deposit upon our humanness of fifty centuries of differing social, religious, and political experience. That same fellow is subject to a whole world of circumstances and considerations that I will never encounter, checks and rules and customs that disguise the fellowship of our feelings. His choice of a bride is always decided by the older members of the family. Several dozen uncles, aunts, and cousins, with great and grand pas — to say nothing of parents — must discuss the advantages of having such and such a daughter-in-law, and give only a secondary consideration to the desires of the groom-elect. He escapes a lot of responsibility. Not only is he not responsible for the choice of his wife, but the onus of her support is shared by the entire family connection who has chosen her for him. If he goes broke, they must rally to his assistance, and it is easy to see how he can so blithely accumulate the usual large family. While this dense unity of the family must sometimes be irksome to flaming youth, it has its advantages as the years roll on and the little ones need shoes.

Once in a while, Romance intrudes her irresponsible presence into this incubative atmosphere. A man falls deeply in love with a woman whom the family council will not tolerate. Elopement is out of the question in Japan — the whole force of patriarchy and a ruthless public opinion is against it. A tragedy ensues. The man and the woman kill themselves — it is 'shinju,' the suicide of frustrated lovers. It is characteristic of such an ordered psychology that a measure so desperate should have a name and a definite pigeonhole in the social schedule.

When a rigid patriarchal system is reënforced by the

worship of ancestors, enshrined in a religion, and isolated on an island, the result is a conservatism, of strength incredible to Western minds. What we call our conservatism is a mere beginning compared to the Japanese article, and our social conventions are vague suggestions in comparison to the time-honored mandates of Japanese custom.

Yokohama, November 15. Things are comparatively expensive here in Yokohama, so I am living at the Merchant Marine Y.M.C.A. at one yen a day. I would like to live in another Japanese hotel, but I stay here, where a certain amount of English is spoken, until I can speak Japanese better.

The manager is Japanese, and his son, Maki, who works here in the evenings after school, has become a close friend of mine. Like all Japanese schoolboys, Maki wears a black uniform with brass buttons, and keeps his hair shaved quite close to his little round head. Last night he came up to the dormitory where I sleep and sat down on a bed to talk. I am the only occupant of the dormitory at present, so we were completely alone. Maki's natural sociableness was augmented, I think, by a desire to practice his English on me, and his narrow dark eyes glittered with eagerness to tell all about his life at school, or, in fact, to converse on any subject.

'All we schoolboys mus' learn English,' he said. 'It iss required. We like to do it even if it iss very, very difficult. We want learn all about America. We want un'erstan' American moving pictures an' books, an' all about machine things in America. It iss very, very different in America. We mus' learn. Japan wondiful country, but not so rich like America.'

It was the study by the Japanese of applied sciences and of military and industrial organization that first made necessary a knowledge of the Occidental languages. This knowledge unwittingly opened up a world of Western ideas to

young Japan, which awakened to the possibilities of life
outside of old Japan's traditions. There was a revolt led
by the plastic minds of young students against the exclu-
siveness of Japanese doctrines. The revolt is still going on.

'We have strikes in school,' says my black-eyed friend.
'If we do not like the teacher, we all agree we will not come
to school. An' if we do not like our studies, we have strike
also. That way we get good teachers and good schools.'

This is an example of the subservience of the individual
to the active force that public opinion is in Japan. So solidly
do people think alike in this country that practically nothing may be accomplished without the sanction of public
opinion, which, being the will of the great mass of the people, ensures a practical democracy.

There are some German sailors here in the Marine
Y.M.C.A., who are a very cheerful bunch, and hang around
all day playing chess, reading magazines, and conversing,
with frequent guttural ejaculations. With the Japanese
they don't get along well — being too blunt and harsh of
speech. Dodi, our Japanese waitress, doesn't like them at
all.

It is easy to be too frank with Japanese people, for they
are not accustomed to frankness and are easily hurt by it.
What would be for us a friendly bit of advice or a trifling
criticism is apt to be taken by them as a cruel insult. They
are used to extreme tact and politeness, which are necessary
in such a closely knit society; skillful in compromise, and
very sensitive to any friction or interruption in the
smoothness of their social relations, they register disapproval only by the most delicate suggestions and obscure
hints, never by blunt declaration of annoyance, as is commonly the practice in the West.

Japanese people always appear pleasant, hiding their
true feelings with perfect self-control, and thus are often
very puzzling to foreigners from the Occident. When you

speak to them, they smile agreeably, nod, and try to convince you that they understand you completely, although it frequently turns out that they haven't the vaguest idea of what you were talking about. Friction, to them, is something to be avoided, at all costs.

One should never say to the waitress, as the Germans do to Dodi at the breakfast table when their eggs are not soft enough for their liking, 'Ach! diss arggs iss us hard us a rochk. Kunt cha gif us some leetle sorfta, eh?'

It hurts her feelings very greatly to be addressed thus. It is much better, if you want to express dissatisfaction, merely to smile and hesitate a little before starting to eat. Just that slight suggestion, even if you have thanked her profusely for bringing the eggs, is sufficient to tell her exactly how you feel, and she will do her very best to set the matter right as soon as possible.

This Oriental politeness and roundabout way of expressing themselves is, I think, frequently the cause of Japanese people being considered dishonest, or unreliable. It is true that they are inaccurate, perhaps due to their racial irresponsibility as individuals.

But, allowing for this inaccuracy, my experience gives me the impression of their being extraordinarily honest. Conductors of the trolley cars leave it to the passengers to pay their fares — and the fares are invariably paid. Frequently you hear of the loss of a gold watch, a piece of jewelry or money in some public place, and of the finder's returning it to its rightful owner by advertising it in the paper.

My schoolboy friend told me of a little boy who, last year, found a five-yen bill in the park. He secretly kept it for eight months. At the end of that time, his conscience troubled him so much that he confessed all, and turned the money in to the police. Such things happen often among the Japanese. Their multiple and minute business transactions are so vague that there would be chaos without personal honesty. We, on the contrary, with our wholesale scale and more accurate system of checks and contracts, do not depend as much upon individual honesty as do the Japanese, who make it the basis of their commercial and social intercourse.

November 17 — *Yokohama.* I never knew what patriotism could mean to a people until I realized the patriotism of Japan — which is a religion. It explains a great many of their apparently egotistical and insular ideas.

The steamship captain whom I met in the Y.M.C.A., who loved to dress up in his uniform and have his picture taken, and was always bragging about his ship, was most obnoxious. But when I got to know him, I realized that he did not so much want to add to his personal prestige as to promote public recognition of the steamship line that he represents, and which, in turn, represents Japan.

I remember how devoted the Japanese in Honolulu were to the interests of their native country, though some of them had been away from it for twenty years; how, amid the widespread intermarriage of races in the islands, they kept strictly to their own blood; how they almost worked their children to death by making them go to a Japanese school in the afternoon, when they had been to an American school all morning; and how they would invest their savings in the industries of Japan, rather than in the often more remunerative industries of Hawaii.

This almost maniacal patriotism seems inconsistent with the extensive adoption of foreign ideas and institutions by Japanese industry and government, until one becomes familiar with the Japanese philosophy of jiujitsu, which means, literally, 'conquer by yielding,' and which is so evident in Japan's national and foreign policies.

Just as jiujitsu is a system of physical defense perfected

by a people of small physique, so the jiujitsu principle is logically applied in the national policy of this race lacking individual initiative. It seems almost inevitable that the Japanese, small, and weak as individuals, should adopt this philosophy that the best way to conquer is, not by opposing force with force, but by a deft and subtle compliance; by using the strength of the enemy, to bring about his downfall. This, to my mind, is typically Oriental thinking; thinking in smooth curves rather than direct, as we do in the West; leading your enemy's strength in a curve to your objective, rather than opposing his strength with your own strength, in a straight line. The Japanese wisely use the strength of alien nations to further their own ends.

The public baths here in Yokohama certainly are good for an evening's entertainment. I went to one last night with two of the German sailors. This was a very public bath, where men and women were separated only by a curtain which divides the tank in half. It is a sort of huge wooden bathtub, full of water so hot that you can hardly stand it.

You are supposed to wash yourself spotless before entering, by successive soapings and rinsings with wooden dippers provided. And the rules also state that you are not supposed to go or to look on the other side of the curtain. It was for the infraction of this rule that we were attending the public bath.

The tank was already full of people and, after rather perfunctory rinsings with the dippers, we lost no time in piling in with the crowd. Our enthusiasm was only temporarily affected by the terrifically high temperature of the water, for, after we became acclimated, my snorting Teutonic associates and I set excitedly about grabbing at the pink limbs which intermittently revealed themselves beneath the curtain. This activity was observed with scandalized amusement by our Oriental companions, looking on through the veil of rising steam.

At length one of the German boys made a catch — which was announced by desperate splashing and squeaking sounds from behind the barrier. Though dismayed to some extent by the commotion he was causing, the boy pulled vigorously, gradually drawing a girl into view, feet first. Friends of the unfortunate were evidently rallying to her rescue, for our sailor began to lose ground and called us to his assistance. The tension increased as our side gained once more, till it was apparent that there was danger of the victim's drowning unless she was released. With victory in sight, however, the Germans entertained little thought of abandoning their sport — and the struggle grew more and more desperate.

But all at once a new factor had to be reckoned with. A husky Jap — one of our own bath mates — had apparently recognized the object of our efforts as his wife or daughter. Splashing through the steam, with fierce ejaculations, this new adversary reached the center of action and, with a ferocity which only filial piety could instigate, wrenched the startled Germans from their catch.

Thus came an end to this good solid Teutonic fun, and we returned to the Y.M.C.A.

November 20. I've said that the Japanese are a courteous race; that they carry it to the point of deception, and that they are mentally inexact.

Today I wished to go to the Russian Consulate to see about my passport.

'Where is the Russian Consulate?' I asked a native official in the Japan Tourist Bureau at the railroad station.

He beamed upon me from behind the counter. The whereabouts of the Russian Consulate were apparently a mere detail in the vast store of his knowledge.

'You go, sir, a leetle ways down thees way, and soon you go a leetle more ways down thees way, sir' — he waved his hand zigzagging imaginatively through the city of Tokio outside the windows. He smiled benignly, and talked on and on, and became enormously informative and with increasing benevolence. I went forth and followed his directions carefully, but they brought me to no Russian Consulate. Evidently I would have to inquire of someone else.

Along the street came toddling a professorish-looking Jap in large spectacles.

'Where is the Russian Consulate?' I asked him, hoping that he was the fount of wisdom implied by the specs.

He looked at me distractedly, so I made signs that I wanted to know in which direction to go, and repeated the words 'Russian Consulate.' Without hesitation, he pointed north, down the street. In order to make sure that he understood me, I then showed him a card on which the Y.M.C.A. proprietor had written 'Russian Consulate,' in Japanese. He perused it a moment with a countenance more profound than ever and then turned and pointed up the street, in exactly the opposite direction from that which he had previously indicated. I thanked him, and he bowed politely and passed on.

Rather dubiously, I started south, up the street, when, hustling along through the crowd, came a young fellow in uniform who appeared to be just out of school. He must be very well-informed on all subjects, so I stopped him.

'Where is the Russian Consulate?' I asked.

'Russian Consul—' He thought a moment, deeply. 'Oh!' he said, suddenly, 'down there! It ees down there!' And he pointed north, down the street along which I had just come, and, bowing graciously, continued on his way.

Either the professor or the schoolboy must be mistaken, if not a liar, so I sought a solution of the problem in an intelligent-looking Jap, dressed in European clothes, who was standing among a crowd of people waiting for a trolley.

To my 'Where is the Russian Consulate?' he first impulsively pointed to an approaching trolley. Then, seeming to have grown doubtful, he began to consult his neighbors, who had sociably collected about us to look on and offer their various morsels of wisdom to the mystery. They all seemed to agree in the end — that I should board the trolley with them, so I complied and, one and all, we scrambled into the thing and buzzed away, winding intricately on some new and entirely inscrutable course. My guides were extremely polite — and equally as extremely vague.

'You mus' go a leetle thees way, and then a leetle more over thees way, and then you mus' ——' and so on they jabbered most convincingly and with great interest.

But as we bumped along, I grew discouraged, and forsook the trolley-load of discussion, and found myself on the street again — Buddha only knows where — pleased by the friendliness of my late companions, who had even offered to pay my tram fare, but still completely in the dark as to how to get to the Russian Consulate.

In my desperation, I resorted to the gentler sex.

'Where is the Russian Consulate?' I asked an old lady. Her purple kimono was of heavy silk and her high hair was gray in streaks. She smiled understandingly, and, without the slightest uncertainty, indicated a new direction for me to follow. Superlatively polite, she even insisted upon accompanying me for several blocks, to make sure that I did not go astray. Then she left me, as had the others, bowing graciously and apparently completely happy in the thought that she had done her duty and done it to perfection. I proceeded exactly as she had indicated — and kept on proceeding — but nothing either Russian or consular could I find.

Although a little despondent, and a trifle dubious about Japanese integrity, I persisted.

'Where is the Russian Consulate?'

Stopping every likely person, I grilled them to their innermost marrow in my effort to unearth an answer to the deepening problem. As before, all were most unctuous in their courtesy and all were most profound in their inaccuracy. Few made any sign to show that they didn't understand English — and none ever admitted not knowing the exact locality of the Russian Consulate.

At last I met an intelligent-looking boy on a bicycle who could really speak good English. He said that he was going 'right by the Russian Consulate,' so I decided to run along beside him. This I did, and we went for miles and miles, zigzagging discursively through all sorts of streets. I realized that it was no wonder that nobody had known the way to the Russian Consulate — the strange thing was that nobody had been willing to admit it. A perfect example of the Oriental desire for superficial compliance.

After about twenty minutes at a pretty healthy pace, I began to think that this was another wild-goose chase, but my companion kept assuring me that it was 'only a little ways more,' so I kept on. He seemed to be untroubled by my having to run miles beside his bicycle. Perhaps he thought me an ex-rickshaw man.

At last — I could see my destination! I had really found a somewhat accurate Japanese! Arriving, I bowed low to this prodigy on the bicycle, and proceeded up the drive to the Russian Consulate office.

I found afterwards that this building was scarcely half a mile from the railroad station from which I had started on my search — three hours before.

When I finally got back to the Y.M.C.A., it had become as cold as Greenland. Sleet was coming down in dense splurges before a gusty gale. Our stove had not yet been assembled for the winter, and our frail domicile didn't provide much of a refuge from the icy blast outside. We shiveringly engulfed our supper, and amid Teutonic grumblings we made an early hibernation under the covers in our little dormitory.

Among us is a lanky darky from Abyssinia. He has a face like a tarsier, with huge bulging eyes and woolly hair, and he appears frightened to death all day long. Before going to bed, he writes mysterious messages on a piece of paper in the weirdest of hieroglyphics, and he sleeps kneeling down on all fours, with his head completely buried under the blankets.

Tokyo — November 22. Here, in the home of an old friend with whom I'm staying in Tokyo, the most interesting feature of our house is the bathtub. Previously, I have known only the method of the six Japanese ladies at my hotel and the community tubs. But this is the most usual private home method, and the apparatus consists of a small oval-shaped wooden tub about four feet long and as many high, made like a barrel. It is kept full of terrifically hot water, which is heated by a fire-box or stove enclosed in one end, and has a smokestack out of the top. A cover is kept over the water to preserve heat when the tub is not in use. It looks like an early model Stanley steamer, without wheels.

As in all Japanese bath procedure, you are supposed to make yourself immaculate with the help of a tiny tin basin, before mounting the vehicle. Then you are at liberty to get in and reap your reward; a nice hot soak. Of course this is all designed for the Japanese, and so, with me, there are certain attendant difficulties. In the first place, I have a terrible time getting into the thing — what with the scalding heat and all. Then, with my knees doubled up tight under my chin, and my eyes getting blearier and blearier with the dizzy temperature, I stay wedged, and gaze ahead at the smokestack rising up before my blistering nose. I listen to the crackle of the fire, the soft purr of escaping steam, and the gentle chug-chug of the heating machinery — and wonder how long it takes to be boiled alive. There is absolutely no way of cooling the water — you just have to grit your teeth and bear it.

Everyone tries to get the first bath, before the water — which does for the whole family each night — has become too hot. The lack of central boilers and the difficulty in heating water has preserved this primitive bathing custom in Japan, even in the homes of the best people. Like all communal benefits, it exacts a high sense of public spirit in the individual. It is a point of honor to make yourself spotless with the tin basin before you climb aboard.

Last night I felt a real earthquake. I was brushing my teeth when I became conscious of a tremendous shudder coming up from the depths of the earth. Doors slammed, windows rattled violently, and things fell off shelves. I could hear the heavy supporting beams of the house crunching and twisting under the strain, and got an unpleasant impression of the roof quivering in its struggle to balance itself on the tops of the walls. I held on to the tub until things were quiet again. The disturbance didn't amount to much, really, but at such times you never know what it is going to amount to.

The Ginza is the big shopping street of Tokyo, the busiest place in town, and is densely lined with hundreds of little shops, very cozy and full of fragile goods, with families industriously arranging them, and selling them and shouting out their merits. It is crowded with a seething stew of Japanese life — rickshaw men in their leggings and strange, thumbed sneakers; newsboys on the corners jingling their little bells — Japanese newsboys are not allowed to shout; old women with their strings of little children out shopping for peanuts; gaunt coolies carrying huge loads suspended from a pole across their shoulders; hundreds of different kinds of shopkeepers; and every variety of bicycle, cart, wheelbarrow, wagon, or other small conveyance that was ever invented, all loaded to the skies and whizzing like red ants on their several and innumerable ways. Everybody is talking and singing, and bustling and making a racket, and having a good time.

I saw some laborers repairing a sidewalk with their little pickaxes, singing a chant together and swinging their tools exactly in unison: a method very practicable with Orientals, who in every way seem so disposed to coöperation and harmony.

Little shops in tents along the curb with small ovens where oysters, fish, and frogs' legs are cooked and sold. Some merchants, not to be bothered with tents, spreading out their wares — teacups, toys, silks, fruits, lacquer boxes — right on the open sidewalk, to be viewed and handled by all. This is Japan — and the goods, fingered by a hundred people at the edge of the street, are as safe as if they were in the vault of a bank.

Here is a man carrying two bulky glass display stands suspended from each end of a pole across his shoulders, weaving with uncanny skill and alacrity through the saunterers. There are sixteen chairs loaded on that flimsy bicycle which a young coolie is merrily peddling through the traffic of a narrow side street. The chairs are dangling around his ears, hanging from his handlebars, clustered on his mudguards — and they are full-fledged chairs with four legs and a back. Believe it or not.

Evening. This is the Ginza by night—a brilliant mass of Japanese lanterns and more colorful than by day. The lights are soft blues and pinks and greens, glowing from behind skeins of Oriental hieroglyphics and designs. Even the traffic cops wave only delicate paper lanterns.

Going down a side street, as you pass the little houses and look in through the frail latticed windows, you will see families, sometimes shivering with the cold, yet busily engaged in carving more intricate pieces of dainty furniture, arranging their thin woven screens, sewing minute representations of Japanese life upon silken kimonos, and weaving microscopic designs into tiny baskets of straw — all without a thought of the howling cold outside their flimsy walls, with only a small glazed pot of glowing charcoal for warmth, and a bowlful of rice and fish to feed their empty bellies. Beauty comes first — comfort last, always. They would rather freeze than submit to insensitive brick masonry. They would starve before they would give up their frail teacups and decorations of painted silk and carved bamboo. It is hard to believe, but it is true. It is proved here under your eyes.

Yokohama again, November 24. I have been leading a very unhinged life of late, rampaging around Yokohama with two fellows named Will and James, whom I found here at the Y.M.C.A. when I got back from my visit in Tokyo.

We had a rickshaw race yesterday, which no doubt brightened the lives of those privileged to observe it. The most difficult part of the performance was to persuade the rickshaw men to let us have their rickshaws. We had to bribe them heavily and fill them up with red wine from a neighboring beer joint before they finally consented, and retired to warm themselves over their hibachi on the street corner.

The course was two blocks — down to the edge of the canal, and back again. The rules were that you had to choose a coolie whom you would pull down to the canal, and who, in turn, must pull you back to the finish line. Jim, being undersized, insisted on this, because he said he needed something to counteract the disadvantage of his shorter legs; also it was supposed to make the contest one of skill rather than mere brawn, for if you picked a light coolie, you would be handicapped when it came to his pulling you, whereas if you chose a heavy one, you would have a hard time at first.

We started off by picking our coolies, which we did very carefully, each of us giving his candidates several time-trials up and down the street. This was very difficult, as the coolies all wanted pay for it, and also every minute would add another hundred to the steadily growing crowd of spectators.

At last all was ready and our coolies chosen, who, according to the rules, got into the rickshaws, though reluctantly. We lined up and started. At first I got the lead a little, but my coolie, being somewhat alarmed by my pace at the start, tried twice to jump overboard, so I was delayed, and reached the canal far in the wake of my dashing opponents. Here all was confusion, with each coolie dismounting from his rickshaw, and each of us trying hurriedly to explain to them what they were to do next, and promising large sums on arrival at the finish line.

We all hopped into the rickshaws and got away on the back stretch in a bunch, and, with vehement encouragements to our coolies, drew steadily nearer the finish, where the whole street was jammed with excited spectators. I could feel my coolie pulling gamely forward, but Will, strange to say, surged by us with a wild burst of speed from his desperate-looking coolie and outdistanced us by a wide margin. James, however, fell to my rear, and I could hear him pleading frantically with his coolie to keep going, that he hadn't earned his yen yet, and similar urgings.

We finished amid wild cheers from the mob. The race was over, and Will had won. We paid off our exhausted men, and, struggling through the crowd, set out homeward to the Y.M.C.A. We couldn't figure out — James and I — how Will had gone away from us so easily on the home stretch. His coolie was only a little bit of a thing, too.

The mystery cleared up only late in the evening when Will admitted having secretly given his unsuspecting coolie a long drink of Pluto water just before the start.

The next night we went again to the beer joint where we had bought the red wine for the coolies. There we met three nifty Japanese girls, daughters of California Frank, the proprietor. Their names were Mary, Frances, and Haruko, which last, strangely enough, means 'fresh peas.' Perhaps California Frank had an eye to future business with American sailors when he named his two older daughters.

We had a good meal, followed by dancing with the girls to a phonograph. They said that Haruko, who was only fourteen, did not know how to dance. She was extremely bashful, but I finally cornered her behind the kitchen stove, and found her entirely satisfactory as a dancing partner. What her feet did made no difference — as they never came within a foot of the floor.

November 26. Will, James, and I are now staying at an inn on the shore of a lake near Mount Fujiyama. We arrived yesterday afternoon, having decided to explore this region on our way south, and we are living in a rural edition of Oriental luxury. We wear only Japanese clothes, which, although they are not very commodious — my kimono falling a considerable distance short of my knees, and my geta about size two — are the most comfortable draperies we have ever known. We find, after experimenting, that one can robe oneself in complete Japanese dress inside of five seconds, there being only the three-foot-long padded kimono with string around the waist, and the two diminutive sandals, with not a button, hook, lace, or buckle in the outfit.

The Japanese food here is more humane than that pernicious stuff I got in Kobe. They even have meat with it, and sometimes good skiako stew, and curry. Although the weather is chilly, our quilted kimonos keep very warm the small part of us that they conceal. For further warmth, we must repair to the community tub downstairs, and submerge in its steaming water with the other inhabitants of the place, who are so diverting that we emerge only when our skins have become as white and flaccid as boiled cabbage leaves.

Taking baths seems to be the great indoor social event of Japanese country life. The tub is a common meeting-ground for the whole neighborhood, and tends to stimulate man's interest in and understanding of his fellows. You are apt to be on intimate terms with your townsmen, and their wives and children, after a few years of spending an hour or so in the tub with them every night.

Will, James, and I have adopted certain conventions which bring us into closer relations with our native acquaintances. One of them is our vow never to sit down to a meal without first shaking hands with the cook. This, while it at first bewilders the cook involved, gains us ultimately many friends, and also — we have found — improves both the quality and quantity of our food.

I have also discovered that there is great social value in the way the Japanese keep from freezing to death in winter in their rickety houses of sliding paper panels. Last night, in a very cold room downstairs, I saw a lot of Japanese crowded around their hibachi, which was sunk in a depression in the floor. Squatting on their thick mat with their toes nearly in the fire, they held out their kimono skirts over the rising heat in such a way as to divert it directly to their bodies. They seemed entirely comfortable and warm. Although their freedom of movement was necessarily limited, and the situation lacking in certain elements of Occidental propriety, it was unquestionably cozy.

Today, during our hike through the countryside, we were close to the dazzling cone of Fujiyama, which we could see now and then looming between the clouds. We climbed, through long grass and bamboo, along its lower slopes. The going was hazardous, as we would come suddenly upon earthquake cracks, sometimes ten feet deep, hidden in the long grass.

At sundown, turning from the presence of the great white monster, we pulled into a near-by town on the railroad, to have a soak in the public bath before continuing our journey south. This proved to be a bath of high-test sociability, being exceptionally crowded. As we got undressed, we were looked at, as usual, rather wonderingly by our native associates, and I think they realized that such intimacy was not the rule with us, for the girls all cheered when we pulled off our pants. We rinsed ourselves with practiced skill with the little wooden dippers, and I made for the steaming tub, already full of soaking yellow forms. Will and James couldn't stand such hot water, and lingered on the brink, so I submerged without them — and it was just as well. The tub was four feet wide by six long, and about four feet deep. I counted eleven other occupants besides myself — six old men, two kids, one old lady, and two young ladies. Believe it or not.

November 28. I left Will and James at Kyoto, back-trailing alone, southward, in third-class cars, on my way to Nagasaki and southern Japan. It costs next to nothing to travel this way, but it is very crowded and the sleeping is difficult. Anyone can use any means he is capable of to get his sleep — even to lying all over his neighbors, or putting his bare feet against the cheek of the old man across the aisle. I am the only passenger, apparently, who cannot repose in perfect comfort on a plush seat, four feet by two.

I have met some soldiers on this train, who are very friendly and intensely interested in the photographs I showed them. I explained each picture as well as I could by sign-language, the few words of Japanese I know, and by pantomime. They liked the pictures of the submarine man's daughters especially, and soon over half the car-load was crowding around, trying to look on, and all very politely asking to be shown the pictures they had missed.

I tried to satisfy them all, explaining more and more elaborately as I went on, until I was giving a regular public illustrated lecture *à la* sign-language. When it was over, there was a great and most polite show of enthusiasm by my soldier audience, much bowing, cries of 'arigato' and 'sayonara,' and even presents of tangerines and peanuts. It is very touching — this generous capacity for showing appreciation.

I was struck also by how much better fed and healthier these soldiers looked than the average man on the street. In a population increasing one million a year, with nowhere to go, there is none too much to eat in Japan.

Contrary to the general impression, Japan has a smaller army in proportion to its population than many nations that escape the stigma of militarism. The proportion of men trained to arms being but 2.27 per cent, while that of France is 15.4 and Italy 14.3 per cent. My impression is that Japan is an over-uniformed, rather than a naturally militaristic, nation.

All schoolboys, and the large majority of young men in the country, are in a uniform of some kind or other which has nothing to do with the army. I know from my school-boy acquaintances that, in spite of the intense patriotism, military training is not popular, and I notice that soldiers have to fight for trolley car seats just like anyone else. They are not deferred to in any way by the general public.

At about midnight we reached Shimonoseki. This is the southeastern point of Japan's main island of Hondo, sep-arated by a strait from the southern island of Kiushu, on whose broken western coast is the great port of Nagasaki, and the China Sea.

On a ferry, and through harbors that were, even at that late hour, full of lights and motion, I crossed to Moji on the other island, where I boarded at midnight a train that was still more crowded than the last.

At first I could find no room anywhere to sit down, but I finally discovered a few empty square inches among some slumbering schoolgirls near the end of the train. One little girl about sixteen was seated beside me, and the others were sleeping soundly on the seat opposite.

They were all dressed in dark uniform dresses, and all were completely dead to the world. Every now and then the little girl directly opposite would be waked as the train started with a jerk, for her head lay right against the hard, wooden seat arm. I gave her my sweater for a pillow, which she accepted without even opening her eyes.

At sunrise, everybody woke up, and I soon became good friends with my schoolgirl bunk-mates. They spoke a little English and I mustered my few words of Japanese, and to-gether we proceeded to improve our respective vocabularies. They also insisted that I take breakfast with them, which

repast they produced from several little bundles. During
the meal they diligently undertook to teach me a well-
known Japanese song beginning, 'Poa, poa, poa.' I did my
best with Poa, and they then insisted on my singing the
'American national song' as a return courtesy. Unhappily
did I try to render 'The Star-Spangled Banner,' of the words
of which — to their horror and to my own — I could remember only the first two lines.

My little friends were very kind to me, and twittered with
enthusiasm and understanding. Their sensitiveness was
extraordinary. Japanese, as children, are given much consideration, and protected from criticism and slight, such as
Occidental youngsters are inured to, so they never need to
build in themselves a shelter of hardness against the world.

Nagasaki. It was from Nagasaki that I had planned to take
ship immediately for China, and I arrived here this morning. This beautiful harbor, surrounded by mountains, is
full of lateen-rigged junks and sampans and liners — and,
on arriving, I set out to see the town.

Later. I have been obliged to postpone taking ship for
China, and I am writing this in the police station. Enter-
prisingly, I took several pictures of a part of the harbor
which turned out to be in the fortified zone, and, having
committed this crime right in front of police headquarters, I
was arrested by the water police.

The Japanese method of arrest, being replete with Oriental subtlety and tact, is extremely interesting. Nothing
could be more frictionless — one almost glides into arrest.
For a long time I didn't realize I was being arrested.

First, a very unpretentious little fellow strolled quietly
over to where I stood on the wharf, and, after looking casually about for a minute, asked me in an innocent sort of way
what I was carrying on my belt.

'A camera,' I replied, and, seeing his obvious interest, I pulled it out and showed it to him.

As he was examining it, a second passing stroller noticed it and came up to see what it was. He, too, seemed intensely interested and asked me if I had been taking any pictures lately.

Then there appeared still more passers-by, all of whom, in the customary Japanese manner, exhibited excessive curiosity and made multitudinous inquiries: what kind of camera was it — how much did it cost — where had I taken the pictures — what was I going to do with them?

Finally, when some dozen craning spectators had gathered around, one of them asked me if I would go out in a boat with him; he wanted to take me down the harbor a way to where his office was. Trustingly I complied, and we boarded the chunky craft, accompanied by the larger proportion of the onlooking crowd, and chugged off among the fishing-boats.

I marveled at the hospitality of my guide, but thought little of the fact that most of my companions were in uniform, until, on questioning one as to the nature of our destination, he told me we were going to the office of the Nagasaki water police.

'We just want to find out why you take pictures of Nagasaki Harbor,' he said; 'we must be careful, you know; there are Reds in Japan.'

Thus was I placed under arrest.

On arriving at the police landing, I was escorted before a very pretentious-looking little inspector, who lost no time in investigating my case, amid politely interested spectators. He searched me scrupulously for communistic papers, unpacked my baggage, read my letters, and even as much of this diary as I had written at the time. He was worried, at first, about some notes on Bolshevism I had collected, but, after reading the diary with the help of an interpreter, he decided I was all right.

The canny little fellows are very merry and polite all the time, though most thorough in their investigations, and all day they have questioned me about my past and future, trying their best to detect inconsistencies in my replies. It is really very entertaining here in the police station.

After my trial, which exacted nothing from me but patience, the police chief, a stubby little Jap, took me solemnly aside and said to me, 'Weel you, sir, now go out, please, for walk weeth me? I want show you beautiful gardens an' beautiful temple on Nagasaki mountains. You weel like, I am sure.'

I was surprised, used to Japanese courtesy as I am, at this extreme expression of amenity on the part of a high disciplinary officer. But I accepted without hesitation, and we started off.

My comrade, clad in a black cape and the neat black-striped trousers of the police uniform, was very dignified and at first not disposed to informality. He frequently noticed people he knew among the passers-by, and to each he bowed, graciously and very low. For a few especially favored ones, he stopped and repeated his low bow several times, smiling paternally the while, and audibly drawing in his breath through his teeth. This sound is believed by the Japanese to express great pleasure. It occasionally gave way to short, energetic grunts, which in Japanese indicate, I am told, that a thrill has just been received.

As we progressed side by side, these brief human contacts seemed insufficient to satisfy his social appetite, and he began to drop into little shops on the way, to gossip awhile with shopkeeper acquaintances. Talking more and more, and descriptively waving his short arms in an ecstasy of solemn twaddle, he kept introducing me to his effusive friends, who knew not a word of English.

Having waited philosophically at some half a dozen stores

and booths while he chattered on, the chief and I at length reached a height above the city, where, passing under a high torii, we entered the shrine gardens.

As we strolled beneath the great carved roofs, he was very silent, and I wondered what my distinguished companion was thinking about. Presently, leading the way with his stately five-feet-two toward the edge of the slope, he said, 'Let us now, sir, seet down,' and he indicated a terrace where some girls were selling peanuts and candy. He had evidently been longing for further social activity. We took our places at a small table, and the girls approached us with their wares.

'We weel have some peanuts, sir,' he said to me, 'you like them'; and smiling affably to the fair venders, he bought a large bowl of the nuts, and set to work shelling them and graciously handing the kernels over to me. Now and then he would converse in dignified tones with a stocky elderly woman, who seemed to be in charge of the establishment. I also shelled peanuts and, as the chief was politely giving all his shelled nuts to me, I, in return, gave all mine to him, which he accepted with solemn gestures of gratitude.

The situation seemed to grow more and more ridiculous as we continued our peanut party, and we kept up the constant exchange of nuts, for never once did my friend relax his expression of grave majesty. As I shelled faster than he did, he of course got the most to eat — so, perhaps, after all, there was method in his courtesy.

Our return at twilight was punctuated by the same frequent visits to small shops, finally culminating in a tea-party with a very pretty little lady in a phonograph store. Here we were treated to a weird concert of Oriental orthophoneticism, while we warmed our fingers over a hibachi and sipped green tea.

We returned to the street an hour later. It was night, and, as we started down through the fantastic lantern-

*My Peanut Party with the Chief of Police in the
Nagasaki Shrine Gardens*

lighted ways, among the moving crowds, my black-caped companion looked up at me.

'You weel come weeth me, please, sir,' he said; 'I show you good place where you can live. It is house of friend of mine. You weel like very much.'

A rambling house, of cheap and rather mongrel appearance, situated on the Bund, was the abode alluded to. At the door sat a very wrinkled and kindly looking old woman, to whom I was presented with extensive bowing and gesticulation. Whereupon, to my astonishment, my friend of the police suddenly bade me farewell, and vanished into the darkness with a last spectacular flourish. I was left stranded in front of this benevolent old dame, who assumed, apparently, that I was her guest, and immediately ushered me into her house.

We entered a sizable living-room, which, although Japanese in general structure, seemed to suggest an influence from the West in its solid old walls of smooth paneling. Some half a dozen girls ranging from two to four-and-a-half feet high, a young boy with a baseball bat in his hand, and an old man, stood and sat about the room, gazing at me in a wondering, though not inhospitable, manner.

The old woman, undoubtedly the mamma of the household, smiled at me and, with gracious bowings, indicated her large brood, introducing them: Fudiko, Hotso, Pupeki, Kancko, Immoto, little Mimi — sisters — and Papa, and Neesan, the brother.

Not knowing what to expect next, I bowed in greeting to this stocky assemblage, receiving in return friendly smiles and gentle murmurings in Japanese. Then, before I had time to think, I was led by mamma out into a sort of back yard, and told I was to have a bath.

'Allai nasai. Yoroshi?' she said as she helped me off with my clothes and bent me over beside a steaming hot home bathtub.

'Anata K'rega s'ki des' — you weel like thees. You weel not min'e old mamma to wash you,' she said, picking up a scrub brush and soap and dousing me with steaming water. 'You no min'e old mamma.'

I didn't feel entirely sympathetic with this cleansing treatment, but there seemed to be no way out of it without seriously hurting somebody's feelings or violating the family traditions.

Just as if I were a baby, mamma set to work, scouring my ears, back, stomach, and everything else, and nearly scalding my eyes out with the red-hot water. I don't think she had ever before in her long career cleaned quite so great an area all in one job, for I heard plenty of grunts and panting before she was through.

When she had done and I had safely wedged myself, as far as I could get, into the barrel-like tub, Hotso was summoned to stoke the fire which I could already hear crackling, just beyond my toes, in the small end of this ovate contraption. Of course I yelled at Hotso to please have mercy — as I already was beginning to feel warm sympathy for broiled live lobsters — but through the steam, I could see her chubby form ruthlessly performing what she considered her duty. She apparently took my protest for a gesture of polite concern over her efforts, and totally disregarded me except for a coy smile between throwing sticks into the furnace.

At supper, which immediately followed my evening purgation, we had skiako, rice, and fish. I was now clothed in kimono and slippers — thoroughly comfortable as far as they went — and we ate in the kitchen under the most informal and Oriental circumstances. The conversation was entirely in Japanese, while everyone squatted on the floor and prodded the food into their mouths with chopsticks as fast as mamma dished it out. Papa and Neesan were not with us. The men of a Japanese family always seem to absent themselves from the women when outsiders are present.

November 30. There are two beds in my little room upstairs, and this morning, when I awoke, I discovered that Fudiko had slept all night right beside me in the other bed. No one seemed to think anything of our being alone together all night, so I guess this is perfectly customary — and I agree that it is a most delightful idea.

I am getting to feel more and more at home in this atmosphere of hospitality. Everyone treats me like a prince. Mimi is frightfully cute and wants me to have a peanut feast with her on the mat floor of mamma's room, which is, incidentally, the family bed. Fudiko insists that she is my big sister, and Hotso the same, and they all laugh a lot about it because they are so little.

Fudi is really an attractive girl — smooth, clear skin, even features, and, as compared to her sisters, a fairly slender figure. She apparently has also a number of intimate men friends.

The outstanding one is a very intellectual Hindu gentleman who abides at Singapore. He speaks no Japanese, and she no Hindustani, so they communicate in English, the diplomatic and international language of the Orient. But, knowing only eight words in English, Fudi is not much helped by it, and I suspect her bond of affection for the Sikh is based more on spiritual and physical kinship than on any kinship of the mind. This morning she asked me to write a letter in English to this gentleman for her, and explained to me in Japanese what I must say. To make her ideas clearer, she showed me her last letter from him, which was indeed intimate and most revealing as to their personal affairs. In it he pathetically beseeches her to come to Singapore, to 'forget her native land'; but Fudi, possessing the traditional Japanese patriotism, will not go. She sends him lots of love, but is firm in her patriotism, and makes an ultimatum by telling him he may have her *in Japan*, or not at all.

I have also discovered another factor which does little to simplify Fudi's espousal problem. I was playfully lifting her up by the elbows this morning when she suddenly asked me to go easy, saying, 'Noh, noh!' and, patting her stomach significantly, 'Baby-san. Noh, noh!'

I didn't like to inquire more deeply into the matter, but, as Fudi is unmarried and obviously in no way embarrassed by her state of affairs, it is apparent that Japanese girls — as long as they are not defiant of their family's wishes, nor disloyal to their country — are extremely free in their actions.

Although there are powerful conventions and traditions and checks on the conduct of a Japanese, these have to do, almost entirely, with his external relations with the world — his filial piety, his worship of ancestors and family tradition, his patriotism, his social courtesy. Public opinion in Japan is very tolerant in all personal matters — religion, sex relations, eating and drinking, style of clothes, etc.; in fact, as long as a Japanese gets along all right with his family, is not unpatriotic, and is polite in public, nothing but his innate lack of individuality stands between him and a wide range of personal freedom. He never need worry about the scandalous gossip which so inhibits personal liberty in the West. Look at Fudi.

Hotso, on the other hand, is not nearly so popular among the boys — in spite of her untiring efforts. With the face and features of an embryo hippopotamus, she is on my heels from dawn till dark. I think mamma is responsible for Hotso's apparent devotion. All the other eligible daughters seem to be taken care of as far as their love-lives are concerned. And mamma, being considerably worried over Hotso's single existence, I have reason to suspect deliberately sets this creature on my trail. Mamma desperately hopes that she may — with the aid of Buddha — find somewhere in me a spark of romance that may be fanned into a conflagration of desire for Hotso.

I am getting into the family life deeper and deeper every day, it seems — and, believe me, it is interesting. Never would I have suspected that a foreigner could be on such intimate terms with an Oriental family. But here I am, and getting along even better than I usually do at home. Kipling's dictum that 'never the twain shall meet' makes me less and less impressed with his wisdom the longer I remain in this house.

I won't be here long, though, as I'm leaving this afternoon for Shanghai. Already mamma is filling a great bag full of peanuts and fruit for me to consume on the way. She is very sweet.

Last night after my bath — mine always comes last, because it has been found that I displace the most water — we all had a huge peanut party in mamma's bed, the soft matted floor covered with blankets. Papa was there also, and now and then Hotso would be detailed to fetch some cider for us. Neither mamma nor the girls ever took any, but the old man and I drank heartily and enjoyed ourselves to the full. Little Mimi was very enthusiastic about singing, and she and I sang 'Poa, poa, poa' over and over again to show our good will.

It finally ended up by my spending the whole night there, surrounded by mamma, papa, and the daughters, all in mamma's bed. It was really very nice, and we slept snugly and soundly in our thick kimonos till daybreak.

I realize, of course, that a certain amount of this apparent affection is politeness: remarks such as, 'We like you — We'll all be very lonely tomorrow'; but it can't all be.

When I left for my steamer, embarrassed at being their guest for so long, I insisted on giving mamma a small present of money. This she accepted with a friendly smile, and a perhaps not entirely disinterested request that I come again, and bring friends.

She casually assigned to Hotso the job of carrying my baggage to the dock. It didn't appeal to me that Hotso, who, besides being a woman, was four-feet-three and quite fat, should bear my burdens, and, as the steamer was waiting and as Hotso's strides were six inches long, my sacks and I made the dock far in advance of our small escort. I found a half-dozen ranking police officers, including my friend the chief, on board the ship to say good-bye to me. They were there, I think, partly out of politeness, and also, perhaps, to make sure I had departed.

After a sad parting from the tearful Hotso, who had faithfully toddled along after me all the way to the dock, the *Shanghai Maru* glided out of the crowded harbor among swarms of fish-sampans and other small craft. Even until the very last, I could see the tiny specks of mamma, Fudi, and the rest waving white towels from the roof for 'sayonara.' It was touching, and I climbed up a little way into the rigging to wave in return, much to the disapproval of my clustering fellow passengers of the third class, and the tawny, rope-coiling sailors.

At last the sunny green mounds of land were fading to the northeast, and the molten sun had sunk into the Yellow Sea.

CHAPTER SIX

CHINA

NIGHT was upon us in our cavernous, teeming hold — a long night of undulating disorder and crying of sloe-eyed babies. In the morning I got up early and went on deck to get the air. It was cold and blowing a gale. For the first time, then, I knew why they call this the Yellow Sea. The great seething waves were yellow, as if in a shallow muddy river, and yet we were out of sight of land.

By afternoon, however, we were steaming into an estuary through wide, flat lowlands, where hundreds of heavily loaded junks and sampans lay anchored along the banks, awaiting the arrival of cargo steamers. We pushed our way through a cold wind and past bleak farmlands, seeing numerous mud huts not far back from the banks, which, I am told, are Chinese ice-houses.

After an hour or so there appeared large power plants, with groups of Standard Oil tanks squatting on the flat shores, and then the busy jetties and anchored ships and warehouses behind which lay a great city along the river. We are in the port of Shanghai. Huge steamers are all about us — from Liverpool, New York, Batavia, Cape Town, Rio. Hundreds of little Chinese boats, in spite of the bitter cold, are out trying to catch garbage from the big ships or earning a few cents in ferrying someone across the stream.

The water traffic is unbelievably dense — every sort of craft, from the foreign freighters and British battleships and bulky sailing barges to tiny rafts crowded with poor, shivering Chinese and laden with absurdly large cargoes of firewood or cabbages. They are almost sinking, while gaunt Chinamen try, with crude poles and oars, to balance them in the raw wind. This great harbor scenes a pathetic struggle on its waters, but the Chinese are well-used to the cold, I guess, for they are clothed only in rags, with bare feet and heads and hands — yet are chattering and cheerful, even laughing among themselves, as they swarm to the scuppers on their scavengerous errands.

Other Chinese boatmen, more fortunate, fly past on the sterns of brightly painted cargo junks, jauntily clinging as their picturesque red sails bend and dip to the squalls. There are no sea-gulls to be seen anywhere. I suppose they all starved to death centuries ago, under the desperate competition of the Chinese.

The Shanghai rickshaw men are ragged and squalid beyond description, and as frantic as starving rats. I tried to walk away from the dock, but they hounded me so, and grabbed my arms, and so begged and howled, that I could hardly move, so I succumbed and hopped aboard one of the frail vehicles, with my baggage, and started for the Sailors' Home.

The man in the shafts was a thin figure in ragged blue cotton pajamas. He was barefoot, and the only covering on his scarred shaved head was the tattered skeleton of a skull-cap. But he didn't seem to mind the cold a bit, and dashed onward over the hard pavement quite merrily, not even bothering to sidestep icy puddles which lay across our path.

Like all Orientals, he insisted that he knew just where I wanted to go.

'My speakee Eenglish — savee all same,' he would say whenever I tried to direct him. 'My takee you all same.'

He seemed terribly afraid of me, yet even more afraid that I would think he didn't understand, and would abandon him for another, and that he would lose his chance to earn the ten cents Chinese money — four cents American — that was the fare. He fairly cringed whenever I opened my mouth to speak, and took me all over the water-front in circles before I could make him listen at all. Not a hair did he turn at the biting gale. All the wretched creature thought of was the four cents he would get when we reached our destination.

We finally arrived, and I gave him twenty Chinese cents — twice what he expected — for I thought he sorely needed it. The rapacious soul, supposing me to be ignorant as to the usual fare, then cannily tried to make me believe that I owed him fifty cents. That, I am told, is the way of Chinese rickshaw men. If you show them the slightest kindness, they regard it as a sign of weakness and, far from being grateful, they try to exploit you.

Shanghai is an international city. In the heart of this great China port is a strip owned by the French, a British and International section, and a walled Chinese reservation. The predominating language seems to be English — at least most of the signs are written in English; but the population includes every race and nationality on the face of the earth. White Russians and British are in great abundance, there is a good supply of Frenchmen, Americans, and Hindus, and not a few Germans, Italians, Turks, Japanese, and Australians, beside many other nationalities.

The cops are burly hirsute Hindus, who must look formidable to the obsequious Chinese. Everyone you see on the street seems to be of a different race, all speaking their various languages and wearing their various styles of clothes.

Just before I reached the Sailors' Home, there was an accident in the traffic, in which a White Russian, being pulled by a Chinaman in a rickshaw, was run into by one of the dodging, rubber-tired, Shanghai trolley cars driven by a Jap. A Sikh cop was called to the scene, but could not settle the dispute until two Australian bystanders pinned the blame on a bus-driver, who turned out to be a Swede.

Sailors' Home. Almost the first thing I saw on entering this ancient dwelling was a familiar face. It belonged to Gus, the fellow who brought me sandwiches when I was in the brig on the ship coming down from Alaska. He had much to tell, and it seemed great to see him again. Later, I ran across another friend — this one from Cambridge, Massachusetts. It isn't hard to believe what they say about this place: that you will see everyone you've ever known if you stay long enough in Shanghai.

December 6. After a rather itchy night at the hands of some sociable bed- and other bugs, I started in a rickshaw to catch a train to Hangchow, a hundred per cent Chinese city which is about four hours' ride away. To direct my coolie to the station, I made vivid imitation of the noise of a train, and was none too sure of its effectiveness as the cringing individual, like all his kind, said only, 'My savvy, my savvy,' and trotted onward in a manner utterly desperate and irresponsible.

In the station at last, the crowds were tremendous — ragged, chattering Chinese by the hundred, all with great bundles. Some of the bundles would become separated from their less bulky owners, and much hysterical jabbering and scrambling would ensue. Everything was turmoil and confusion — and bundles. The law, I think, limits the size of hand luggage at eighty cubic feet, or four hundred pounds in weight, but the law apparently cannot be enforced.

The temperature of third-class cars in China in winter is nothing to make a song about. A raw wind blows through them like a blizzard, and you have to rely on animal heat from your ragamuffin buddies to keep from freezing. We all huddled on four parallel benches which ran the length of the car — and were a merry bunch considering the circumstances — not bashful about snuggling in each other's laps.

Once in a while a man would come around selling crackers and green tea in thimble-cupfuls. It was almost a necessity, and cost next to nothing, so we all indulged heavily, making the usual Chinese sucking and blowing noises as we guzzled. Some of my comrades were frightfully accomplished in the art of spitting, and some did things that made me less unhappy about the fresh breeze, however cold.

A Chinese woman with a baby seemed to think nothing of merely holding it out over the aisle on certain occasions, and, on more serious occasions, she held it out of the window. All in all, we were an informal party.

Outside the open window we could see, drifting by, a flat

country with little mud farmhouses and fields of frosted cabbages and rice straw. There were strips of woods here and there, and meandering stream-beds, but for the most part it was an open lowland, a great flat valley and delta, which the centuries of rain and wind from the rough mountains to the west have carried through the gorges to pile here inch by inch. The ground was frosty in the crisp morning light — this ground that is so fertile that it is called the 'Garden of China.'

On all sides were evidences of ancient civilization, irrigation canals, old paved paths, and wide expanses of grave mounds. As we went further, gently sloping hills appeared, and these were veritable forests of graves. The cemeteries extended frequently over many square miles of good farmland, becoming, I should think, no meager liability to the neighboring landowners. But a grave is sacred above all else to those ancestor-worshipers, and they will never transgress its sanctity.

This characteristic — this blind adherence to tradition in various forms, this superlative conservatism — is, I believe, responsible for most of the poverty and backwardness of these Asiatic peoples. It is so in Japan — in the extreme suspicion which the humbler laborers, especially farmers, hold toward any new or more efficient tool or machine — and it seems even more so here.

There is no national consciousness here — no national ambition strong enough to counteract the Chinese peasant's religious mania to follow exactly in the footsteps of his deified great-grandfather. This religion frustrates all efforts at progress, abhors everything new, binds the vision of a people essentially to a past which, no matter how bad, they consider perfection.

Hangchow was at one time the seat of government under the emperors. It affords a realization of the religious extravagance of these people. No matter what you want to see, they show you a temple; and you can't turn your eyes without confronting another temple. These are not cheap, hastily built structures, but as gorgeous as they are ubiquitous, and their façades are dazzling with red, purple, and gold.

In one place I saw a gigantic temple in process of construction. It was of reënforced concrete and its cost must be comparable to that of any great cathedral of Europe.

I also witnessed, within a vast shrine garden, an elaborate service for the repose of a departed soul. This pre-burial ceremony was on its sixth day, and due for many more, the exact number being decided by a special high priest who names the burial date. He is considered an expert on the art of interpreting the moods of the gods. Daily — until the day he makes his decision — he is consulted as to whether it is yet the politic time for the burial. Considering the large fee received by this pontiff each time his invaluable advice is given, it is easy to understand why Chinese corpses remain so long above the ground.

A long procession of priests in silken robes marched about the garden, occasionally halting to set fire to baskets of paper money intended to finance the deceased on his jaunt to kingdom come. They also ignited paper knights on horses, paper models of cattle, food, of junks — in fact, of everything that might be of service to a lonely traveler in the Chinese hereafter.

As the priests trooped on and on in serpentine arcs, setting fire to all sorts of paper absurdities, waving their mysterious charms and performing other ceremonies, they seemed to be a bit absent-minded. Poor fellows — after six days of it, they must be pretty thoroughly fed up.

Chinese gods are not accredited with very acute powers of observation. Paper models can be passed off on them for the real thing with no trouble at all, and the most superficial of solemn appearances is tendered confidently as genuine reverence.

Beyond the garden was a mighty hall containing statues of revered dead. These were meticulously sculptured, and all coated in real gold leaf. There must have been two or three hundred of them, and they were life-size.

After all these squanderous displays, how can one wonder at the poverty of the Chinese? The only people who appear to be well off here are the priests, and a few of the less hide-bound merchants. I went through the private garden of one of these last, and saw its bridges and fish pools and chiseled masonry. It was but a part of his luxurious circumstances and was open to the public at a certain hour each day — to add, I suppose, to the owner's prestige.

Then, walking along the lakeside, I saw numbers of raw-boned farmers out on their rafts, grubbing in the icy muck and water for a little fertilizing water-weed. They were almost naked, and gaunt with famine.

Such are the contrasts of China.

Farmers constitute about ninety per cent of the population. They are, as a class, wholly illiterate, and densely ignorant of all but the most primary principles of agricultural science. To make matters worse, they marry early and raise the large families necessary to filial piety. And then, for the coveted honor of having five generations living within the same walls, they restrain their boys from going out to earn a living, and make them struggle along on the local resources.

When droughts or floods come, they make no attempt to prevent or to prepare for their recurrence, but, with cheerful piety and in great numbers, they dry up or drown. The patriarchal system was deified to preserve Chinese civilization — not to advance individual well-being. It is tough on the Chinese farmer.

In the heart of bustling Hangchow again, I visited an old

Chinese pharmacy, where gruesome drugs and lotions are for sale. They sell mud pills, and, out in back, keep a pen for deer, from the antlers of which they make a very popular powder for prolonging life. Mud is a very important element in this pharmacy. Besides the pills, the building, floor, and counters are all made of mud — as are most of the houses in rural China. It is an excellent building material, easily got at, cheap, warm in winter, and cool in summer.

Also of mud, and twenty feet high, is the wall around the missionary's home where I went to tea. 'To keep out the rebels, who sometimes rampage through these parts,' he said casually.

Walking back to the station, through alleys, narrow and winding and pitch-dark, I would come to a dim, lighted window, and could see the huddled Chinese within. In their bare, dirty, mud-floored room, their squalor revealed by the light of a feeble candle, grouped darkly on the floor, eating or working, they are apparently most cheerful and merry together, and always chattering sociably.

I can't help but admire their spirit. They are well-mannered though low-born, they have poise and even a certain dignity in spite of their squalor, and they can smile in the most overwhelming adversity.

On returning to Shanghai, I arrived in the middle of a riot—not a bad riot, but the Chinese kind, full of vituperation and jabbering. Soldiers were trying to disperse a mob of laborers from around the railroad station. As it was after midnight, and the riot in a dull stage of its development, I went home to bed. Next morning, I read in the papers that it had been a communistic uprising, and that, after I had gone home, the jabbering had given way to some excited shooting in the safe and insane Chinese manner.

Shanghai, December 7. Yesterday I met, through a friend,

Loy Chang, a thin, neatly dressed, modest individual, who is the right-hand man of the Nationalistic finance minister. We had tiffin together, with several other Chinese politicians of the Nationalist administration. I found Mr. Chang had been educated at Harvard University, and that many of the men present — and others in the Nationalist government — had been to Harvard or Yale. We sat around a big circular table of Chinese food, and listened to stories about the rebels.

The food consisted of curries and suey salad mixtures, which appeared in a continuous stream until we were stuffed. They then passed around hot towels, to wipe off the guzzle splash, which is inevitable when one eats as we do in China.

Chinese table etiquette seems kind of exotic on first acquaintance. It involves a great deal of gurgling and a frank exuberance of mastication. Appreciation of the host's food must be expressed beyond shadow of doubt. With this in mind the guests submerge all restraint in a demonstration of gastronomic lust. Lest the host feel slighted, they take pains to maintain a high standard of recklessness in their gobbling and gulping, which sounds, the while, like a herd of cows getting out of a swamp. Resulting indigestion is indicated by formal belchings and polite regurgitations.

The man I sat next to, a Chinese labor administrator, besides being no slouch with chopsticks, was a most garrulous personage — and keen. His eyes, which have developed great flexibility, due to the spasmodic pressure upon them from within as he raves, seem to be a sort of thermometer of his brain. By watching closely the dilations of his bulbous eyeballs, you can read between the lines of what he is saying, even when it is in singsongy Chinese.

Although not excessively fat, he is round in every possible sense — shoulders, arms, legs, head, nose, ears, eyes — and how he loves to talk! His attitude is distinctly paternal. He has been connected with various rebel war lords at one time and another before he became affiliated with the Nanking outfit, and of these past acquaintances he seems violently proud. For Feng, the present outstanding rebel general, he feels particular admiration.

'General Feng — he good fren' of mine,' says the labor administrator. 'I on his staff — long time. Way up in Taiyuen two years ago. We very poor then — famine. Feng, he had hard time to get food for the soldiers. Sometime caravans of camels with provisions come across Mongolia from Russia to help, but only in long, long time. Feng, he say, "We mus' grow opium, and sell to get provisions." Feng never let soldiers have opium for themselves, but he grow it to exchange to get provisions. Feng very wise. Feng good man. But sometime Feng very fierce.'

None of these Nationalist government officials seem antagonistic to the rebels, but are inclined to take them as a joke. Although these men are, of course, back of their own government, it is mainly for the sake of stability, as they all admit that the Nanking régime has many weaknesses, and that Feng could probably do just as well.

In spite of their casualness, however, they are extremely shrewd in their methods of promoting in China a democratic and centralized form of government. They realize that it is a long way from the rule of village great-grandfathers over illiterate and tradition-bound descendants, to the administration of a president, chosen by popular vote, over four hundred million people of growing education and individuality. In order to tide the people over this gap, an opportunity is offered them to transfer their jolted filial piety and ancestor worship to the Nanking government.

Dr. Sun Yat-sen, father of the Chinese Republic, is becoming a god. His vast but simple tomb is a temple, one of the most beautiful, most sacred in the world. His widow, of the Soong family, is the sister of Mrs. Chiang Kai-shek, wife of the president, and also of T. V. Soong, the finance minister, and is related to other members of the cabinet, most of whom are of one blood. It is to this privileged administrative family of Soongs that the Chinese people are encouraged to transfer their filial allegiance until they reach a condition of mind in which they can listen to teachings that 'exaltation of the past is superstition' without going completely berserk.

As far as I can make out, the political upheavals and interminable civil wars in China have, to date, affected the mass of the people not at all. The only effective government that the Chinese have ever been generally conscious of is the local rule of the patriarchs in each community, which rule is not changed in the least by the campaigns and varying fortunes of the war lords. The central government is not, and never has been, more than a remote, impersonal symbol. The Chinese emperors gesticulated and exploited, rather than governed. When the emperor's tax collectors came around, the people submitted, as they would submit to a flood or a famine — as they always submit to every impersonal form of oppression. Except through indirect taxes, the people had practically no contact with a central power.

When an army takes possession of a province and deposes its governor, the people are only passively interested; this happens often and matters not the slightest to them or to their real sovereigns, the village great-grandfathers.

Once in a long while the soldiers do a bit of ravaging here and there, but everybody is used to bandits, who are always lurking in the open country, and the ravaging is hardly noticed. It is always necessary to travel in force when going from town to town, as a protection from bandits, so a few rebel soldiers as an added menace are immaterial.

All in all, China is not nearly so unstable politically as it seems if you judge by reports of revolutionary activities.

Official bulletins, and especially newspaper reports, in China are absurdly exaggerated. After a skirmish, each army delights in fabulous accounts of the desperation of the struggle, the destruction wrought, and the numbers of slain. This is natural enough, for self-respect, 'face,' the possession of reputation and public esteem, is an inordinately important thing in Chinese psychology.

Without it, neither an army nor a man can succeed, so it is as important to the armies as to their leaders that the battles should be represented as terrific — the slaughter immense — and the results vital to the cause.

Newspapers coöperate, for obvious journalistic reasons, in these extravaganzas; so it is no wonder that a few military scrimmages are heralded as an Armageddon, or then some.

The truth means little here; the great virtue in this super-social country is 'face.'

'Face' is the possession of reputation and public esteem. It is the standing, the approbation a man commands in the minds of his associates. 'Face' is a Chinaman's self-respect, and self-respect is as precious to him as is ours to us. It depends, however, not, as does ours, on a man's knowledge of himself, but on the estimation of him by his neighbors.

If he loses their regard — if he loses 'face' — he is utterly undone. This is a logical development in a civilization based, not on the individual, but on the subversion of the individual to public opinion and mass convention.

As 'face' is essentially a false standard of worth, it has developed along the lines of superficial appearances. 'Face' has come to mean, not what his fellow-men think of a man, but what they appear to think of him.

It is on this insecure basis that the Chinaman builds his dignity — his self-respect. One must not forget this important fact, for Chinese life and Chinese psychology seem alien and inexplicable unless you understand this conception of what a man values most in himself. If you have realized this racial idea of 'face,' you will see it working through all things Chinese — in private and public life, in domestic and foreign policy, in social and commercial standing.

To lose 'face' is so serious a matter that, when a Chinese has been caught at some nefarious undertaking, and has ducked behind a screen of bluster and transparent lies, his friends, always, and sometimes even his enemies, will politely accept this fabrication — although the discreditable facts be as obvious as the neck on a giraffe.

From rickshaw coolies and house boys, right up through all grades of the social structure to China's national attitude toward foreign powers, this idea of 'face' is the basis of Chinese psychology. To lose 'face' — to admit individual inferiority or to accept the idea that you have failed in Chinese standards of personal dignity — is what Chinamen — or China herself — hates and fears more than anything in life.

To accept a gift, for instance, to the Chinese way of thinking, is a concession, and carries with it a dangerous implication of inferiority for him who accepts it. To maintain sure self-respect, he must take the offering disdainfully, gloating haughtily over the submissiveness of the giver.

The rickshaw man, accordingly, if you give him in pity more than his fare, immediately makes further and exorbitant demands upon you — to save his 'face.'

Even the central government, in dealing with foreign powers, conforms to this tradition. With great condescension does China accept the surrendering by the powers of their extra-territoriality rights on Chinese soil. The more these treaty rights are generously relinquished, the more China demands and the more haughty becomes her manner.

She regards any renunciation of extraterritoriality as a sign of weakness in the foreign powers, and believes that soon China will be ruling the world. When the United States tells her that it wants 'not a foot of Chinese land but only China's good will,' the Chinese pretend that we realize their 'great power' and desire their favor as protection for ourselves.

It is absolutely necessary for them to pretend this — to save their 'face.'

Very late at night, on my way home through the dark labyrinth of streets, I saw hundreds of scrawny rickshaw coolies wandering about in the darkness, looking for fares. It was after one o'clock and the streets practically empty, yet there they were, gliding like vulture ghosts through the shadows, hunting for a crumb.

Outside a little bar into which an English sailor had gone for a drink of beer, I counted nineteen of them, waiting, pacing tirelessly back and forth in the cold, in the forlorn hope that he would use them when he came out. He might stay in the bar for hours, and the chances of any given one of them getting him as a fare — if he used a rickshaw at all, which is not likely — were about one in a thousand; yet even that faint possibility kept them there, hovering up and down, up and down, straining their ghastly skeletons hour after hour through the bitter night — on this most barren hope of a Chinese ten-cent piece.

It was pathetic — and terrible.

On the Sado Maru — bound for Hong-Kong — third class. I am now in the bowels of this small Japanese ship, steaming down the coast toward the South China that I must see. I have a tiny compartment with a Chinaman and a Hindu. The Chinaman is very mysterious. He spends all day playing a sort of solitaire on our table with weirdly marked disks of red and white bone.

The Hindu, with dark eyes and the customary long black beard, is a very agreeable fellow. He says little except his prayers, and them very regularly and often. But he smiles a lot, and hunts for bedbugs with the highest standards of sportsmanship. I like him very much, but neither of us can make the Chinaman out at all.

The Chinaman, when he first gets up in the morning, looks fierce and dominating, but, as the day wears on, he looks meeker and weaker till, in the evening, his vitality is so low that he seems scarcely to breathe at all — as he slowly, slowly shifts around his disks of bone.

I wonder about him — this strange being. What is he — what can be his part in life? I wish he spoke English.

At the entrance of Hong-Kong tall islands rise before you — brown grassy mounds, bulging above Gothic cliffs of black rock. Here and there are Chinese sailing junks, heeling to the northeast breeze as they tack through the canyon channels. Built for vast cargoes, they are wedge-shaped with wide, high sterns and a tiny platform at the top where a sailor stands at his long rudder or tightens the sheets of the broad bamboo-ribbed sail above him.

The cliffs become pink and light gray — the sun has come out, and we are in a big arena of bare mountainous

THE PRINCIPLES OF CHINESE CHARACTER WRITING

Chinese Characters (Simple)	Meaning	Probable Original Forms	Chinese Characters (Compound)	Meaning	Probable Original Forms
日	SUN		旦	SUNRISE [SUN ON HORIZON]	
月	MOON		明	BRIGHT [SUN AND MOON]	
山	MOUNTAIN		林	FOREST [TWO TREES]	
木	TREE		東	EAST [SUN BEHIND TREE]	
天	GOD		友	FRIENDSHIP [TWO HANDS]	
人	MAN		古	FACE [MOUTH WITH EYES AND NOSE]	
女	WOMAN		言	WORDS [MOUTH WITH SOUND WAVES]	
子	CHILD		話	SPEECH [FACE AND WORDS]	
手	HAND		好	GOOD [WOMAN AND CHILD]	
口	MOUTH		安	PEACE [WOMAN UNDER ROOF]	
宀	ROOF		妒	JEALOUS [WOMAN AND DOOR]	
魚	FISH		奸	TREACHEROUS [WOMAN AND HAND]	
户	DOOR		妖	UNCANNY [WOMAN AND GOD]	
井	WELL		㛰	FIGHT [TWO WOMEN UNDER ROOF]	

家	HOME [A PIG UNDER A ROOF]	衣裳	CLOTHES
屍	CORPSE	上馬	TO GET ON A HORSE
議 政 國 會	PARLIAMENT ← Compound Word →		[DISCUSS – GOVERN – COUNTRY – ASSEMBLY]

Chinese writing is ideographic, not phonetic. Therefore, although it is used in Japan and all parts of China, its pronunciation varies with the numerous dialects. As there can be no alphabetical index or dictionary in this writing, literacy among orientals is slow in spreading.

islands, at which all manner of ships, large and small, are docked. And on one especially lofty island, against its mountain-side, lies the crowded city of Hong-Kong.

It is warm here, being south of the Tropic of Cancer, and the mountain-side gullies are filled with a mixture of palms, vines, and evergreen trees, sultry in aspect, but cooled by the strong sea breeze.

In the main part of the city, near the quays, are tall modern buildings, but where the precipices rise, in the background of the city, the streets become steep, winding trails, and only the most tenacious little houses can cling to them.

Hong-Kong, being an English settlement, is garnished extensively with sporty-looking old Britishers in sun helmets, being carried about in stretcher chairs by two husky coolies, one in front and one behind, who walk along with measured step. The spasms of the supple bamboo poles across each shoulder keep the dignified passenger in a constant state of rising and falling, while the primitive vehicle croaks out a hoarse 'oomph — oomph — oomph' with every stride.

Hindus here, as in Shanghai, seem to be given the jobs where physical power is requisite. They are cops, ticket-takers, watchmen, doormen, bouncers — anything which will capitalize their burliness. And very impressive they are — as they stand with arms folded, gazing at you out of somber, deep-set eyes.

Many things are different here from North China. Not only is the climate warmer, but the people are of a slightly different race and speak a different language. They are as Chinese as around Shanghai, but the foreign component in their blood is Malay rather than Tartar. Their eyes seem less narrow, and they look more shrewd.

I have been watching a great gang of coolies engaged in constructing a big building in the middle of the city. Their working methods are characteristically Chinese. Unlike Occidental laborers, who are comparatively business-like and serious when at work, these Chinese are always chatting and joking in a highly sociable manner.

They never hurry and are never anxious to be effective. Their chief aim seems to be companionship. Needless to say, they don't do much work, and you need ten of them to fill the place of two or three Western laborers, but their pay is so low that they are well worth while to the employer — and so, everybody is satisfied.

I marvel at the amount of joy they seem to get out of life. It is very hard to understand at first, but I think they win to it through the elements of leisure and sociability. Never do they get worn out, or nervous and irritable, because they do nothing according to schedule or under pressure. Their pace and path are their own, and they are surrounded by their friends.

When, for instance, a coolie has the job of wheeling bricks from one place to another, he does not set to work and steadily and mechanically plod back and forth with his wheelbarrow, more or less unconscious of the rest of the world, as we do in America. No; he keeps in close touch with his fellow workmen — he is always joking and conversing with them.

If he feels a little tired of pushing his wheelbarrow, he sets it down and talks for a while, and perhaps gets somebody else to take it until he is rested. He changes his task often, relaxes often, and is always chatting. This, I think, is why he can work for such long hours, and is content with such meager compensation. As long as his Chinese self-respect is shielded from any rude impact, like a driving foreman or a rigid time schedule, all he asks is to be among comrades. It is very simple — and he is happy.

In the world there seem to be three main forms of what is considered necessary to happiness. One, as in America, is material possessions; the second, as in the tropics, is leisure; and the third, as here in the Orient, is companionship.

Hong-Kong — December 11. Today, as I was on my way to the dock with some luggage in a rickshaw, a Chinese boy on a bicycle ran into my coolie, cutting the latter's foot. The bawling-out that resulted was stupendous — such ferocity of expression, such waving of arms, such language! The coolie's resentment was that of a man crippled for life, and in a fury he kicked the frightened little boy, and wouldn't let him have his bicycle. Humiliation to personal pride could apparently be redeemed in no other way.

The boy, for his part, saved his 'face' by blaming someone else who, he claimed, had pushed him into us — and so the squabble continued.

Finally, my coolie, to bulwark further his threatened 'face' in the eyes of the onlookers, pulled a piece of paper out of his pocket, sat down right where he was in the middle of the street, borrowed a match from a bystander, and set fire to the paper. I wondered what in the world the fellow was up to, but he let it go out again straightway, and then, while all the crowd were offering their jabberous versions of the causes and cures of the difficulty, he rubbed the ashes carefully and thoroughly into his wounds. Having thus indicated the seriousness of his injuries, and being further sustained by another long and fierce harangue at the depravity of the little boy, his 'face' was saved. We then went on our way.

They tell me that of all the cities of China, Canton is the most utterly Chinese. It is admittedly one of the most densely populated places on earth. To make things more interesting, there is a war going on a few miles north of it, and I am very anxious to see what a Chinese war looks like.

So last night, after dark, I set forth for Canton, an overnight journey by boat up the river from Hong-Kong. The wharf where I embarked was strewn with the ragged bodies of sleeping coolies, whom I had to step over before reaching the gangplank of the *Fatchan.*

Soon we were off and weaving among little shadowy islands in the blackness, while the lookouts chattered on the bridge, perhaps discussing the prospects of meeting pirates — not unknown in these waters.

The Chinese lookout system seems strange after the one I've been used to. Instead of having one man pacing drearily back and forth by himself, they, as would be expected, have three or four who stand in a little group and jabber about things of interest seen ahead. This is another example of how Orientals can change a dull and lonely duty into a cheerful social event.

With the morning appeared Canton, and never have I seen such a crowded place. There is more of a vortex of minor industry here than even in Shanghai. Canals are jammed with sampans, loading, unloading; people are living in them and eating their breakfasts of fish and cabbage, tossing the scraps to their little brown chow dogs.

I boarded an empty sampan to look it over. They are wonderfully made crafts. The roof, cylindrical as on a covered wagon, is made of woven straw and bamboo in sliding sections which telescope within each other, and the small space in the stern not reserved for cargo is full of intricate shelves with pots, pans, tools, food, and cordage.

Although the canals and street gutters in Canton are intensely septic, most of the people, especially the girls, have on clean clothes and seem to be healthy.

Certainly everyone gets plenty of exercise. I have never seen busier people anywhere. Every soul is doing something intensely, either carrying a load, often two or three times his own size, on his back, or selling something, or building something. Even the women, when not carrying babies, have great bales on their shoulders. I saw one with a load which must easily have weighed two hundred pounds — a tremendous bundle of bamboo.

The whole street seems a congested mass of motion and cheerful chattering and singing. And there are a lot of jingling and humming and clanging and tinkling noises. Each kind of sound means something. The barber makes a twang on a certain kind of spiral-shaped wire, the book-seller rings a little bell, the meat man blows a horn, and so on; so, if you want anything, it is very simple to find it. All you have to do is to remember what kind of noise it is advertised by, and your ears will lead the way.

In addition to all the mechanical noises, there is a great deal of singing by the laborers who carry loads and who sing — to gain coördination in their work — simple chants of a monotonous rhythm.

As everywhere in China, there is a local coinage here. The only way, as far as I can see, to tell what a piece of money is worth, is to hold it up in front of a coolie. His eyes will, of course, begin to bulge, but you will notice that they bulge more at the sight of higher denominations than of lower. So, after a little experience of relative bulging, you can tell pretty accurately what each piece is worth.

In spite of its squalor, Canton is beautiful. It is full of vegetation of many kinds, winding canals, old stone arches, and temple ruins; and the people themselves are picturesque in their graceful boats and crude ox carts.

Walking through the quaint, busy streets, I set out to the northward toward the open country, to see something of the Nationalist army which is said to be engaged in a fierce war with the rebels a few miles from here. The narrow, muddy alleys presently led to broad roads, the squalid by-standers dwindled in numbers, the plastered houses became more scattered, as I approached the outer limits of the city.

There were many soldiers wandering about, most of them very ragged and clad in uniforms which would scarcely pass, at home, for an imitation of a Boy Scout's outfit. Their caps were made principally of cardboard — a very poor quality of cardboard at that — and their coats of a cloth resembling cotton gauze smeared with brown paint. It is no mystery to me that Chinese soldiers are in rags after the first rain.

As I came at length to a large crossroad, I saw several dozen soldiers waiting beside a supply store. They glanced at me suspiciously and I could hear them jabbering with one another, speculating as to my purpose and intentions.

In a few seconds they all started in my direction, trotting in huddled formation, and with their bayonets held out before them. I was apparently about to be taken by storm, for, having no weapons but a pocket knife and an innocent expression, and not knowing whether the raiders were rebels, bandits, or Nationalist soldiers, or what to do about it whatever they were, I was in no position to make a stand. Surrounded, I was ordered to put up my hands, while four of my captors went through my pockets, and the others, in a most distrustful manner, kept their guns trained on me.

My little camera seemed to cause the searchers great worry. None of them could diagnose it, and all displayed great caution in handling it. At last, however, one old fellow, who seemed extraordinarily versed in worldly wisdom, convinced them that it did not contain high explosives — and so I was allowed to go on my way.

Except for the groups of soldiers who were wandering about in the outskirts of the city, I could see no signs of war anywhere. The alleged 'great battle' against the rebels, now in process half a dozen miles distant, was apparently functioning without either aircraft or artillery. Utter silence was broken only by an occasional squad of bedraggled Chinese soldiers, young boys in faded cheap uniforms, trudging drearily home from the 'battle.' All looked tired and irresponsible, but I saw no wounded anywhere.

A missionary acquaintance of mine who has actually witnessed a Chinese 'battle' says that the opposing armies remain a mile apart and excitedly blaze away at each other. 'Their guns,' he says, 'have an effective range of about half a mile.'

The country around Canton impresses me with its vast emptiness. I've always heard that this was one of the most thickly settled spots in the world, but it is surprisingly wild and barren. The hills, being no good for rice or cabbages, seem to go to waste and remain a wilderness of dry grass, ideal for grazing land. But conservatism and tradition prevent what would be, here, a novel enterprise.

In the evening, I went to a Chinese theater: a long room full of people, with a slightly raised stage at one end, without scenery or curtain. The acting was practically all pantomime, and plenty was left to the imagination of the audience. The orchestra looked like a bunch of carpenters, sawing, chopping, and hammering away on most primitive instruments, but the music was strangely soothing, with a sort of monotonous Oriental fascination.

Between the acts they passed around steaming towels to wipe our faces with. Very refreshing after breathing that stuffy atmosphere the whole evening.

Some of the acts lasted for hours — so long that the actors seemed to be in need of recess. I noticed especially two young Chinamen who were supposed to be prisoners chained to a post. Having arrived at a rather fidgety state, they began to edge slowly toward the side of the stage, dragging the post with them. Gradually, in short wriggles, calculated to avoid being conspicuous, they made over to the end of the platform, where each in turn, with the utmost solemnity, and entirely without furtiveness, leaned over the edge and relieved himself. Then they wriggled back, as dignified as ever, to their position in the center of the stage and continued with being prisoners chained to a post.

None of the animal exigencies common to mankind seem to embarrass the Chinese at all. Calling as little attention to them as possible, the poised Chinaman ignores, without attempting to conceal, these unlovely occurrences.

A fat man in the front row of the balcony thought nothing of spitting intermittently over the rail upon the audience. Too gripped by the intense excitement of the play was he to consider the effect of his casual indulgence upon the unfortunates below. No one in the theater had a greater air of dignity and refinement.

Next morning as I boarded the train for Kowloon where I could take ship for Manila, I noticed a Chinese family, an old mamma and three boys, who had been carrying baggage into the train for a Hindu Gentleman. They had evidently succeeded in bulldozing him into giving them more than he should, for I saw them gloating in predatory glee over the handful of coins they had received. It is queer the way Chinese go almost wild with the joys of overcharging.

CHAPTER SEVEN

THE PHILIPPINES

Manila, P.I. After one day of steaming across the vast, sultry, millpond of the China Sea, I awoke early this morning in Manila Bay. It is hot. The country seems very similar to the Hawaiian Islands except that it is flatter and there is more of it.

Manila is still a Spanish city in appearance and atmosphere, with old buildings of smooth plastered masonry, with courtyards and balconies. The people, while obviously Orientals, show unmistakable traces of Spanish blood, and the women wear bright shawls and dresses of Spanish lace. Much here besides language and religion has come from far-off Spain.

I drove from the dock in a little top-buggy, like a black sunbonnet on wheels, drawn by a diminutive horse. There were hundreds of buggies like it in the streets, and many automobiles, and occasional big carts pulled by water buffalo. These animals are driven by a rope tied to each horn and waddle complacently along flapping a hairy ear on either side. It must be a dry life for a water buffalo — this hauling loads of bamboo through hot, dusty streets.

Finally my buggy went through a tunnel piercing the

staunch old Spanish wall, and my little brown driver pulled up to a crumbling plastered gateway. He said that this was the cheapest lodging-place in town.

I found myself in a patio full of clotheslines, chickens, monkeys, and flower-pots. Up the stone stairs on the broad balcony sat the landlady, a fat, dusky old dame, fanning herself in a rocking-chair, surrounded by an assortment of timid-looking children. The house inside is made of white-washed old boards, and is one big, high-ceilinged room with six-foot partitions to form little compartments for sleeping.

The proprietor's family make rattan and bamboo furniture in their 'factory' on the other side of the patio. The kids don't take their work very seriously and wander about playing with monkeys. Sometimes I hear the landlady teaching a boy of six to say 'Gimme money' whenever he sees a stranger. This innocent tot, being dressed in the height of pathos, must add much to the family income.

This old Spanish house is charming. Last night I took a bath, with two big buckets of water, out in a little alcove off the moonlit balcony while, across the patio, the family made music and the little girls danced on the wide piazza at the head of the stairs. The abundant vines, flower-pots, old mossy stone posts in the balustrade, and beyond, the Filipino girls dancing, made a picturesque setting for my prosaic activities. This family must have Spanish blood in their veins, so well do they fit into these beautiful Spanish surroundings.

Although they are exceedingly thoughtful and hospitable to me, I cannot get on nearly as intimate terms with these people as I enjoyed with my Nagasaki friends. Compared to the Japanese I've known, these Filipinos are cautious and unconfiding. This is due, I think, to the innate inferiority complex that is so prevalent among Filipinos that it can be considered a dominant racial characteristic. It is an inheritance from the long subjugation of their proud race.

Like other Orientals, they are not individualistic, and their touchy pride is not that of an individual, but a mass feeling. Denied normal expression, this pride of theirs takes odd forms. They incline to aristocratic appearances, and love to wear silk shirts, and will 'high-hat' foreigners if they can, though perfectly polite if you are careful of their feelings.

They are like the Japanese in that they have a strong national consciousness and a patriotic desire to see their people politically free — not because they feel badly governed, but from national egotism. It is the implication in foreign domination that they are an inferior race that rankles, more than any sense of actual injustice. Except for this inferiority complex, they are very like their cousins the Japanese — patriotic, clean and neat, idealistic, sensitive, and honest.

Very susceptible to suggestion, they are easily led. They love crowded living conditions and will bunch together in the most cramping proximity, even when there is plenty of room. As far as I can see, they have a very optimistic philosophy, and feel that it is only a question of time before they attain their national aims. In the mean time, they take their fun where they find it. Very fond of music, gambling, and revelling, they make the best of things — while watching with satisfaction their increasing self-government.

In the Manila Public Library today, I read some books and articles by Filipinos, full of their native idealism, and in which they discuss with frankness and intelligence their own national traits. They ascribe their touchiness and pride and their weakness of suggestibility to the fact that long domination has denied them a chance to evolve and form a stable character of their own.

In speaking of their adaptability, one of these writers says:

'What may appear to other Orientals as a weakness may really be our strength, if we can preserve the good that is our own — the valuable and useful practices and ideals which our people have learned to cherish — and at the same time gradually absorb from the civilization of the whole world those things which, through experience, have been found either useful or beautiful. It may be our good fortune that our people, as well as their character, are the product of the influences of both East and West, for they may thus contribute a world outlook and point of view which will help mankind to attain those conditions of good understanding, good will, and justice, for which it has been struggling from the beginning.'

Yesterday morning I set out to see something of Filipino country life. On the train for Bauan, one hundred and twenty-eight miles south of Manila, I joggled along over a soft, low, rolling meadow land interspersed with frequent groves of tall bamboo and occasional herds of long-faced water buffalo wallowing in the swamps.

We passed through spacious rice-fields, and sometimes vast stretches of sugar-cane. Much of this country could be taken for Hawaii, with occasional little sugar mills, and always, not far to the eastward, that irregular mountainous horizon, barely seen over the feathery tops of bamboo clumps, and silhouetted in hazy purple against the empty, torrid sky.

The station platforms are lively with long-haired Filipino girls selling eggs and fruit from wide baskets on their heads. In the cab of an engine on a siding, the Filipino engineer and fireman are singing gleefully together as if they hadn't a care in the world. Even the responsibilities attending a modern locomotive can't repress the Filipino spirit of child-like merry-making.

Sometimes we come to great hilly palm jungles, where

copra comes from, and sometimes rubber trees and coffee bushes, until finally we draw near to the coast again. The Filipinos in this train seem to be farmers and poultry men. Judging by the noise, there must be at least fifty hens and other fowls in the car.

As an example of the Filipino's love of being crowded, on the seat opposite me sits a man with two roosters in his lap. Wedged in on either side of him are two old women, one holding a hen and one a baby. The next seat back of this Oriental congestion is entirely empty.

I have made friends with a fellow who sits beside me. He has the usual Filipino black eyes, dark, straight hair slicked back, smooth cocoa-colored skin, and says he is a law student. He is highly unoriginal in being interested in the question of the independence of the Philippine Islands. All educated Filipinos, when not thinking about food, money, or the cosmic urge, are thinking about independence.

'It isn't fair,' he says, 'for the United States to deny Filipinos their independence and, at the same time, to refuse to grant them representation in Congress' — this being a popular plea for independence broadcast by Filipino politicians. In this and in all he subsequently said, my legal friend voiced the ideas held generally by the intelligent Filipino.

'The islands,' he said, 'have now a good, stable government administered almost entirely by native Filipinos, and I am positive that the Filipinos are able to govern themselves, entirely unaided by the U.S.A.' He admitted that they had nothing to complain of in the present government other than their lack of representation, and the injury to their pride imposed by dependency. This last was so great as to make happiness impossible to them as a nation.

There are Americans living here who say that the Filipinos are hopelessly irresponsible, and incapable of governing themselves. But I am not so sure.

My diminutive friend asked me, as we swayed and rattled into Bauan, his home town, to take lunch at his house, and I accepted.

Bauan is a small village by the sea, made up of the usual thatched huts on bamboo poles, and swarms of brown people. In the streets wander, I suppose, every sort of domestic animal known to man — except elephants. When the drenching May-to-November monsoon hits these settlements, it must be fine for the water buffalo — and I suppose the turkeys and pigs go upstairs.

Walking up a narrow lane of flimsy huts, we came to a house on a side hill, surrounded by tattered green banana trees. Several small brown children, their loose white clothing barely covering their dusky torsos, leaned, gazing at me, over the straw-woven window-sill. A little dog was playing with a goat at the foot of the door-ladder, and we had to push a couple of hens off the rungs as we ascended. Animals were everywhere.

On reaching the top, I find myself in a sizable room and surrounded by the stumpy relatives of my attorney friend, all gazing suspiciously and intently upon me. My friend, in his neat European dress, contrasts strongly with his wrinkled mother in her loose-hanging drapery, and with the multitude of scantily clad children of all sizes.

Introducing me briefly to his mother, whom he treats rather disdainfully, he asks me to sit down at the table for lunch, while the old woman nods, timidly receding into a far corner. My host has an attitude toward his family which plainly says, and with pride, 'Look at this guest I have brought home. Note what a man of the world I am.' He hardly deigns to look at these cowering spectators at all. But to me he maintains a most gracious hospitality. I am probably the only foreigner who has ever been in this hut, and it is obviously an occasion.

As we seat ourselves, a couple of black pigs — the kind

known as 'razor-backs' at home — come wandering in from the uphill door and sit down under the table. Neighbors' children appear and join the swarm of onlookers till there are at least twenty kids standing around, watching my every move. The meal is very good — mostly fruit and nuts — but you have to be careful not to let things get too near to the edge of the table on account of the pigs. Every time you drop a crumb there is a wild rush for it, and the brutes are very careless and clumsy in their movements. More than once I think the table is going.

Afterwards I thanked my host for his very real hospitality, and set out on a hike cross-country. I followed a winding muddy lane in which wandered herds of hairy, black swine, and sometimes Filipino farmers in huge sombreros returning from the fields. Everyone I saw seemed excessively timid and afraid of me. I would smile and make signs of friendliness, but only the very boldest dared smile in return. Most of them stared open-mouthed and edged suspiciously away.

I crossed a corn-field lined with scraggly hedges of castor-oil bushes and long grass. There were beautiful sparsely wooded hilltops about, and valleys patched and dotted with bamboo groves and densely leaved trees. All the foliage was glaring with the most vivid greenness, and full of the tangled vines and creepers of the jungle. The heat was fierce, a luxury of living warmth that deadened thought. Sleepily, I sat down in the grass on a knoll, while crickets chirped and trilled about me, bees hummed faintly, and tiny, brightly colored birds cocked their heads from near-by bushes, pausing in their sweet ecstasy of song.

I could see the deep blue ocean far down to the westward, and, way-way off, a great mountain range on another island, Mindoro, in the Sulu Sea. Miles away in the little village could be heard the mellow tolling of the schoolhouse bell in the old Spanish belfry ——

I awoke, and ambled into the midst of a great bamboo jungle. With the breeze, the thousands of slender yellow-green poles moved weirdly with a sound like creaking cordage. Farther on, I came to a hut where two dogs slept in the sun and a woman washed clothes in a tiny pool. Within six feet of them I passed — unnoticed.

Back in the village, I finally persuaded, by a long and delicate process of friendly gestures, some little school kids to toss their ball with me. After we once got going, their suspicions disappeared altogether, and, before I knew it, practically the whole population was on the scene, cheering and clapping their hands.

One little boy wanted me to play pingpong. These children all know some English, so conversation is not difficult.

'I would like very much to play,' said I, whereupon my diminutive and dusky companions led me to a hut over on one side of the street, where, under the great matted eaves, stood a pingpong table, complete in equipment, but about one third the usual size. The whole swarm gathered about, steadily increasing in numbers, and pressed so close that we could not make side shots; but there was tremendous enthusiasm from the spectators, and laughter and applause when the ball bounced off one of their little brown heads.

This friendly merriment over a childish game is sincere. But don't think, for a moment, that it is more than one facet of the character of these people, which includes every complication of Oriental psychology.

The ancestors of these laughing villagers were Malays, a fierce, ungovernable race of pirates, conquerors, and traders along the equatorial shores of Asia, whose swift praus were the terror of these uncharted waterways.

Mohammedan in religion, fatalistic in philosophy, they swarmed upon these sultry coasts — human embodiments of the fierce vitality and swift destruction of the environment that bred them.

They overran the entire Philippine archipelago, driving the Negrito aborigines into the mountains — but not before they had received an element of Negrito blood into their inheritance. Later, a steady infiltration from China further modified their Malay characteristics, and gave an agricultural permanence to their occupation.

Spain's conquest of these islands was as ruthless as anything in their remote piratical past, but it varied with locality, and she never entirely subdued the southern group. To this day, they remain Mohammedans, living in small warlike tribes.

But for centuries, upon the bulk of these primitive little brown people her hand lay heavy, while her religion and social mould closed down over their primitive customs.

Here, then, was a nicely complicated little racial, religious, and political problem; and it was into this that the United States, in 1898, most innocently and unintentionally barged. For a generation since, we — as devoid of conquering ambition as any great nation has ever been, we with democratic ideals and good intentions — have struggled to negotiate a people of Oriental psychology and tropical temperament, mixed in blood, primitive in development, utterly alien to us in thought, and warped by centuries of subjugation.

In our bewilderment at being here at all, we automatically applied the process we were accustomed to use in frontier lands: eliminated opposition to our intrusion, and then proceeded to institute American ideas, in spite of the fact that no Americans lived here or wanted to do so.

During this long period of unwelcome benefaction, of instituting schools and sanitation and roads and parliamentary ideas, we have constantly questioned our right to be here, and our Filipino beneficiaries, stimulated by improved conditions and more general education, have joined us enthusiastically in that doubt.

In the mean time, here we are — seeking an objective too much a part of erratic national idealism to be understood by other nations — in a long task which could have been negotiated consistently only by a subtlety we do not possess or a ruthlessness we are not willing to employ.

We uncomfortably realize that our government here is unsupported by our basic national principle that 'Governments are instituted among men, deriving their just powers from the consent of the governed.'

But the authorities tolerate this discrepancy. They assume that a future Filipino nation will award to our present government a posthumous consent of the governed — in the light of a prosperity and independence made possible and secure by this period of American tutelage.

So here we stay — somewhat self-conscious and apologetic — and looking forward, along with our Filipino friends, to the happy day when we will go home where we belong.

My pingpong game came to a satisfactory conclusion. In every color of the prism, the sun was sinking into the Sulu Sea. Dusk was stealing from under the banana trees, along the ragged street of thatched houses, when I took my leave of Bauan. Mothers called to their children, chickens flapped up to roost, the sultry dark closed down upon the warm, rich earth.

Sharing the innocent excitements of a game with merry children is ended. Bauan, with the tropic night, withdraws itself from me into its own remote life — which I cannot share for long — which perhaps no white man can fully understand.

CHAPTER EIGHT

NORTH CHINA

On board S.S. Tjikembang. At Hong-Kong, on my way north to Peking, I boarded this Dutch ship *Tjikembang*, bound from Java to Shanghai. Her name, when properly pronounced, sounds like stumbling over a milk bottle in a concrete entry, and means 'Flower River.'

There is one missionary aboard, and the other passengers are Dutch, Javanese, Hindu, and Chinese. Only Asiatics are allowed to go steerage or second-class, which rule forces me in with the first-class passengers, and for a remarkably low fare. I sit at the captain's table with three Dutchmen and the missionary.

The first meal was very somber — the mammoth Hollanders gazed ominously into space, chewing steadily the while and saying nothing. At the second meal, however, we had beer, and a few gruff observations, mostly meteorological and gastronomic.

This afternoon, driving through a raw, frothy sea — the kind where the wind has come up too suddenly for the waves to rise and the water is all swept with spume — we approached Amoy, one of our ports of call. The sky was black, and the sea almost white with foam under an ill-boding light, while pale cliffs stood out like teeth before the murky hills.

Amoy is a medley of motion and traffic — as are all Chinese ports — gliding sampans, dense throngs in the streets, frenzied rickshaw men, coolies straining under gigantic loads; everywhere the antlike industry of the Orient.

Soon we weighed anchor, and we are now at sea again, ploughing steadily northward into the cold. Night has come. Still continues that mysterious light on the surface of the ocean. The foaming crests, like a million ghosts, are gliding hissing past, filled with a strange green fire. They shine — even to the horizon. Phosphorus I have seen many times, but never the like of this. Even the phlegmatic Dutch skipper is stirred about it.

'Nefer haf I seen such stuff like dot,' he grunts, 'nefer een mine life.'

December 23. We are at the full mercy of the monsoon this morning. The *Tjikembang* is prancing about like a wild horse. The sea has become tremendous, and now roars past us in staggering mountains and valleys. When we have plunged into the depths of a vast watery crater, our whole horizon is but one wave — a wild avalanche bearing down on us — terrifying, overwhelming; a towering mass of water with ruffles of white foam laced across its green immensity.

I lean on the poop rail, gazing at this dappled flood surging just beneath my nose, when suddenly there is a reverberation in the depths — a thunderous shudder, as if the whole ocean were collecting its forces for attack. Then, as if shot out of a volcano, our gigantic hulk is hurled with terrifying force into the sky. There is a cruel sound of stretching, rending iron. The entire foaming world drops dizzily out of sight — I cling to the quivering rail — and in an instant we are among the clouds. Our mighty hull is standing on end. There is a shrill whir of propellers raised momentarily out of water, and our stern seems to whip back and forth in the empty air like a bamboo pole. Hatches crash, heavy chains grind and clang; everywhere is a great straining and creaking, as if our very keel would snap.

Then, with a twisting, writhing, sideways motion, we are dropped hurtling into the abysmal hollows. The wind whistles upward through my hair, salty spray sweeps stinging past, and, with the stupendous splash of sixteen thousand tons of iron, we are all but buried again in the hissing mountains of spume. There is nothing in the world more beautiful, nothing in the world more terrible than the sea.

A Chinaman in a skullcap sleeps in my room. Not once has he been out of bed since we left Amoy, and he isn't sick either. He just lies and smokes cigarettes and gazes at the ceiling, and once in a while he reads a little. Peace is much more to a Chinaman's liking than any kind of exhilaration, which is why opium is preferred to alcohol. The Chinese labor or exert themselves only for tangible reward or to satisfy some powerful tradition — never for the pure pleasure of exercise. A Chinese official in Hong-Kong, who was witnessing for the first time a tennis match between two of his foreign friends, remarked, 'Great game. But why not pay coolies to do it, and sit at ease and enjoy it yourselves?'

Christmas Day. S.S. Hoten Maru — outbound northward from Shanghai for Tsingtao. When I landed at Shanghai, I learned that the railroad from there to Peking was being bombed by the rebels, so I have to go north by sea as far as Tsingtao and from there, by a relatively unbombed railroad, to Peking.

As I had a humble, third-class ticket on this boat, I sought out the most squalid group of humans I could find on the dock, thinking that they must be my companions in destitution. But it appears that my eye for squalor is a bit too keen. These wretches were bound for the fourth-class quarters in which only Asiatics are allowed, and I was shortly summoned upward to the third-class.

It was just as well. The fourth-class quarters consisted of an excessively crowded portion of the well-deck, and were occupied by Chinese, on their migratory way to Manchuria, and who were not in a condition conducive to snuggling.

Vaccination for smallpox, having been recently introduced into China on a large scale, has prevented the dying-off of countless millions of children. Formerly sixty per cent of all Chinese children died of it. In the old days, when a census-taker came to a Chinese hut to count the members of the household, he would perhaps see eight or ten children playing about the floor. On inquiring of the mother as to the number of children she had, he would be informed 'two' or 'three.'

'How about all those there?' says the census-taker.

'Oh, those!' from mamma. 'They haven't had smallpox yet.'

Children, in those days, didn't count until they had survived this inevitable disease.

Vaccination, with other modern sanitary measures, has thus increased the terrific pressure of population in Central China, resulting in starvation, cannibalism, and all sorts of appalling things. This crowd of destitute people are fleeing from these conditions to the wide lands of Manchuria.

Before I left the fourth-class well-deck and its utterly pathetic collection of human beings, I saw a Chinaman with a face that was pure horror. It has been eaten away by syphilis. He has no nose at all; his mouth is a tiny round hole that he can neither open nor close; and his eyes are mere dimples. His whole head is like a formless mass of dough. And there are others ——

One old man, when I first saw him, was evidently in agonizing need of cocaine. By means of a safety-pin he was

trying to inject the dope into his leg, but he shook so violently that he could hardly make a scratch. It was a ghastly
spectacle. When he finally got the stuff in, after what
seemed an age, he calmed down immediately. Then, as I
left him, an indescribably serene smile — like a shaft of sun-
light — formed across his ashen face. He was relieved —
but I cannot forget that monstrous struggle.

I am now in the more bourgeois third-class, but at tiffin-
time there appeared little of interest to an Occidental stomach. A couple of stout Chinese stewards were ladling out a
fetid vegetable substance resembling spinach mixed with
coleslaw. Neither the sight nor the odor of this delicacy
was stimulating, but if I wanted any Christmas dinner, I
must take it as it came. Wading through a mass of clamoring Chinese, I secured a portion of the stuff and was pushing
my way out of the crowd when one of the Chinese stewards
advanced upon me, jabbering hysterically and brandishing
his dripping ladle.

He grabbed hold of my bowl. From the crescendo in his
harangue and the glare in his eye, it was obvious that I must
fight for my recently acquired Yuletide feast. Mine not to
reason why — so I took a firmer grip on the greasy con-
tainer while the other stewards rallied to the support of my

assailant. Just as I was contemplating immediate engulf-
ment of my repast ere it be too late — from the deck
above, came a voice.

'Hi zair!'

I glanced up the companionway to see a young man
beckoning to me with — a piece of ham!

'You, down zair, plees to come up — ve gif you good
deenir.'

Instantly I decided that ham was the better part of valor,
relinquished my hold of the Chinese idea of nourishment,
and hopped up to the deck above. There I found a group
of people who turned out to be White Russians, Eugene
Kirkor, his wife Tamara, and some others.

They were in the midst of a meal of ham, bread, and hot
dogs — to which they generously invited me. To this provi-
dential Christmas dinner, I added some of mamma's left-
over peanuts, and discovered that my friends were returning
to Tsingtao, where they lived, that they had not been in
Russia since the revolution, and that they did not regret
it at all.

'Arr you going to trry to go zroo Roosia?' they asked,
astonished. 'Oh, no! you must not do zat — you vill nefer
get out alife. Ve haf been zair — you must take our advice.
Ze commoonists arr cannibals — zey murdair you — zey
shoot you wenefer zey feel like! You must not go!'

These White Russians were very intelligent, and quite sane
on all other subjects — but mention the communists, and
they became even wilder than they said the communists were.

With a fat, bald, bullet-headed man, one of Eugene's
friends, I played some chess during the evening. He was a
shrewd player, but he had a bad habit of taking back moves
when subsequent events revealed weakness in his position.
In self-defense, I adopted a similar policy.

'I mus' take back zat las' move,' announces Humpty
Dumpty, 'eet was ver' stoopid.'

'Oh, yes,' I reply, 'and I'll take back that fool one of mine.'

'Of courze, yes,' says he, 'and you won't mind, I am sure, eef I take over again my move before zat, also. I made zair a most zerious mistake.'

The game went backward faster than it went forward and became practically interminable.

Never were people more kind to a traveler than Eugene Kirkor and his wife while I waited at Tsingtao for my night train to Peking. Poverty-stricken musicians and exiles as they are, they gave me a big ham and egg dinner, a warm room and their company. Like all the exiled and unhappy of the world, they hope some day to get to America. Such generous hearts would enrich any land.

Among other kindnesses, they show a grave concern about the dangers of my trip north from here.

'You mus' have warm coat,' said Eugene. 'I get you one.'

With that he summons a Chinese house boy and details him to haggle me an overcoat among the innumerable pawnshops which line the street outside.

In and out of the shops we wander — the boy and I — pricing, examining, expressing horror at the high price of dusty old Chinese overcoats. The boy is very young, but, being Chinese, is an expert haggler. We walk out of shop after shop, gradually getting the prices down: three hundred, one hundred, sixty, twenty, ten, five dollars — concentrating only on the most humble coats.

At last we've found a coat, first priced at one hundred dollars, which we've haggled down to three. When we have walked out of the shop four times at this price, we realize that it will go no lower. We buy the coat. Of fairly heavy wool, with short loose sleeves in Chinese style, it is to be my closest friend for many months to come.

Two hours of stampeding around with a lot of frowsy third-class passengers in the station, and being corraled by ragged gold-braided soldiers with daggers, I finally, in the middle of the night, boarded my train — the most dilapidated so far, and icy cold. The lights would not go on, the benches were mere splintery boards, a few inches wide, that momentarily threatened to fall apart, and everyone, of course, had his maximum cubic footage of bundles. With my Chinese overcoat, my baggage was further swollen by the possession of a cotton comforter — price, a dollar and a half, and brightly, beautifully pink. These two are to defend me from the northern blizzards.

Nowhere was there space to lie down, but, feeling my way along in the darkness, I came at length to an especially corpulent old Chinaman — a veritable fountain of animal heat. I snuggled up to him as close as I could, and was quite warm and comfortable, though the smells and sounds and squalor would have been tough on one who had not long since become accustomed to them. My bunkie proved potent as a central heating plant. When chilled, I merely turned my cool side toward him.

It was so dark that I could see very little, but I could hear plenty, and smell even more. Every now and then there would be a thud as something gave way and deposited one of our number on the floor; then boisterous laughter all down the car — good evidence that cheerfulness was with us. It is marvelous how these people can thrive and be merry under such wretched conditions. And it must be a great advantage to have not the slightest feeling of repulsion about an old lady in filthy rags leaning against you and spitting opium juice on the floor, or a greasy gent of Moby Dick proportions, such as was with me, sliding into your lap from the other flank and emitting shrill snores in an unearthly soprano. You have to hand it to the Chinese; and with it all, they have dignity and poise, and great self-respect.

I could not sleep. The night was a long, dreary nightmare, though somewhat illuminating at intervals. Dawn found us in a flat country covered with snow. Peering through the frosted panes, we could see grave mounds scattered over the bleak landscape, and mud huts, few of which — even among the humblest — were without 'pailou' arches over the doorways and other evidences of a cultured heritage.

While changing trains at Tsinan, a picturesque, windy town whose people, with red, windburnt faces, are larger and healthier than the Southern Chinese, I fared forth to find something to eat. This town is pure Northern Chinese. With the exception of a bank and one or two legation buildings, there is no sign of any foreign element in this primitive place, and no restaurant to be found.

Rawboned women, so tall and strong that they are almost indistinguishable from their husbands, haul heavy wheelbarrow loads across the windswept causeways. The bleak rolling country is of grayish-brown earth, the low houses are built of it, the people are dusty with it, the streets are rutted deep with its mud.

At last I found, on the outskirts of town, a little shop of earthenware jugs where the proprietor, in sign-language, said he would sell me some eggs and green tea. Meanwhile, he regaled me with talk about extra-territoriality — all in elaborate sign-language — and the latest news about the rebels, who have just completed a good ravage in these parts.

Some communist propaganda posters in town are attributed to them, and have caused great excitement. Such things as these posters are bad for the Chinese. They stimulate in them no desire for constructive effort, but merely the contagious idea that extortion from those who have achieved prosperity is the poor man's only — and therefore justified — means of salvation.

The railroad again — this train for Peking. More scrambling. More squalor, and of a colder variety. There is no stove or heating arrangement of any kind whatever in the cars, and the windows are seldom shut. The passive Chinese, too bundled in rags to feel anything beyond the fourteenth layer, counting outward, like to have the windows open so that they can reach out and buy fritters and tea at the stations without having to leave their seats. As a result of this, the temperature in the car is well below zero.

Peking — December 28. Today at noon we came to a stone wall forty feet high and twenty feet thick. The train passed through it by a tunnel; a minute later we pierced another and similar wall. We were entering Peking, the ancient city for whose defense these stupendous barricades were built.

Here in Northern China everything is different from the South — language, coinage; the people are a different race. Walking out of the Peking railroad station, I found myself in a wide square, full of the usual swarms of jabbering rickshaw men and cab men, who have small closed cabs drawn by a woolly horse. Each rushes at you with both hands and both feet, explaining to you in passionate desperation that he will take you to any place you name, and much more cheaply and quickly than you ever dreamed possible.

Eight miles over the bleak plains outside the city, there is a little town called Haitien, at the foot of the Western Hills. Toward it, in a skimpy rickshaw with my baggage in my lap and my pink comforter around me, I started on an icy jaunt. I was to visit some English friends of mine who are teachers in the great Yenching University of Peking.

It being a long trip, my rickshaw coolie had a relief man who trotted behind while awaiting his turn in the shafts. Streets full of traffic, trolley cars, rickshaws. Jogging steadily onward we turned off the thoroughfare, and began to wind through narrow alleys, sometimes barely five feet wide, rounding sharp corners, when we would come suddenly upon an old woman carrying fagots, or a barber, knife in hand, leaning in the cold over his fat, squatting patron. On either side are high mud walls, hiding squalid dwellings from which come the sounds of children laughing dogs barking, old men jabbering, and all manner of strange Oriental odors. On we go, winding, dodging through the alleys of Peking.

I was about frozen by the time we had passed through the great pailou arches of the city gates. These are always double, and arranged so that you make a right-angle turn in them, thus excluding evil spirits which, according to the Chinese theory, always travel in straight lines.

Five long miles more across a bleak, windy, flat country, getting colder every minute, till, shivering in every vertebra, I would have given anything to have changed places with the coolie, but couldn't because I was too cold to move. At last we reached the house of my friends, a beautiful old place, once the home of a mandarin prince, and surrounded by tile-topped walls and double pailous according to custom.

Here is the highest society I've experienced since the Governor of Hawaii — charming, cultivated people who are professors or missionaries, often the same thing out here. Among them I am spending a nomadic week and, as their wide hospitality involves a superabundance of guests, I find myself at times in my old place — sleeping on the floor with the pink comforter. This possession is becoming more valuable to me all the time, though it isn't as pink as it once was, and I can still smell my fat Chinaman at one corner and the opium lady at another. My friends look somewhat askance at it, not realizing its true worth.

December 30. You should see the way a Chinese traffic cop settles a dispute. When an accident occurs, instead óf taking down license numbers and handing out a summons in a righteous rage, as American cops do, the Chinese policeman asks each party to express his views on the situation then and there, and listens patiently to the ensuing session of jabber and frenzied debate. The flocking spectators must have their say, too — in fact, there is much to be said by all. At last, after an hour or two, when everyone's 'face' has been well saved and public opinion has been defined, and it is clearly understood that no one was to blame, the cop works around very diplomatically until he can bring about a compromise satisfactory to all involved. This may require all day, or all night, as the case may be; but he is a poor cop who does not effect it eventually, when the affair is settled for good.

Subservience to the law is easier for people devoid of individuality than for those, like us, who have so much of it. A Chinaman subscribes to public opinion, where we submit to it.

December 31. I met Will and James again yesterday, and they are now staying with me here in Haitien. It is great to see them, and to exchange stories of our recent adventures. The English girls here are very, very conservative, and are shocked when we tell our adventures in too vivid detail — but we make a great effort to broaden their tolerance.

The Chinese girls in Haitien are the most beautiful in all this country. They even have sex appeal to foreigners, which is practically unknown in the rest of China. Jim says he thinks our presence here for the last few days, which no doubt has had a stimulating effect on the girls, is largely responsible for their unprecedented comeliness.

Last night, Will, James, and I went into town on what purported to be a party — and spent the evening singing hymns amid a large assortment of missionaries. Foreign society in Peking is very high, and is famous throughout the world for making you wear boiled shirts to tea. But it is divided into two groups: the legation and business group, and the missionaries. I find myself — God knows why — among the missionaries.

Missionaries are pioneers of the many influences from the West that are seeping into China and undermining the traditions that have bound her for so long. I wonder how much the Chinese are helped by this occidental reformation movement which seeks to supersede the great moral force of Patriarchism. A man who has lived almost a lifetime in China says, 'The hopeless feature of the present situation is that the growth of wholesome new ideas is infinitesimal as compared with the collapse of old moral standards.'

When Chinese tradition and its discipline are removed, the people go wild. One Chinese boy here, heir to thirty centuries of tradition, and who has recently been taught that its constraint is an evil, wrote home the other day to his father in the country, recommending him to 'get rid of that woman you are living with. She has bound feet, and is old, and no good anyhow. Why don't you come here to the city and get yourself a nice young one and enjoy life for a change?' This certainly seems a heartless way for a

Chinese boy of patriarchal heritage to be speaking about his own mother.

January 1. Why does Manchuria draw northward almost a million Chinese every year from their ancient homes in the South? I am curious to see this promised land, this so-old country that, under modern methods of exploitation, offers hope and opportunity to the wretched Chinese. On my way into Siberia, I shall go through as much of Manchuria as I can.

With that purpose in mind, I am now on the train for Tientsin, on the first short leg of my journey, and I am sitting beside the very prettiest Chinese girl that you can imagine. She has the color, and somewhat the contour, of a ripe peach. But she is sensitive-looking, with big, soft brown eyes, and she can speak a little English and a lot of sign-language.

Soon after the train started, she pulled out of her bundle a huge bag of chestnuts and we had a feast, to which I supplied a few raisins, bought in Seward, Alaska. Then the neighbors joined in, donating more chestnuts and a few rather haggard oranges, and we were all very gay. We called it the New Year's dinner.

It's wonderful how friendly Chinese will become in a short time. These people, who have never seen each other before, and who, a minute ago, were buffeting each other for seats, now are as companionable as roommates in a girls' boarding-school. They ask me all sorts of questions: my age, nationality, destination, and purpose in life; and are very interested in my answers.

One of the old men, by finger sign-language, tells me he is seventy-three — they are very proud of old age in China, for the older you are here the more divine you are. I kid this old man about his great age, making motions of digging a grave and of putting a corpse into it. He retaliates by waving his arms, dancing, and punching his fat benchmate to show his virility.

Everything is done in a spirit of good fun, and there is constant hilarity and smiles on all sides. This, by the way, gives me a clue to the reason why Chinese have such slit eyes. I think it is because for ages they have smiled so much. They are always in good spirits, and as they beam, their eyes wrinkle at the outside corners a little and get narrow.

On train, two hours out of Tientsin. On and on again toward Mukden. This is cold! I don't know whether I can live through tonight or not. There are twenty hours of it ahead, and it is worse than camping on the open steppe. The icy wind made by the train is terrific. I find that my Chinese companions wear fur-lined pajamas and fur haori overcoats; so they have advantages over me. They persist in opening all the windows at every station, as well as often between, and never think of closing the door. I don't believe the word 'stove' has even been introduced into their language as yet. Their hardihood is phenomenal — fur or no fur.

I have my pink comforter wrapped around me. It is something — but leaky in spots. What there is of my Chinese overcoat is all right, but the sleeves are very short and open — the Chinese use them for muffs — and all the buttons have by this time snapped off. I see some shivering ahead.

The severe cold also causes great trouble with the toilet arrangements, which are none too good anyway, and results in the most obnoxious smells as the drains get frozen up. All provisions for privacy have long since fallen apart and the accumulating emanation is in plain view of everyone in the car. The scene is hardly fit for more detailed description.

We are now in the country of the great China Wall. The ground is bare and windswept, with thin, clinging splotches of snow here and there, and grave mounds and bleak plains punctuated with frequent ranges of steep brown mountains, all very bare and immensely cold.

In each little station, the peddlers still flock to our open windows, and shove their wares upon the sills, hollering hysterically, 'Yao booyao!' while emitting from their cracked mouths dense clouds of steaming breath. They specialize in little roasted chickens covered with some sort of brilliant red varnish, which they sell to us in quantities, very cheaply. And, of course, there are the usual cherries and fritters. On trying fritters, I found them stone cold and full of grime and cinders from being lugged around the dusty station — probably for months.

It was dark by half-past four in the afternoon, as we rattled slowly northward over the rickety track. A long grisly nightmare was beginning. There seemed nothing to do but just sit and try to keep from shivering, but my icy joints soon grew pretty numb.

As the night wore on, we stopped frequently at small stations, and the number of my fellow passengers decreased rapidly, bringing animal heat to a huge premium. The car now was occupied mostly by bundles — and it is a tough job to get any animal heat out of an icy hamper of tea-kettles or a tattered sack of bamboo and cabbages.

I was seated beside a Chinese doctor who could speak a little English, but he was scrawny and, though extremely nice between spits, he was no solution to the heating problem. You might as well snuggle up to a wire fence. And so the minutes crawled along, now slipping two or three at a time, now stopping altogether with a cruel pitilessness, and the hours loomed ahead like Arctic winters, always, always ahead — a grisly, intangible mirage. Horrible!

Mukden. Was it good to see Mukden! It was morning and clear as a bell, and I don't know how cold, but we were here — Mukden! I walked out of the big open station, desperate for a place to get warm. The tattered rickshaw men clamored, as usual, like famished wolves, and a long row of frosty cabs stood behind as many little furry horses with icicles hanging from their steaming noses.

I hated to discriminate among the poor devils with their rickshaws, and I needed exercise to get warm anyhow, so I ignored their clamoring and trudged stiffly into the bleak street with my baggage, to look for a hotel. I was wild to see a stove, but the houses at the street sides looked about as cozy and hospitable as icebergs. Today is one of the New Year holidays, and all shops are closed. Being unusually cold and windy, almost no one was on the streets.

I had troubles. My hands began to give out on me. My baggage, containing all my earthly possessions, which have been accumulating steadily since I left New York, is by no means light and my mittens are full of holes. Soon my fingers were so numb that they felt like iron hooks. Knowing, after my Peking experience, that a rickshaw is the coldest, most exposed, and most cramped mode of winter travel in the world, there was nothing to do but trudge onward, hoping for a sign of human habitation in that bleak expanse of frozen front doors and polar façades.

Trudge... trudge.... At last I see a signboard — written in Russian, Chinese, and English. It is a Japanese restaurant, and it is open! With my fingers almost dropping off, I fight my frigid way across the street. I reach the door and swing inside. Warmth! After almost twenty-four full hours of sitting in temperature well below zero and with very inadequate clothes and practically nothing to eat, I was so exhausted by cold that the warmth of the restaurant was actually *refreshing* to me, not merely soothing or vitalizing, but refreshing as a cool drink in summer is refreshing. I never before knew that one could be actually refreshed by heat.

'Konnichiwa, plees weel you haf something to eat,' says the stocky, black-eyed proprietor. 'You haf jus' come to town, stranger, yes?'

'Yes, I'm on my way to Harbin,' I reply. 'Kudasai, may I sit beside your stove?'

When thawed out, I had quite a conversation with my Japanese host — until it was time to take the train for Harbin. It is useful to know a few words of Japanese in this part of Manchuria. There are many Japanese, with large economic interests here.

On train to Harbin. What a contrast to the Chinese cars are these Japanese third-class coaches in which I'm going on to Harbin! These have double windows, plush seats, heat, toilets, spittoons, and even porters who come around to clean up the floor once in a while. They are better, I should say, than the average day coach at home. The only drawback is in the habits of the Chinese who fill them.

It's strange about these Chinese. They seem more broad-minded and unprejudiced than the Japanese, and are very clever about many things — and you'd think they could spit straight with all the practice they get, but I haven't seen one hit the bucket yet. People who are wise on Chinese trains pull their feet under them when they hear a throat being cleared.

This must be a flourishing country in summer-time, this Manchuria. Though the fields are now all bare and crusty in the icy winter wind, you can see, from the soya bean stalks bristling to the horizon, from the frozen withered poppy stalks stretching endlessly over the hills, what an exuberant crop must grow here in warm weather. It is said to be the richest opium and soya bean country in the world, and it yields many vegetables besides beans too. This fertility, it must be, that is appealing so strongly to the famine-stricken Chinese in the South; that is drawing them northward till every ship and every train is crowded with them — crowded with their families, and their children and their grandchildren, and their bundles.

There is still plenty of unoccupied land here. The settlements are little more than isolated farmhouses or tiny railroad stations — but very picturesque. They look like castles, with high turreted walls around them for protection against the roving bandits. There is real feudalism in this country. The central government doesn't amount to a beanhill here, and bandit armies roam unmolested across the countryside, plundering what and wherever they can.

Harbin — January 3. This morning at nine o'clock, and with the temperature at twenty-five below zero, we arrived in Harbin. The snow was dazzling in the early sunshine, and the town seemed cozy and friendly after the monotonous rolling hills and the vast bandit-infested bleakness of the open country. But this air is certainly the coldest thing I ever felt. I wondered why all the horses were so white, but found they were coated with frost outside their fur — frozen sweat. Their nostrils are like steam valves in this biting air. The hardy creatures are left standing out all night, and aren't bothered by it in the least.

Leaving my baggage in the station, I pulled my woolen cap down over my ears and set out to find a place to live. Along the street, past restaurants and cabarets and banks, everybody's breath rising up in little puffs like a donkey engine, to be blown away by the wind.

Harbin seems like a hundred per cent Russian town at first. Signboards are all in Russian, and everybody speaks Russian. Little droshky cabs, piloted by heavily bundled and bewhiskered old men, rumble through the streets, and dainty cabaret girls with brightly painted faces step snap-

pily down the sidewalks. They seem to take this intense
cold as a matter of course.

Not knowing a word of Russian, nor a soul within a thousand miles, I feel very much alone in this lively atmosphere.

January 4. Today I am feeling less lonely, as I've just been
calling on a White Russian girl, named Bellia Korsakov,
whom Will told me about. He must like her pretty well, too,
because the last thing he said on the subject was, 'Go easy
now, gol durn ya.'

When I finally found her house, 36 Pekarnaya Street,
entered the double outside doors, scraped the frost off my
coat, and rang the bell, a little girl, about twelve years old,
came to the door, and murmuring something in Russian,
ushered me within. Then there appeared from down the
dark hall, another older girl, also very small and wearing a
shawl and Russian high felt boots. She was blonde, with a
rather squirrel-like face, and a bleak, windswept look, but
was as pretty as anything I've ever seen. This was Bellia
Korsakov.

'Plees come een. Plees seet down.' She showed me into
her sitting-room, a rather humble little place, where, on a
table, were two typewriters, numerous books, papers, drawings, and other evidences of intellectual and artistic activity.
The room obviously served also as a bedroom and dining-
room, and in the corner on a shelf I could see the shiny
chasuble of a small ikon, standing beside a candle burning
in a red tumbler. I was just beginning to get acquainted
with Bellia, who was telling me how glad she was to have
escaped out of Soviet Russia two years ago, following a
dozen years' terrific hardship and persecution, when in came
her parents: the mother, a squatty lady with a very kindly
face, and a father of bushy red mustache, aristocratic
goatee, and fiery blue eyes. Neither of them spoke English,
so I made as Russian a bow as I could, and kissed the lady's

hand, while Bellia, as interpreter, explained to them who she thought I was.

'Sadeetis pazsholista — Vui kooshete? Please sit down — Have you eaten yet?' said the old man with a wistful twitch of his bushy red mustache.

'Marousa! Marousa!' cried Bellia, calling the little girl who had opened the door for me. Marousa appeared — she was evidently the servant — and began industriously and timidly to set the table for dinner.

Meanwhile Bellia, with the help of her mother who speaks French, continued to tell me of their experiences in escaping from Vladivostok, and of how they had worked as peasants in the fields in order to watch their chance to get across the border into Manchuria. On learning that I am on my way into Soviet Russia, all three broke out with vivid descriptions of the horrible experiences I would have. I would very likely have all my baggage stolen, I might be arrested, this and that calamity would befall me — all this coming at me in three languages, Bellia speaking in English, her mother in French, and father in Russian.

The meal was delicious — deep dishes of soup with meat at the bottom, and ham, Russian bread, and tea. It never seemed to end. 'Plees, plees, some more ham, chi peet, pazsholista, plees,' they kept saying. And as I accepted, they kept reaching over to the samovar for another glass of tea, or sending Marousa to the kitchen for more bread. Everything in the house was offered to me before they would let me arise from the table.

Afterwards Bellia showed me some articles and poems she has written in English for the Associated Press, of which she is a correspondent. She certainly has brains. The education she has given herself, when you consider the obstacles she has been up against, is almost unbelievable. Not being a communist, she had no peace while in Russia — what with blackmailers, tax-collectors, government officials, and others — and her schooling was of the very scantiest — and most irregular. And yet, in spite of everything, she can now speak at least five languages fluently, including English, which, although she has never lived anywhere where it was spoken, she knows well enough to hold down her steady job as Associated Press correspondent. That in itself is remarkable enough, I should think, but she is also a civil engineer, and intimate with every science from calculus to geology. In addition, she is an accomplished dancer, can draw and paint, and plays both the piano and chess with consummate skill.

This little house where Bellia lives is a boarding-house. In the next room are some cousins of hers, a family of Georgians, very dark, black-haired, smooth-skinned, brown-eyed. In order to help me to get a lodging, Bellia introduced me to one of these cousins, a young boy named Maxim Byadula who is studying engineering. Maxim, thin, dark, keen-eyed, artistic-looking, said he could find me a cheap hotel — so together we set forth into the night.

After trying several places, finding them too expensive, haggling unsuccessfully, and nearly freezing our ears off in the wind, we decided on a little hovel run by a scrawny Chinaman, who lives in a closet under his stairs.

January 6. This is a very nice hotel in some few ways, and the best we could find for a reasonable price. Its chief favorable feature is that it has sealed windows, 'to keep out the cold.' But it is not without limitations, namely: 1. Very little heat, the source being two stoves, one about four feet in diameter situated in the lower hall, and the other, an insignificant contraption located in the Chinaman's closet. 2. Not a drop of water in the house — the toilet-room, being designed for water, is now a perfect horror, not having been cleaned out since the freeze-up in October. Incidentally, people carry their own toilet seats in this country for obvious sanitary reasons. These portable seats are usually made of beaver-board or cardboard. You also, of course, always have to supply your own toilet paper, which is unknown here. 3. No mattresses on the beds, nothing but rusty coiled springs to lie on. 4. No blankets, pillow, nor any sort of bedclothes. 5. Very stuffy atmosphere, due to the sealed windows and the fetid toilet which contaminates the whole building. 6. Excessively inquisitive neighbors who come around and ask questions in sign-language and Russian, and try to get me to give them passports to America. Outside of these details it's a charming hotel.

The Chinaman is the only reasonable person in the house, but even *he* is a bit eccentric. His closet under the stairs is six feet by two, and contains, besides himself, one stove, one old mattress, one bookshelf full of Chinese papers to be consulted when lonesome, two hooks from which hang dark-colored woolen rags — probably apparel belonging to the Chinaman — and one cracker box, employed by day as a chair. This cozy location of the Chinaman is strategic, as it is his duty to know at all times who is in and who is out of his hotel. Those who go either in or out must tread the stairs which form his private roof. All he has to do is to rush quickly out whenever he hears footsteps, note what is going on, and then, returning, stir up the fire and doze off again till the next occurrence of thunder overhead.

Almost no one in Harbin speaks English, so I am learning Russian fast. This is very important, for I must know how to haggle. Here, as in all China, haggling is an advanced science and in wide practice. When you buy apples, for instance, the salesman starts at sixty cents an apple and you must bid him down and walk out on him a few times, till you get him down to the proper price of three for ten cents. Everybody is very friendly, but they all follow this tradition — the numerous unsqueamish Chinese jabbering away in their best pidgin Russian.

There are lots of soldiers about the town, and sometimes wagon trains of provisions go creaking by. Refugees, who have come in from the country on account of recent warfare, have to live anywhere and be thankful for a roof. Some of the places they are forced into by the extreme cold are horrible beyond words.

Down near the end of my street, there is an old boarding-house where several dozen have taken refuge. But it can scarcely be called a refuge now, because a terrible epidemic of typhus has broken out among the inmates. They are dying like flies, and yet more are driven by the ghastly cold to enter the gruesome dwelling every day.

Some few prefer to take their chances on camping out in the street, but that is little more enticing. Today's paper here says: 'Harbin's Morgue contains no less than thirty-two corpses, collected during the three Russian Christmas days on the streets and in refugees' asylums, frozen to death or with relapsing fever...'

January 7. Today I took a walk down the Sungari River, a vast prairie of rough ice. There seemed to be no limit to the ice's depth. Sometimes I looked down cracks that were easily twelve feet deep and the ice seemed to go on down even beyond that. The wind was stinging. I could feel my nostrils crisp with frost inside, my lips with icy varnish, and the intense cold of air when it plunged into my lungs.

There were some dozen heavily bundled Chinese coolies at the river's edge with sleds, earning a meager living pushing people across to the small settlement on the opposite bank. When they saw me, they became much excited and began to holler, 'Tolka! Tolka!' — pidgin Russian for 'Push! Push!'

Partly because of the cold and partly because of stories I've heard as to the fate of other wanderers, I did not go far from town. There are numerous bandits lurking on the outskirts of the city. One fellow, a few days ago, inadvisedly ventured a few hundred yards from the railroad track just out of town, and was seized by bandits who immediately hurried off with him, one at each arm. Very luckily for this fellow, two Japanese sharpshooters happened to be walking along the railroad, and they neatly picked off the bandits who had hold of his arms, causing the rest to flee. And so he was saved. Others who have strayed have not, however, been so fortunate.

Coming home, along the busy droshky-crowded streets, every minute added to the whiteness of my coat, which came from the freezing of my breath.

January 8. The only human being at my hotel with whom I have any language in common is a large, wall-eyed Jewish lady, who claims to have once lived in Chicago, and who speaks a sort of pidgin English flavored with German, Russian, and Jewish. She seems dedicated to woe, and her conversation is confined to the lugubrious details of her mother's recent death and the deplorable lack of luxury at our hostelry.

What her privations may be I know not, but I am sleeping

in my overcoat and the pink comforter. The other night
I had a bad dream and woke up about four A.M. with a
smarting bruise in the stomach, as if I'd been jabbed with
a spike. At the same time I heard a queer sort of twanging
sound. I was very startled at first, but soon realized that
evidently as I lay sleeping on my latent couch, suddenly
one of the bed springs sprang!

January 12. The Russians here seem very serious-minded,
and no wonder, after what most of them have been through.
From Bellia and her family, Maxim, and other of their connections, I hear every day more horrible and gruesome tales
about the Russian Revolution — about the famine of 1920,
when whole towns were subsisting on dry grass for months
at a time; when cannibalism spread till parents were eating
their own children to hold off starvation another week or
two.

The Korsakovs were among those seriously affected by
the famine, though their worst troubles came later when the
blackmailers and grafters got after them. Many times Bellia, in her wanderings, had to ride freight trains, sometimes
in fifty below zero weather, and once, when Bolsheviki came
to search the house for her father whom they intended to
shoot, Mr. Korsakov was forced to conceal himself on the
roof. Finding nothing, the communists assumed that
Korsakov was out, and decided to wait until he came home.
They remained over a week. Meanwhile, the unfortunate
Korsakov lay on the roof, without food or water, and not
knowing what had become of his family that they did not
give him the signal to come down.

Having escaped that time, months later he learned that
Bolsheviki were again after him. He sold all his valuables
to buy a single diamond which he cemented into a hole in
one of his back teeth. Thus equipped, he succeeded in
crossing the Manchurian border and arrived in Harbin,

where he sold the diamond for enough money to establish himself in business. Bellia and her mother, left alone in Russia to face the blackmailers and secret communist police, eventually got here to Harbin, and the family was reunited.

It is fortunate for escaping Russians that Manchuria is a relatively undeveloped country. Once they cross the frontier, they find themselves in a land more progressive and full of opportunity than any in the East. Their problems are difficult enough, God knows, but far different would be their fate if they emerged into the crowded and famine-stricken provinces of the rest of China.

The Soviet Russian Consul is back in Harbin today after a year's absence. I am trying to get a visa from him in order to enter Russia, but he is now so busy with important matters that I must wait a few days until he has more time.

Last night the Korsakovs invited me to go with them to dinner at the house of some friends of theirs who, it turned out, are comparatively prosperous and who gave quite a regal party. The conversation was in Russian — except for a little boy who could say 'Thank you verry much,' and kept repeating this for my benefit. Almost all the men present had aristocratic bushy red mustaches and talked on deep subjects with occasional hearty chuckles.

Most of these White Russians are excellent linguists, but they don't like the sound of English words especially *th's*. Bellia's mother says the word 'health' has a most unhealthy sound to it.

Often I talk with Bellia in the evening. She is so intelligent and charming that it is the hardest thing in the world to go back to my drab hovel. She wants very much to come to America some day. She says, 'if I can get to America I'll be so happy I can take th' earth by its axis and turn it round. ... T'ree quarters of the Americans I've seen all have beeg round spectacles. Maybe I'll have 'em too when I get to America.'

January 15. Venus is a laughing goddess. Men, no matter how bleak and starving they may be, must have her and her laughter with them. Last night I took in a Harbin cabaret. It was a very shabby building on the outside, but warm and hospitable within, bright scarfs draped about the walls, wool caps and heavy fur overcoats hung on hooks here and there. There was spirited music from a small bushy-whiskered orchestra, and young fellows in tuxedos and with bleary eyes talked seriously with red-lipped girls at little tables. Everyone was drinking vodka or dancing in the meager bit of open space between the tables.

One of the girls, in a black and white dress with a red shawl, danced solo. Delicate of physique, thin, but thoroughly feminine and well-rounded, she was one of the most beautiful women I've ever seen. Her beauty wasn't of the doll variety as in Japan, nor was it the least wishy-washy.

She was strong. She had endured her share of hardship in life, and her jaw was firm, her steel-blue eye keen and steady. Her cheeks and lips glowed with the red blood streaming within them. Her whole being seemed exuberant with vitality. She was all there.

The reckless hardship of this country gives to many of these Russian girls a beauty which seems to emanate from the backbone out, different from the ordinary surface prettiness which covers a flabby interior. Theirs is *real* beauty.

January 16. I rejoice in my Chinese overcoat. It helps considerably in my dealings with the Chinese. Not that I can ever hope to deceive anyone into thinking I am a Chinaman, but my coat gives me a certain kinship with these people by virtue of its raggedness. And it is a wonderful help in evading the beggars. Some of them, after observing my costume, seem to be in doubt as to whether to ask me for money or to give me some.

This Soviet Consul in Harbin is so interminable in his delays about my visa for entering the U.S.S.R. that I've decided to go down to Seoul in Korea and get a visa from the Soviet Consul there, who may not be as busy as this Harbin fellow.

From Seoul I can go north up the Korean coast, and enter Siberia at Vladivostok.

CHAPTER NINE

KOREA

January 17. *On the train for Seoul, Korea.* I am now rattling southward toward Seoul, among little valleys of bean- and paddy-fields, walled by steep wooded hills. Korea, in its rugged topography, is very like Japan.

The train stops frequently, and Koreans, a queer-looking lot, in the white robes and Happy Hooligan hats of their topknotted ancestors, troop in and out of the car.

Long ago, the Tartars who used to roam the Siberian steppes wandered eastward, and, in the manner of traveling men the world over, they mated with Chinese, Mongols, Malays, Tibetans, Siamese, or anybody they could persuade to be Tartar-conscious.

These Koreans are one of the queer results of the Tartar's indiscretions. The men look absurd. They all have weak-hearted, straggling beards and drooping mustaches, and their preposterous little black hats are of varnished horse-hair, tied on the tops of their round domes by a string under the chin. These hats originated as coverings for top-knots. Most Koreans have discarded the topknots, but hold on to the hats, which they consider a sign of aristocracy.

My glee over the get-up of the Korean beau is suddenly

dampened by a thought — after all, is he much more ridiculous than an American in a derby hat, or a British guardsman in a bearskin shako? To the eyes of an ancient Greek, would he appear any more absurd than the average American commuter — I wonder ——

It was about midnight when the train arrived at Seoul. As I came out of the lighted station with my luggage the usual swarm of natives scrambled for the passengers' baggage, and I observed among the rickshaw men that ultra-Korean mode of transportation known as a 'jiggie.'

To the uninitiated eye, a jiggie looks like a chair without front legs and with straps on its back, through which, when he has loaded its seat with baggage, the jiggie man may slip his arms and raise it upon his shoulders. This done, off he trots — no doubt believing, in his simple, topknotted brain, that his jiggie is the last word in transportation.

At any rate, a jiggie man, unhampered by the comparatively bulky rickshaw, can grab and pester to great advantage, and I was set upon by a mob of them when, carrying my luggage, I fared forth from the station to find a cheap hotel.

Jiggie men, like their rickshaw brothers, are always solicitors for various hotels, and apparently, from their wild hospitality, receive a commission for every guest they are able to seduce. Each of my retinue of clamoring jiggie men has his hotel to which he wants to lure me, and each holds up fingers to indicate how many yen I must pay for a night's lodging. They are all desperate. At last I have auctioned one of them down to one yen. Too tired to haggle further, I accept his offer, give him my stuff, and go with him up a dark winding street to his hotel. The other jiggie men still follow, pathetically trying to lure me away.

The hotel, constructed of bamboo, is built in Japanese fashion and, after a hot soak in the common tub, I retire behind my sliding partition to sleep on the matted floor.

In the morning I climb a steep hill from which I can see the whole city of Seoul — miles of low bamboo buildings with here and there a modern stone or brick structure rising above the sea of gray tile, and all surrounded by a circle of baby mountain peaks lifting into the haze.

The schoolboys of Seoul have just staged a big strike. There is general hatred here of the Japanese, who govern these people in an atmosphere of almost constant friction. The Koreans are of quite a different blood from the Japanese, and resent the rule of the proud, stocky little men from across the channel.

The striking schoolboys, wishing to make a greater commotion than would be caused by a mere student protest against Japanese oppression, proclaimed themselves communists backed by the Soviet Government, and carried red banners which said, 'Hurrah for the Proletariat!'

None of these demonstrating school kids come from proletarian families. On the contrary, the fact that they are going to school testifies that they are more well-to-do than other children. Like many communist sympathizers, they have no conception of what communism means, but use its name to promote any rebellious campaign they may have undertaken.

I had arrived in Seoul in midnight darkness, and it was appropriately dark when I again took the train for Gensan, northward on the coast, from where I was to take ship for Vladivostok.

This Korea, the 'Hermit Kingdom,' and its life seem to be held in a dark isolation. Even from the rest of the Orient, Korea is withdrawn, aloof, in its remote esoteric culture, and its suspicion of the world outside.

There is something very remote about these people in their voiceless but obstinate antagonism to everything new and everything not Korean. Undoubtedly, if you lived here, you would break or wear through to contact with their thinking and feeling. But just what is going on under these topknots and Happy Hooligan hats is certainly a dark mystery to an itinerant Western understanding.

So it was appropriate that I should leave Seoul in the same darkness in which I arrived. And I was far on my way northward when, the next morning, I looked out of my third-class window at the sunrise.

We were already among the Diamond Mountains, their delicate massed peaks dazzling in snow, with folds of dark pine forest rolling down to disappear in the sea to the eastward. It was still hours before we would get to Gensan, where I was to take the boat to Vladivostok, and my sleepy eyes ached under the cold and brittle glare of this wild country. So I told the little conductor to call me when we got to Gensan, and clambered back up on my shelf to sleep.

When I next woke, we were already eighty miles beyond Gensan — the conductor had either forgotten me or had not understood my sign-language, and I felt quite peeved with the black-eyed, wistful little fellow. But I find that I can still catch my boat for Vladivostok at a small fishing town called Seishin farther along the line, which the train will reach some time tonight.

We are running through little valleys along the beaches,

our progress punctuated by a series of tunnels piercing the intervening cliffs. Fishing villages — little clusters of mud huts, each with its reed-fence enclosure and usually a rack of drying mackerel — come several to the mile. There are many paddy-fields, too, and little brown cattle bearing towering loads of reeds and straw along the slanting hill trails. White-clothed villagers gaze at the train; women with huge trays of fish on their heads, men building sampans for the spring. At every station, crowds of passengers fill the car aisle, all talking and gesticulating, and lugging trays and bundles of fish. Many get off and many get on, and so it is always crowded.

Seishin — January 21. Last night I had a tough time getting a place to sleep. At ten o'clock and not many miles from the Russian border, we pulled into Seishin where I am to catch my boat. Little or no railroad station was visible in inky black Seishin, and as the lights of the train faded, with rumbling diminuendo, into the distance, I was left, with my impedimenta, in utter darkness beside the track. I could see only the vague outline of the inevitable squad of jiggie men as they surrounded me with their expectant jabbering.

None of them could understand either my Russian or my Japanese, and my sign-language in such darkness was of very doubtful effect. But, after a desperate attempt to indicate 'hotel' in every way I could conceive of, the jiggie men seemed suddenly to understand.

In the blackness, some two hundred yards down a shadowy street, could be seen a dim light. Pointing to it excitedly, the jiggie men started in that direction, urging me to accompany them.

As we drew near the glimmer, it proved to come from a tiny building and I wondered what sort of lodging-house it might be. Entering, I found three uniformed, black-eyed

Korean cops seated around a stove and deeply engrossed in conversation. There were a few bookshelves, files, and desks in the room, all stacked with papers. I was in the police station.

On trying to converse with these gentlemen, I found that they spoke nothing but Korean, and knew even less Japanese than I do. They were too bewildered by my unexpected appearance out of the night to be able to understand sign-language, and they gazed, incredulous, muttering to one another until, having perceived that I was a foreigner, one of them called up a number on the telephone. In a minute, having made connection with his party, he beckoned to me to speak with this person.

'Hello.'

'Dobri vecher,' came the reply in a woman's voice. I was evidently speaking to a Russian lady who had just been roused from a sound sleep. Her tone was anything but hospitable. Knowing but a dozen words of Russian, which did not include the words for 'hotel,' 'night's lodging,' 'bed,' nor even 'sleep,' I began to rack my brains for the best method of procedure. My problem cannot be appreciated by anyone who has not been called upon to talk sign-language over a Korean telephone, in the middle of the night, to an angry Russian lady he has never seen, while surrounded by a crowd of staring, jabbering jiggie men in a police station.

Although I gave the irate lady a vivid imitation of snoring, in hopes she would understand that I needed sleep, I don't think our conversation was, on the whole, very enlightening to either party. Evidently she thought I was insinuating that she snored for after another half-minute of rapid Russian which didn't sound like compliments, she hung up.

Amid the crowd of jiggie spectators in the police station I somehow found a pencil and paper and drew a picture of a hotel, making signs to show my ignorance as to how to get to such a place. But the wary Korean cops, who had grown suspicious during all this fracas, now refused to answer my questions until I had first satisfied all of their prying curiosity. I drew extensive maps and diagrams to show where I came from, where I was going, and why; diagrams descriptive of how much money I had, and pictures illustrating my noble character.

In the end I was placed under the care of the oldest of the jiggie men, who loaded my sacks upon his jiggie and scampered off into the darkness. Watching the dim outline of his black topknot against the snow, I followed closely until, after several minutes of mysterious wending, we came to a lighted doorway of bamboo latticework. A hotel. Paying my ancient companion of topknot and jiggie, I pulled off my shoes, entered, and was received with the customary amazement. But my troubles were at an end for the night.

This morning, along the street of crude wooden fish warehouses where ragged Korean fishermen jabbered in the doorways, one of the first things I saw was a Ford Sales building, tin and modern among its archaic Oriental neighbors. Looking for somebody who spoke my native tongue, I went in.

'Good morning.'

'Goud morrneng,' responded the Russian sales manager, tall, thin, dark, of aristocratic features. Talking further, I learn that his name is Viktor Yankovsky and that his family and connections are Russian refugees out of Siberia — the only Russians living in Seishin.

'Then the lady I spoke with over the telephone last night must be a relative of yours?' I ventured.

'Ah,' says Viktor, 'vas zat you?' Of course the lady had told the whole family of her adventure.

Hearing my side of the story and realizing that I am not the communistic menace feared by his kinswoman, Viktor invited me home for lunch.

The Yankovsky house stands among the Korean fisher-men's huts on the top of a hill. It is scarcely distinguishable from other houses around it, except for its size and its slightly more exotic appearance. It looks like fifty back houses huddled and jumbled close to one another, tacked or tied together with string or wire as the case may be, and thoroughly patched all over. Apparently as each additional cousin turns up after escaping from Russia, or as more children are produced by those already escaped, old man Yankovsky just orders more back houses.

Some of the houses, I find, are bins of salt in which fish are packed; some contain firewood, old bear hides, or tools and supplies. The Yankovskys, to support themselves, have become a family of fishermen and hunters. Every-where about the rambling collection of mongrel back houses wander the family hunting dogs — wolfish brutes with heavy fur for combating the mountain blizzards, great long-toothed hounds with hanging ears, every description of large-size fighting dog known to man — all lounging about, asleep against a barrel of salted herring, lolling about on the parlor rug with feet in air like a kitten, or drooling great jowls on the rough floor under the piano.

The walls of the living-room are covered with magnifi-cent skins and furs — tigers, leopards, boars, and other animals. Siberian tigers and leopards are larger than their cousins in India, and have much heavier and more brightly marked coats. One of Yankovsky's tiger pelts, over ten feet long, is the most magnificent skin I have ever seen in my life.

Lunch-time. We all sit down to one long table, thirty of us, and drink venison soup. This is followed by boar meat, roast pheasant, caviar, and one's choice of a multitude of vegetables cooked to the czar's taste.

I sit beside the lady I last encountered on the other end of a Korean telephone in the middle of the night. Mrs.

Arbatov is her name, and though she speaks no English and is a bit suspicious, she appears pleasant and unrevengeful. On the other side, Anna Yankovsky, who speaks good English, has been to Shanghai, is aged twenty-two, blonde, artistic, intelligent, attractive.

At the head sits the old man himself, manfully straddling his chair, stocky and solid of build, gruff, proud. He once owned a domain of thousands of acres near Vladivostok. The blood of nobility is in his veins, he is still the head of his family, and even exile and this rickety, rambling shack cannot humble him.

During the meal we listened to band music from a radio, but the music frequently gave way to violent oratory. We were getting the broadcasting station at Harbarovsk. The speeches were taking place at a Bolshevist mass-meeting in anniversary commemoration of Lenin's death. The chief plea of the orators, some of whom were women, was to live up to the promises made to Lenin before he died, and to carry on his spirit. It was in Russian, of course, and we could hear the wild cheering of the communist audience; but later the main points of the propaganda were repeated in Japanese, Korean, Chinese, Mongolian, English, and Esperanto.

January 22. Today I broke up a fight. There was a big crowd around two furious jabbering Koreans on the street who, in the Oriental manner, were being mutually smothered with vituperation without once laying a finger on each other. Although they were almost down one another's throats when I joined the group, everybody—even the combatants—instantly forgot about the dispute and turned open-mouthed to gaze at me. I am getting used to this now, but it is still rather disconcerting.

January 23 — Fusan Maru. Last night my little freight

steamer, bound for Vladivostok, weighed anchor in Seishin Harbor. Viktor Yankovsky having rowed me out to her by moonlight, I was escorted into the hold by an old Japanese steward carrying a lantern.

Third-class gets the hold apparently, a vast dirty expanse lined with vaguely shaped bales, sacks, and crates. Some two dozen drunken Chinese and Koreans were camped, huddling close to one another in a corner. You don't often see Orientals drunk, but they're pretty lousy when they are. Nearly as bad as some of the boys back home. One of the old Chinamen is reading to himself aloud, as they always do, in a weird, singsongy voice varying from a hum to violent high-pitched jabberings. It lasts for hours and sounds like an old priest singing a long series of chants.

I choose a large bale of straw on the other side and, pulling out my comforter, roll up in it for the night. A cool draft seeps between the folds. There is a rustling in the hay beside me. Two large rats scamper boldly forth. Reaching the middle of the cleared space, they stop to gaze about, sniff, and prune their whiskers. I am used to rats by now and don't mind them much, as they generally keep out of my way, but these creatures are quite annoying — they have too much self-confidence. Although I douse my comforter in camphor oil, which is supposed to be bad medicine for all vermin, I can hear and feel the creatures scuttling about my legs all night.

Today we anchored off a little fishing town — a long crescent-shaped beach lined with hauled-up fishing boats, at the very northernmost point on the Korean coast. All the Koreans and Chinese with whom I spent the night have gone ashore and I am now the only passenger on the ship. This boat is a freighter and passengers are a minor consideration.

They are excessively slow about unloading here. It has

taken these people fourteen hours to unload sixty tons of cargo into some scows which pulled up alongside, a job which the same number of American sailors could have done in an hour and a half. The Orientals are too leisurely and sociable, and have too little initiative, to be efficient. When the hook gets caught on a strongback, instead of just kicking it loose, they begin to hold a convention about the best way to fix it, and the winch-driver comes down into the hold and consults, and the debate is long and furious. Finally they reach a compromise and, fastening a rope around the hook, they all get together and pull it free. Then the winch-driver has a good laugh about how Wei Leng nearly fell over backwards when the rope slackened and, his witticisms being well received by all, he leisurely climbs back to his winch. What is time to these heirs of the ages!

I am solitary now, in my quarters in the empty, freezing hold of this little ship. At meal-times, the wizened and dignified old steward appears at hatch number one, and clambers down the ladder to leave a bowl of sticky rice and cold, oily Oriental vegetables on my table, a bale of straw. As I negotiate the sticky rice, all is silence save the faint swish of water outside our iron hull and an occasional scurrying rat. The rice gone, I contemplate the cold, oily vegetables with a sigh, and speculate upon the destiny of the unfortunate Japanese crew who exist exclusively on this diet. No wonder they never grow up to the size of normal human beings.

January 25. Last night, on our northward course again, it was very rough, and cold as the devil. When I could stand it no longer in the drafty hold, I sneaked up to the warm officer's messroom, and spent the rest of the night on a comfortable upholstered bench, unbeknownst to all.

CHAPTER TEN

RUSSIA

THIS morning the whole ship is coated with frozen spray, and, at dawn, when our winches started up, the air was so cold that the steam enveloped the ship in a dense white cloud. At ten o'clock, drawing nearer to shore, the floating ice-cakes became so thick that the sound of our hull's cutting through them resembled a bunch of workmen scraping a city sidewalk, and now and then could be heard the deep concussion of an extra large piece being forced beneath the surface.

Then suddenly a mighty impact shook the ship. We had struck something solid! The pack-ice of Vladivostok Harbor. With a grinding shudder we slowed down — but continued slowly to plough our way onward through the crunching, writhing débris of ice. Bare bleak hills could be seen to the north and west forming, ahead of us, a small harbor. Vladivostok. Soviet Russia.

A fat little pilot boat draws near us, ferociously bucking the big white chunks. As she comes alongside, we can see flying, the communist flag — all red except for a white crossed-hammer-and-sickle in the corner. The 'Gay-Pay-Oo' — Soviet Police — come aboard to inspect my visa, money, and baggage. Husky, raw-faced men, they all wear warm sheepskin coats and wool boots, and are very polite.

It takes us nearly two hours more to get to the dock, about a quarter of a mile away, in spite of an icebreaker's frantic struggle to remove the jam which keeps accumulating between us and the wharf.

As I finally go down the gangplank, thinking principally of where I can most quickly find some food, I notice long-shoremen carrying loads into a near-by Chinese freighter. Women and girls can be seen standing about here and there, bundled up with drab-colored woolly shawls over their heads, and high boots. But I miss that atmosphere of light-hearted bustle so prevalent throughout the rest of the Orient. There is no joking or laughter. The air is full of grimness. The attitude of the women and of the longshoremen is deeply serious.

Walking up one of the rough cobblestone streets of the quaint city, which is formed of tiers of brittle little wooden houses sprouting out of the bare steep hills, I pass many people, almost all blond, dressed in black, gray, or brown, and trudging along with no noticeable 'joie de vivre.'

I am quite inconspicuous among these bleak people, as my costume is even less elegant than theirs. Beneath my Chinese overcoat, my once white flannel pants are fresh from being slept in for forty-four nights in succession. And my shoes, which I have worn constantly for two years, have an expression of grim fatigue.

January 26. I am staying for three and a half rubles a day at a little place called The Third Communal Hotel, on the corner of Lenin Street and '25th of October' Street. A ruble is worth about fifty cents.

The lobby is twelve feet by six, of old dust-stained plank paneling, and as dark and gloomy as a dungeon. In the creaky hall at the head of the stairs roams a decrepit hag with a red rag around her head, who makes beds and sweeps. My room is distinctly proletarian, although the old iron bed has a mattress and bedclothes. Its nearest approach to bourgeois luxury is a very warm but unæsthetic comforter made of dishrags sewn together with grocery-store string, and stuffed with wornout stockings, mittens, neckties, and underwear — the buttons left on.

I had learned from Will that there is living in Vladivostok a plumber, one Ivan Ratovsky, who has twice been to America, and who now owns a shop on Lenin Street. I visited his place this morning. When I opened the rusty door, I saw three young men in high boots and leather breeches apparently taking an inventory of the stock of pipes, tools, and hardware which were piled in dusty confusion on the shelves and benches.

'Where is Ratovsky?' I asked.

They did not know, and did not seem to care. Going into the shop next door, I met an old man, who got Ratovsky on the telephone and persuaded him to come down and see me.

In a few minutes a tall man of about forty, dark, unshaven, grim, very hardy and intelligent-looking, came striding down the street. He entered, unwinding an old black scarf from his thin neck, and shook my hand.

'Hello,' he said, with a smile that took some effort. 'It iss pleasure to meet an American once more. I was in America, the last time, two years ago. I wish I was there now.' He went on to tell me that only yesterday his shop and stock, worth six thousand rubles (about three thousand dollars), had been confiscated by the Soviet Government.

'The communists arr in there now,' he said bitterly, pointing next door. 'They are counting up my goods.'

He seemed too discouraged and sick at heart to talk further on the subject, so I asked him no questions.

'Let us eat,' he suggested. 'The best restaurant in town is just around the corner.'

'Isn't it rather expensive for you now?' I ask, thinking of his recent loss.

'Oh, yes, very extravagant,' replies Ratovsky, with an ironic smile, 'but I might as well eat in the best restaurant because the communists will soon take all the money I have, anyhow, and the more I spend now, the less they will get.'

Ten minutes later, with a little aristocratic soup in his stomach, Ratovsky is feeling well enough to talk more about his troubles.

'The government,' he says, with acid eye, 'has no right to take my shop. Do you know what they did? They taxed me ten thousand rubles. Now, how can I pay ten thousand rubles when my store and stock — all I have — is worth only six thousand rubles?

'They know that. They know I can't pay the tax. That is why they imposed it — so they could take my shop for not paying taxes. If I had sixty thousand rubles, they would tax me a hundred thousand. This is the way they do with everybody.' He gave numerous instances of his shop-keeping friends having all of their goods confiscated which in most cases led to their imprisonment through inability to pay subsequent taxes...

'I have been in prison twice myself,' he continues. 'It iss no joke. We get only one kilogram of bread a day. Sometimes a little soup also, and the quarters are terrible — cold, and filthy. It was before my second trip to America. I had to spend four months in jail. The communists suspected me of something — I don't know what — and it took them four months to find out I was innocent. Then they let me go. I come back to my shop, and find I have lost all my trade.

'If you are not a communist, they treat you like a dog. Nobody can save up any goods or money now. It is all taken by the communists. Nobody is doing work seriously. The only work you can do which the government approves is to work in factories or other places under government management. No matter how hard you work, you will be given only the barest necessities of life; one pair of shoes, two kilograms of bread a day, and just so much of this and that. Everything is measured — even the amount of floor space you can take for living quarters. Nobody has ambition any more, because what is the use? That is why Russia is poor. That is why everything is so scarce — food, clothes, merchandise, everything. It is that way all over Russia. I am a storekeeper, so I know. I used to order merchandise from Moscow, Leningrad, Odessa, Harbarovsk. Now they have none. There is a shortage of necessary goods all over Russia.

'The only people,' he continues drearily, 'who enjoy life at all are the Communist Party members. Anyone who has ever owned private property is automatically barred from the party, and even those who join must go through a hard test lasting three years. Everything is against those who have, in the past, been leaders of economic affairs — the private traders, manufacturers, and merchants who had enterprise enough to build up their business. Now this enterprise is suppressed and little or nothing is brought to fill its place. All ambition is drowned in government discipline and government laws.

'The laws are so rigid that they are very hurtful, even to the Bolshevik's own interests. The government fishermen here in Vladivostok, for instance, often waste a great part of their catch because there is no salt for preserving the fish. The big salt merchants have been taxed out of business.

'And there are many other cases. The workmen who take the places of the suppressed experienced producers, are never as well fitted for their jobs, and never have as much real interest in their work. How can they, when it means just a way of passing an eight-hour working day, instead of a road to prosperity?'

Such is the stuff I got from Ratovsky. The communist ideal, according to him, disregards some of the fundamental laws of nature, such as 'that the fittest shall survive,' 'the Lord helps those who help themselves.'

'Who,' he asks, 'can enforce the communist principle: "From each according to his means, to each according to his needs?" Who is able to measure means and needs? And who, also, will agree to another's measurements of his means and needs, even if they could be measured accurately?'

There seems to be no halfway about a man's position in Russia. He must be either Red or White, and whichever he is, he soon becomes violently bitter against the opposing side. In this fundamental issue, the Whites consist principally of older men — conservative, weary, bewildered by radicalism and change; the Reds are young people — idealistic, hopeful, exalted. Ratovsky's talk fairly illustrates the usual White Russian state of mind.

January 27. When I next called on Ratovsky at his house, he was very despondent. He told me he had just received a tip from a friend warning him that he was going to be arrested within two or three days.

'I can't stand the idea of going to that horrible prison again,' he said, with the look of a doomed man. 'I'll go crazy in there. Nothing can stop those communists. I'm done for now.'

He pointed to his humble cot in the corner. 'That is not my bed,' he said.

Indicating his little table on which lay three books — 'Those are not mine. Nothing in this house is mine. All these things and many more I have bought with money earned in plumbing — but yesterday the communists came. They said all my goods are taken over by the government, but that I may continue to use the most necessary of my

furniture. Then they took my pictures, my clock, my arm-
chair — everything of value.' With a sigh — 'They have
everything but my life. Soon they will have that.'

The poor fellow, tough and strong as he was, looked sickly
pale. He had apparently resigned himself to a communist
prison to the end of his days. His jaw rested limply upon
his heavy collar. His eyes were as dead as glass.

'If I could only get away,' he said hopelessly.

Suddenly he looked up.

'How far is it,' he asked, 'to the Manchurian border?'

I got out my map. 'About thirty-five miles,' I said.

'I could walk that distance almost overnight,' said
Ratovsky. He was thinking deeply now. His eyes grew less
glassy. 'Yes, I am strong. If I left here at sunset, I could be
far away by morning.' His fingers were nervously ploughing
his hair. 'Of course,' he said, 'if I was seen by the communists, they would be hard on me — they would probably
call me a counter-revolutionary, and shoot me.'

'But,' said I, 'there must be plenty of room for hiding in
this country.'

Ratovsky's eyes brightened. 'Yes, yes,' he said; 'I could
rest in the forest during the day, and walk at night. I'd
keep away from people and roads — I'd work toward
Harbin or Seishin — I could get employment in Harbin...'

It was beautiful to see hope come to life in this crushed
and woebegone man. 'Yes — yes,' he kept saying to himself. 'Yes — I can do that — yes, I will do that.'

We talked for a long time. He seemed to know almost
nothing about the country west of Vladivostok, but dis-
missed the question of bandits by saying, 'I have nothing to
fear from them — I don't think my appearance will tempt
them to hold me for ransom.'

Returning toward the Third Communal Hotel, I saw a
platoon of young communists marching along the street,

bayonets fixed, and singing lustily. No one paid the slightest attention to them. I guess it is an everyday occurrence. I've spoken a few words with various communists in restaurants, and all have been very pleasant, though very serious, and rather suspicious of me. They seem sympathetic about individual store-owners and people like Ratovsky who are being sent to jail. They admit that such people are being wronged, but they say that these are merely the unfortunate victims of laws which were made for 'the good of the majority.'

Almost everybody seems poor, however, even more so than the average Russian refugee in Harbin, who isn't any too prosperous. And food must be very scarce, for I often see kids steal the leavings off of restaurant tables.

Everywhere in Vladivostok I notice lack of interest in jobs and much inefficiency. There are not enough trolley cars to carry all the people who want to ride; restaurant waitresses take hours in bringing the food; I had to wait in line an hour and a half to get railroad tickets. No one is quite all there in his work.

At four o'clock I stopped in to see Ratovsky, who was in a state of great excitement. Realizing the danger of delay, he had made plans to depart at sundown. He was studying his map. His equipment was spread out on his cot: two sweaters, a woolen scarf, cap, mittens, matches, a small loaf of bread, three packages of raisins, two cans of beef, compass, map, pocket knife, and all the money he had left — twenty-two rubles.

It was now quite dark. No time must be lost. Stowing his supplies in his pockets and on his belt, he donned his sweaters. We shook hands.

'Good luck, Ratovsky,' I said.

We went out into the cold night. The stars twinkled through millions of miles of black emptiness overhead. To the west the pale, frozen bay stretched inland to the hills.

Far beyond lay Manchuria. With a smile and a wave of good-bye, down the little street strode Ratovsky, provisions on his belt, and clothed for a dozen nights unsheltered in the desolate mountains. He is undertaking a reckless adventure. He must go alone, totally unfamiliar with his dangers, in mid-winter, facing cold, starvation, bandits, wild animals, communist police who would bring him back to be executed, and his own fatigue which might leave him to die a horrible death in the wilderness.

I watched him to the foot of the hill, where I could but dimly see him making for the edge of the ice in the darkness. Then he was gone.

On train for Habarovsk. They don't like to speak of different classes of anything in this country, as it is contrary to communist ideals, so they call the various kinds of railroad cars 'hard' or 'soft.' This is a third-class, or 'hard' car. We sleep on shelves of smooth boards arranged in tiers of three. They provide no mattress, blankets, or pillow, and I sleep in my overcoat and the pink comforter.

At Vladivostok, I boarded this Trans-Siberian local train for Moscow, six thousand miles away through the heart of communist territory. I expect to stop off at one or two way-stations to see what is to be seen, and my immediate destination is Harbarovsk, one day's journey north from Vladivostok. It costs ninety-nine rubles, or fifty dollars, to get to Moscow this way.

My traveling companions are a very unkempt and serious lot. The only one of them who seems at all cheerful is the unshaven, bullet-headed conductor who tends the car stove and keeps our tickets under his coat.

There is a big Russian, sitting on the bunk opposite me, who must weigh two hundred and eighty pounds. He certainly is a brute — the kind that is baptized by having a bottle of vodka smashed over his head. He wears the usual cylindrical cap of thick black wool and sports a huge, bushy red mustache. On his hand I see tattooed the crossed-axe-and-anchor of the Soviet Transportation Service.

He is always munching at a large loaf of bread, which he keeps wrapped in an old newspaper beside him — and, as he chews, his whole face seems to go around in circles. On the up-stroke his chin ascends, taking with it his fat lower lip and nose, while the right wing of his mustache describes a wide circle to the right, and then, on the down-stroke, his jaw drops sharply, releasing his nose, and with a violent twitch at both ends the mustache sinks quickly back to the starting position. And then over and over again, like a cement-mixing machine, hour after hour.

Two young communists are sitting on the shelf directly beneath me. At first they looked at me blankly and rather disapprovingly, but after an hour or two, I got them talking and, even in spite of my limited vocabulary, we got along quite well. One is blond, and has the strangest eyes I ever saw — of an insipid yellowish-green color — and the other is dark with thick, curly hair. Both wear striped jerseys under their coats, for they are sailors in the employ of the Soviet Government. Following a month's vacation in Vladivostok, they are going to Harbarovsk to work on a gunboat on the Amur River.

Also, near by, is a peasant lady who seems to hate me. Her name is Sufeena, or something like that, and all day long she sits and scowls.

The windows are frosted with ice curtains, but occasionally through the door I get glimpses of an open rolling country. At almost every station we all rush out to get a drink of water and perhaps fill our kettles and pots, if we have such, or buy a little black bread or ham.

My sleeping-shelf is really a baggage-rack. I couldn't use any of the lower bunks because my feet, which protrude some distance into the aisle when I'm asleep, get in the way

of passers-by. But here on top, they are high above everyone's head, so it is all right, and I slumber in peace among
the bundles. Everything in the train is cramped. Not only
are the shelves much too short to stretch out on, but if you
sit, you have to keep your head bent over, to avoid the shelf
above. If you sit on the shelf above, you still have to keep
your head bent on account of the baggage-shelf above that.
And even if you sit on the baggage-shelf as I do, the roof of
the car will keep your head bent. The only place to sit upright would be on top of the roof of the car, and there, if you
were not immediately frozen, you'd be either arrested or
knocked off by a tunnel.

If all communists are like these sailors, I would not mind
being a communist myself. I told them that I, too, had been
a sailor, and we are becoming fast friends. I have a little
English-Russian dictionary, and it is doing hard service as
we converse ever more eagerly. These boys certainly have
the communist spirit. They are always offering me bread,
meat, sausages, and all they have. I've never yet seen an
inhospitable Russian except Sufeena — and I think even she

might be friendly in time. I took her picture this morning
when she was asleep. Considering her appearance, it was a
dastardly trick to play on any woman.

January 28. I am writing this in the Matross Dom, or
Sailors' Home, of Habarovsk, where my two communist
sailor friends of the train have invited me to stay as their
guest as long as I like. This is fortunate for me, for otherwise I would have to spend at least six rubles a day at a
hotel. Hotels in Russia, being rare, are correspondingly
expensive.

The Sailors' Home is a gaunt, rambling hovel, away off at
one end of the town. Except for the kitchen, each room
contains a large stove and some beds, and nothing else.
There is no bathroom, and the toilet, a ramshackle frame-
work the size of a telephone booth, stands in a snowdrift
about forty yards behind the house.

This is a good-sized town, spread loosely upon the bleak,
gently waving plain. Here and there on the vastness is a
sketchy strip of woods, but, for the most part, the wind has
a free sweep, and in the distance you can see the glistening
crust of the Amur, winding ever northeastward — to the
Sea of Okhotsk and the North Pacific. The streets are wide.
The roof-tops all exhale white veils of steam which fly, in-
termingled with each other, like racing whippets down the
wind. Everywhere in the streets are sauntering young blue-
eyed men, dressed in various government uniforms, with
black wool caps and leather knee-boots; everywhere are
girls bundled in knitted shawls, and old bearded men driving little sleighs of bread and firewood.

Everybody wears caps; never hats. If you should wear a
hat, you would be considered either very bourgeois or a
foreigner, and would be a marked man wherever you went.
It is really wonderful — the raggediest clothes are perfect
attire for any occasion. You never need think of shaving,

brushing your hair, wearing a clean shirt, or any other bothersome conventions. It's superb.

My two sailor hosts are kind indeed to me. Their hospitality extends, beyond mere lodging, to giving me food and showing me the sights. In addition to taking me all over town and answering my inexhaustible supply of questions, they have even offered me money. All this they consider a part of living up to their principle, 'From each according to his means, to each according to his needs.' They are true communists.

Their attitude substantiates my theory, which I've already proved to my own satisfaction, that one can learn more by going about the world alone than with any companion, however pleasant or congenial. If, for instance, I had a traveling companion, I doubt whether these boys would have taken me in as they have. They wouldn't have gone so far out of their way to be friendly and to make me feel at home, because they would have considered me already befriended and in no danger of being lonely.

As it is, however, everything is grand in the Matross Dom. There are girls employed here to keep the place in order. Their clothes are terribly ragged, and their thick black stockings are full of holes — but, boy! They come around early in the morning and build fires in our dormitory stoves, and sweep the floor, and cook soup for us, and wash dishes — they are nice to have around. My sailor friends have a guitar which they play very soothingly, and when they sing their songs, the girls sit around on our beds and listen, and keep us company.

Such an arrangement could hardly exist in any country other than Russia. If girls inhabited any sailors' home of the type I am used to, they could not survive a week. Here, however, the passions of these sailors seem to be intellectual quite as much as physical, and they seem to have deep respect for women. Instead of treating these girls in the usual predatory and irresponsible manner, the sailors seem to prefer to play chess or talk seriously with them. There is practically free love in this country, but you seldom hear of the privilege being abused by these serious-minded people.

This morning I had an economic discussion with the boys, which, though necessarily very crude owing to the narrow limits of my Russian, showed me that none of them had a very accurate idea of conditions in the outside world.

They stated, among other things, that the workingmen of America are so much under the power of 'imperialism' and the 'capitalists' that they have no liberty left, and that it is just a question of time before they will be strong enough to succeed in their revolutionary hopes. Also that the 'Chinese imperialists' are trying to extend their dominion into Siberia, but have been frustrated by the powerful Red Army which defends the workers and peasants of the Soviet Union.

All the boys offer reckless sums for my camera. It is a thrilling luxury to them — any camera is — anything not strictly necessary is. Only necessities are tolerated in Russia according to Communist Party policy. Everything unnecessary, from silk stockings to nail files, must be bootlegged over the border.

I had a ten-cent tube of shaving-cream which has been the envy of all who have either seen it or sniffed it. Many offers were made for this coveted prize. There are other shaving-soaps fully as good and for sale cheaply here, but foreign luxury lends a satisfaction and social prestige that the best local products cannot satisfy. I got three rubles for my tube: about fifteen times what it cost me.

I had lunch today in the 'Rabochi' — workingmen's — Dining-Room with two of my seamen friends. We filled up on soup and 'zraza' and drank much of a syrupy bellywash known as 'kvass.' It was a wonderful meal considering the seventy-five kopeks — thirty-five cents — we paid for it, and everybody in town seemed to be there. Most of them were in the uniform of the Red Army and the rest in dark woolly clothes or heavy furs, lined up in a long file to get their meal tickets. The busy waitresses, wearing red handkerchiefs around their heads, scurried to and fro with bread and bottles and steaming bowls of gruel. It was a great bunch of people... No one too proud to finish up the fish on another fellow's plate after he had gone.

Afterwards we went to a movie, which was intensely communistic in sentiment. First they showed pictures of Stalin, Rykoff, and the other high administrative officers of the Soviet Government. These bushy-haired fellows are a battle-scarred lot. Stalin, dark-eyed, stout, stiffly mustached, his face dotted with smallpox pits, is about as hard-boiled-looking an individual as could be imagined. He has a sort of ruthless look, like Captain John Silver, and glares craftily from side to side out of half-opened eyes.

Having read a little about his past life, I can understand why his face is not as sleek and balmy as it might be. For twelve years before the Revolution, Stalin worked for Lenin as a Bolshevist bandit in the Caucasus. He was arrested again and again, and sent to prison in Siberia — and eleven times, while other prisoners died of starvation, exposure, and disease, Stalin escaped. Each time they would guard him more carefully, but, surviving all hardships, he invariably escaped again.

He has developed an astounding genius for political strategy. On Lenin's death, while the great Trotsky, Zinoviev, and Kamenev were fighting it out for the position of power left by Lenin, Stalin, the humble secretary of the Communist Party, let them fight, while quietly, mysteriously, by roundabout methods, he established, as provincial and district secretaries, men whose loyalty he could rely on. It is one of the most miraculous machinations in history. Dealing with ruthless, suspicious, jealous men, who could have exiled him in a minute if they knew what he was about, Stalin has gradually 'cleansed' the party of his enemies till now practically no opposition remains.

Although these peasant people regard him as merely one of many leaders, and he himself assumes to be nothing greater than the equal of the other administrative officers, all presumably humble 'disciples' of Lenin, Stalin is actually as absolute an autocrat as any existing in the world today. The masses under him do not begin to know his power. For that reason it is all the more secure.

Next came a half-hour of pictures showing the greatest fields of industrial development, the new farming communities in function; and then a magnificent view of some of the Soviet battle cruisers on the Amur, the Red Army in action, and similar incitement of enthusiasm.

It is really a most beautiful thing, this ideal of the communists. No wonder they are so thrilled about it. It is so simple in principle, so uplifting to the long down-trodden masses, and, at the same time, proclaims as its purpose the establishment of a society worthy of the highest aims of the entire world: 'A society in which no man shall have the power to exploit another, in which all men shall work and as workers jointly control their product, and in which humanity, united to the ends of the earth in peaceful productive relationships, shall by science and coöperation subdue all nature to the needs and development of Man.'

It is a marvelous conception. And in these pictures were brought to reality, in the minds of these struggling people, the actual beginnings and great foundations of this tremendous movement. Here was shown 'the largest republic in the world, the largest stretch of territory under one flag in the world, the largest sown area, the largest forests, the largest iron deposits' — all already working in coöperation and sympathy to develop themselves toward an enlightened end.

Lumbermen in the great northern forests, fishermen in the Baltic, peasants on the wide plains of Siberia, miners in Ukraine, factory workers, soldiers, men of the proletariat everywhere, all with one purpose, working, sacrificing, gaining... gaining...

To a vast nation of simple people, it is an exalted ideal. As such, it justifies the colossal effort expended by them. If only their government will hold true to this people's idealism ——

If only its leadership and its methods will be worthy of this people's purpose ——

When the movie was over, we went around to a Soviet supply store, where the boys got me some provisions for my projected journey across the continent. Knowing the commissioner, and the food being for the consumption of a 'rabochi' — workingman — they got it at a huge discount: for less than forty per cent of the regular price.

As we were leaving, we saw the daily meat line at the counter, each man awaiting drearily his turn. This is one of the many still existing inefficiencies of the Soviet system. Everyone must spend an appreciable portion of his day just standing in line. After taking me around and answering my plentiful questions till dark, the boys took me home to have some delicious 'shi,' a cabbage soup, which our fair house-keepers were brewing for us.

I don't know whether my friends act as they do because they are trying to advertise the good qualities of communism, or out of pure friendship. There is no way of knowing. Probably it is a mixture. At any rate, whichever it is, they are far from selfish, whether they are working for Bolshevism or to help me. It occurs to me that communism, when it is applied in good will and liberty like this, is about the same thing as the Golden Rule. But it seems a mistake to attempt to enforce any such code. If the Golden Rule were forced, it would be golden no longer.

On the train again. What I had to go through to get my ticket for this leg of the journey is alone enough to fill two or three efficiency experts' notebooks.

First, I spent half an hour in the waiting line in the town ticket-office, only to learn that my particular kind of ticket was not sold there, and that I would have to get it in the station. So to the station I went and there joined a still longer line of ticket-seekers.

We never seemed to make the slightest progress, and each man who reached the window would stay there talking and waiting a long time before he got his ticket. There was always someone, who had a pull with the soldier in charge, cutting in near the head of the line, so that we at the tail were counting our progress in millimeters. At length, at half-past two, after an hour and a quarter, the ticket-agent went off for lunch, locking the window with a heartless finality.

I hoped the line would break up then, but no, the members all gritted their teeth a little harder and held firm. Seconds ticked slowly by. Minutes. Quarter hours. Hours. We dozed and dreamed, shifting wearily from one foot to another. No ticket-man.

Once in a while a haggard form would drop despairingly out of line and trudge limply away; others would get relatives and friends from the vast crowds around us to relieve them for a while. Some sat patiently down on the floor among their bundles, to blink and snore away the long hours. It was not a cheerful outlook. The ticket-man had apparently closed up for the day. But if some of the others were still waiting, I figured there must be some hope. They spoke Russian. This was their country: what they were used to. They ought to know what was best.

So we waited. And waited — and waited. Four o'clock came. Five o'clock. Six o'clock. The line had now dwindled down to a meager twenty or twenty-five people leaning, dozing, groaning, relieving each other in half-hour shifts. I was beginning to contemplate giving it up as a bad job.

I had no friends to relieve me, and had already been leaning against the same dirty brick wall for over four hours. Nobody seemed to know whether the ticket-man was coming back or not. Most of them seemed to have forgotten him entirely — and were waiting blindly, through long habit, as if it were an accustomed part of their daily lives — rather dazed, hopeless.

At last, all of a sudden, here was the ticket-man again. It seemed like a new day. In a minute the line had doubled, trebled. Everyone was on his feet, hopeful. But, alas, the man was gone again in five minutes: all he did was to get one ticket for an old lady who had toddled up behind him, probably some relative or family friend to whom was due special attention.

Once more, hope sank in the waiting line. People began to come and go. Some seemed to be ringing in very brazenly ahead of those who had been waiting many hours. Two women wormed in just in front of me. Then a man, tall and bony, tried to do the same, as if this had been proved the weak spot where ringers would be assured success.

I decided that this sort of stuff had gone far enough, so I put up a stout defense and kept him off. He tried some more and set up a heavy barrage of jabber, but finally contented himself with the place next behind. He kept growling at me in guttural Russian for some time, but I paid no attention and started making conversation with some of the people in front of me. They asked me a lot of questions: was I a rabochi? — where did I live? did I belong to the Revolution? In an hour or two more we were pretty thorough acquaintances.

It was really getting pretty much of a hardship to stick in our places. The pressure and heat of weary bodies were oppressive. I'm sure there weren't many of our backs that didn't ache from standing in the same position for so long. We had had many ups and downs in hope, but here it was half-past six — night — and we hadn't moved an inch in five hours. What the hell was the matter with this ticket-man anyway? It seemed he might at least have the decency to let us know his plans.

I finally resolved I would stay till the last man had left. I had to get a ticket sometime, and I couldn't bear to let all this effort go to waste. It would probably be just as bad tomorrow. From the way my companions were acting, it looked as if these were little more than average conditions.

Well, we waited some more and some more, and shifted, and ached, and dozed. We were certainly paying for our tickets. When I finally got so hardened in despair that I didn't care whether the man came back or not, he suddenly appeared on the scene and busily set about selling tickets.

At last I reached the window. It seemed like being face to face with Saint Peter at the end of a sad life. I asked him about my ticket. He didn't seem to understand my Russian very well, but a soldier to whom I had previously told my story came to my assistance. Then I learned that there were 'no more tickets to be sold for tomorrow's train.' Cheerful news!

However, with the characteristic inconsistency of Russian affairs, I finally got a ticket on a train which was to leave in 'half an hour.' With a light heart I rushed back to the barracks for my baggage and then I had to wait four hours more for that train.

The frosted locomotive finally panted up to the station in a white cloud of steam, and the bundled passengers rushed out with their bulky baggage. I joined some twenty others beside car number six, where we stood on the freezing platform until the old conductor had seen each of our tickets, and until three sacks of coal for the stove had been shoveled back from the passageway — while the train waited.

At last — ah — we got to our shelves. Golly, was I ready for a good sleep! The man with whom I'd had the fight in the ticket-line was right opposite me, but we both felt so glad to be where we were that we were friends in two minutes. And then, sleep — sleep — good — deep, refreshing sleep.

Morning. There is a peasant with his wife near me with whom I've made rapid friends. They are quite poor and therefore very thorough communists. Vashilii, the man, a wiry little fellow with a dangling wisp of mustache, loves to discourse on the virtues of communism, for apparently he has benefited considerably by it and is exempt from the heavy taxes which the 'kulaks,' the more prosperous peasants, have to pay.

He gave me a long lecture on farm life, religion, and other interesting things affected by communism. He points, in my dictionary, to the words for 'God' and 'gentleman' and says that there are no such things as 'God' or 'gentlemen' in the U.S.S.R., and 'we are glad to be rid of them, and their imperialism.' I tell him that perhaps 'God' and 'gentleman' mean something different in other countries from what they mean here. But he doesn't believe that can be so: none of the magazines or papers give the slightest indication of it.

Ennokenti Gorbchnov, another of my companions, is a journalist illustrator, or political cartoonist for the Soviet Government. Young, fiery, scrub-brush-haired, stocky of build, extraordinarily energetic of mind, nothing can discourage his ardor to do good work for the party. Lecturing didactically on the horrors of 'capitalism, imperialism, and religion,' drawing violent illustrations to emphasize his main points, he is my most ardent converter.

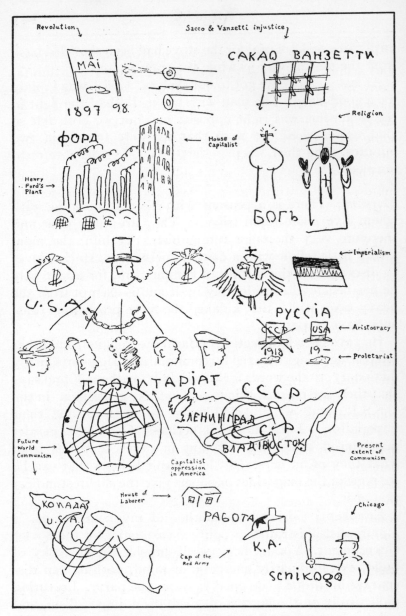

Some of the Drawings of Ennokenti Gorbchnov

In spite of my feeble knowledge of Russian, my companions at first failed to identify me as a foreigner. My limitations in pronunciation and vocabulary were perhaps no more noticeable to them than would be those of a Tajik, an Azerbaijan Turk, a Talish, a Kurd, an Abkhage, a Tat, or some other of the speakers of weird tongues that are included in the Soviet Union.

When my car mates found out that I am not a communist, most of them being rather inexperienced in dealing with capitalists and rather awestruck at finding a foreigner in their midst, they did nothing but gaze at me suspiciously. But when Vashilii and Ennokenti started converting me, the others overcame their timidity and all gathered around to participate in the glories of the adventure. More came from farther up in the car, and raved, and drew pictures, and fingered my dictionary frantically, and asked sarcastic questions — and the situation got hotter and hotter.

Finally, after repeated efforts at relieving the tension by vain smiles, I was forced in self-defense to pass around my great loaf of bread and suffocate their ardor in food until they realized for the time being that, after all, I have the communist spirit, and am in sympathy with the 'rabochi.'

These are very pleasant and natural people except when in debate on the subject of communism. Then they become demons; their eyes begin to bulge, and, uttering strong declarations as to the horrors of the capitalists, accompanied by wild and absolutely fictitious stories about the terrible conditions of workmen in America, they go, to all intents and purposes, violently insane.

Their idea, in general, is that America is like Russia as it was in the days of the Czar, the only difference being that the American aristocrats, aggressive and enormously rich, have developed extraordinary machines and systems of manufacture by which they maintain their power over the vast masses of humble laborers. These oppressed and worthy workmen make up about nine tenths of the population of the United States, but, under the iron dictatorship of the capitalists, who build tremendous skyscrapers, run the government, the press, and control all resources, they are kept in a condition bordering on starvation. They are too ignorant, disorganized, and too much under the influence of capitalist and papal propaganda to actively resist their oppressors. They can only wait and pray for that happy day when their greedy, exploiting, capitalist government shall be overthrown.

This misinformation seems inevitable when you consider the vast gap in heritage, culture, and environment between these people and the people in America. The reading public of Russia, newly literate and receptive, has even less chance to discriminate than have Americans. From reprints of sensational American news, the Russians are told of extensive crime and corruption in America; and from their own Soviet press, which seeks to avoid dangerous suggestions, they are told nothing of crime in Russia. With this contrast for their only guide, Russians are certainly as justified in their fantastic conception of America as are Americans in their usual wild idea of Russia.

February 1. This is a long, long journey, and very cold. Our locomotive and forward cars are all white from the frozen steam which flows back toward us in dense wings of soggy whiteness — as on and on we go with a grind and rattle and crunch of wheels. Always, from sunrise at nine-thirty to sunset at two-thirty we can see our shadow to the north of us waving along on the white snow, a black silhouette of our car, the steam, and the many little stovepipe chimneys sticking up out of the roof.

We have been going through a sort of wavy plateau country, fairly well wooded with pine and wispy birch, for three days — ever since we left Habarovsk. We see logging camps and miners' huts occasionally. Now and then we go through tunnels, but not often, and the country seems to be gradually leveling out and getting barer and bleaker. The boys tell me we have been going through the Klondike region of Asia.

Vukol, our conductor, long-faced, watery-eyed, wearing a limp, stringy scarf around his neck, is a great social referee. He has to get along with every type of human that lives in Russia, and for weeks at a time. Emerging from his base, the coal closet at the end of the car, he sees life in many forms, and both in peace and under stress and strain. With broad outlook and malice toward none, he is always smoothing out difficulties among us passengers.

When the boys get too hot in their efforts to convert me to communism, he comes around and cools them off. Finding that I have no tea-kettle in which to get water, he lends me a pot of his own. He even undertakes the difficult task of teaching me Russian, to put me more nearly on an equal footing with my fellow passengers.

When we make our three-minute stops at the small stations, there is never time for all to get water out of the one dinky faucet, so it is a question of the survival of the fittest. There's not much communist spirit then, I notice. The water is boiling hot when we get it and we often get scalded in the scramble. They never have any cold water anywhere, because, unless it's kept hot, it freezes at once.

We seldom get a chance to buy food, and when we do, it is nothing to write home about. I made an awful mistake this morning as we were making a brief stop at a little shack in the woods. I was eating a nice dish of 'zraza' in the crowded little buffet when the gong rang for the train to start. Foolishly I picked up my remaining meat and dashed out with the crowd — not realizing my mistake till I got into the open air and smelt the meat. It was horrible, and smelt so that I couldn't get it into my mouth. You don't notice such things when you are indoors in these little stations because it is very crowded, and almost everybody takes off his shoes...

The only food we eat in any quantity is black bread. Instead of a crust, this extraordinary bread has bark, like a tree. It is much cheaper than other foods and a couple of good twelve-pound loaves which are five inches thick and four and a half feet in circumference, are enough to last a week. It is wonderful, only ninety kopeks a loaf, and full of whole wheat after you've gnawed through the bark. I eat pounds of it every day. I eat it so much that sometimes I get tired of eating it. Then I eat cake, which I make by sprinkling a little sugar on the bread.

February 2. My latest acquaintance is a burly communist naval commander, returning from Habarovsk to Moscow. This morning he sat beside me on our bench in his simple but impressive uniform, with four gold stripes at each sleeve and brass buttons and red stars, and lectured on the virtues of communism. He told me he was a locksmith, besides being a naval commander, and that he often did a mechanic's job on his ship, as well as commanding it.

'That is one of the fine things about government of the proletariat,' he said. 'No task can be too humble for any man.' I agreed with him.

He went on to tell me about how he had had a hand in overthrowing the Czar, how he had battled thus and so, and killed such and such aristocrats — with much glaring and waving of arms. He got wilder and wilder, and finally even pulled out his automatic when, after brandishing it about a few times, he pressed its muzzle to my head in illustration of what he would do were I an 'imperialist.' Indeed, a soothing companion.

The force of this idea of communism is almost unbelievable. It is much the greatest thing in these people's lives;

virtually a religion. Not otherwise could it possibly have
the appeal and power that it has.

Krupskaia, the wife of Lenin, has written a statement on
'What a Communist Should be Like.' It is typical of the
high aims they have set before themselves. She says:

First of all, a communist is a social person, with strongly developed social instincts, who desires that all people should live
well and be happy. He may be a member of any class in society,
but is more apt to be a member of the working-class, because
life trains workers in knowing their common needs.

Second, a communist must understand what is happening
about him in the world. He must understand the mechanism of
the existing régime, must know the history of the growth of
human society, the history of economic development, of the
growth of property, the division of classes, the growth of state
forms. He must clearly picture whither society is developing.
Communism must appear to him, not only a desirable régime,
but exactly that régime to which humanity is going, where the
happiness of some will not be based on the slavery of others, and
where there will be no compulsion except strongly developed
social instincts. And the communists must clear the road, as you
clear a path in the wilderness, to hasten its coming.

Third, a communist must know how to organize creatively. Suppose he is a medical worker, for instance. He must first know medicine, then the history of medicine in Russia and in other lands, then the communist approach to the problem of medicine, which means: how to organize and agitate wide masses of the population to create from the ranks of the toilers a powerful sanitary organization in the cause of health. He must know not only what communism is, and what is coming, but what his own job in it may be, and his own approach to the masses.

Fourthly, his personal life must be submitted to and guided by the interests of communism. No matter how much he regrets giving up the comforts and ties of home, he must, if necessary, cast all aside and go into danger wherever assigned. No matter how difficult the problem, he must try to carry it out. He fights against everything that harms the cause of communism. Nothing can leave him indifferent. Body and soul he must be devoted to the interests of the toiling masses of communism.

And so, inspired by this most beautiful ideal, my comrades rant on for hours. They never leave me in peace till I agree in the minutest detail, which I always am forced to do in the end in order to get air to breathe. These boys would certainly have a wonderful time with Fatty the oiler. I can see his eyes bulge as he drank in their hair-raising harangue.

Being in Russia is a sort of challenge to one's powers of reason. No matter how hard you try to avoid being fickle, you cannot help but see each point of view — the White or the Red — in a rosier light when you are among the very ardent sympathizers with that point of view.

It is certainly a difficult question to think out clearly, because it involves so many and complicated conceptions: such as Liberty, which means a different thing to the Whites than to the Reds, and Imperialism, and Democracy, which are equally poly-definable.

I try to find the answer by thinking how I would feel if I had been a grovelling 'rabochi' under the czars — and then, on the other hand, how I would feel if I had had the accumulations of ten or twenty years of my struggle to get ahead in the world suddenly and ruthlessly confiscated by a new and dictatorial government.

In each case I feel I have been wronged, and in each case I think I can see how the system which inflicted the wrong could be greatly improved. In fact, if I think it over carefully, I can see how the two cases are peculiarly alike in most respects. Each rebels because he is deprived of a thing which he holds of great value in life. Each calls that thing liberty.

To the Red, liberty means freedom from things undesired — from exploitation by a class visibly superior in wealth and education, from arbitrary bossing. To the White, liberty means freedom for things desired — for individual opportunity, individual expression, a chance to rise.

To the Red, liberty is passive — it is freedom *from* —. To the White, liberty is active — it is freedom *for* —.

The law of the Red is the Golden Rule. He is one of a mass, and to him it is selfish to try to rise above one's neighbors. The law of the White is the Rule of Survival of the Fittest. He is an individual, and to him it is weak to remain on the level of one's neighbors.

Each assumes that the realization of his desires is absolutely incompatible with the realization of the other's desires. Each calls his desires liberty.

As I think it over, it seems to me that both of these ideals are just ones, and not incompatible, and that an ideal form of government, never yet attained by man, would be that form of government which assured to every man these two freedoms. Perhaps these two blood-drenched ideals are the same. Perhaps some future day will see them merged in peace. Certainly it is in Russia today that these two tides of civilization meet in storm.

I keep reminding myself that Russia has been far away from many of the developments of Western civilization —

Chivalry, the Renaissance, the Reformation, Puritanism, the French Revolution, and modern Industrialism. These great individualistic movements of the West have left her relatively untouched in her Oriental and patriarchal subversion of the individual to the mass. The struggle between the Reds and the Whites may be a struggle between the East and the West; between the psychology of the mass and that of the individual.

Between Cheeta and Irkutsk — February 3. The country is leveling out, and sometimes the valleys widen till they are tremendous plains stretching to the horizon — and we go on and on across empty wheat land.

But always, to the north, is that eternal forest lurking in the distance. We may lose it for a while, but it comes back every time — sometimes gradually, sometimes suddenly as we come to a roving range of hills. I don't think we have been really out of sight of it once. The stations are in small farming communities, with scattered houses and barns, cows lounging about, a few horses, and many haystacks. Between lie the vast expanses of wheat. Sometimes the stations are surrounded by gigantic piles of flour and grain sacks waiting to be shipped to the cities.

The station-houses are usually colored red or yellow, and include, in addition to a sizable waiting-room, some sort of a restaurant, a supply counter or store, water faucets, and sometimes a barber shop.

When we are buying bread at the larger stations where we are not hurried, I am much touched by the friendship of my acquaintances. They are so generous — often risking going hungry themselves in order to make sure I do not lose out through my handicap of language. Someone is always making an explanation, or putting in a plea in my behalf at the supply counter, so that I will get special attention.

I get greatest sympathy from the old peasant women, who

evidently are convinced that my past life has been but one long tragedy — that after twenty-two years of starvation and persecution in America, I have come to Russia for relief from oppression. They take it upon themselves to see that I am spared any continuance of my former hardship, and try hopefully to impress me with communistic efficiency and prosperity, and encourage me to have faith in the future.

There is surely no lack of kindness among the Russian peasant people. A traveler who has recently lived in this country writes:

A great many of the former titled nobility and landed gentry have withdrawn into the country, where they owned great estates, and are being provided generously with everything they need by the peasants who expropriated their lands and wealth. The Soviet authorities know about it and pretend not to see what is going on. Time is purging the Russian Revolution of one of its most powerful but degrading motives: revenge. The fact that a peasant can divide his crumb of bread with his former landlord, and the district commissar knows about it and does nothing to stop it, is a healthy sign for Russia.

These itinerant peasants love to look at their maps. One reason, I think, is that the particular map which most of them use is very sympathetic with a communistic point of view. It is a Mercatorial projection map in which Russia and Siberia, being relatively far north, look, of course, much bigger, in reference to the rest of creation, than they should.

My car mates gaze fondly at these maps over long periods of time, murmuring contentedly about the progress of the Revolution, sometimes becoming wildly excited in their harangue on this subject. Pointing to the gigantic area which the U.S.S.R. occupies on a Euro-Asiatic Mercatorial map, they dilate on the great strength of this colossal movement which, in a single decade, has swept 'almost half the world.' They expound on how it is reaching out, out, all the time — across the Indian border, by means of provision trains, and teachers who have dedicated their lives to relieving the poor oppressed of India; into China, by the same method; into Korea; into Turkey; Bulgaria; Poland; Finland; Germany.

Convinced are these companions of mine that the U.S.S.R. is steadily spreading over the whole earth — that there are only a few small countries left: a tiny negligible bit of Western Europe, a few minor considerations like Africa, America, and Australia, which will soon succumb. Then communism will live in peace and prosperity throughout the length and breadth of the world!

You can have no idea how these peasants feel about the world till you look at one of these projection maps. The peasants judge the importance of a country by its area, not by its population or anything else. They overlook the fact that China, comparatively small in area, contains nearly three times as many people as all the Soviet republics and Siberia combined. They forget that the entire U.S.S.R. has a population of only about 150,000,000, which is less than one thirteenth of the total 2,000,000,000 souls who live on the earth. That, in the whole world, only one man in a thousand actually belongs to the Communist Party.

I am amazed that these untaught peasants are so vitally interested in academic questions of government, religion, philosophy, evolution, and science. Where a group of American workmen would be discussing the latest movie or the batting average of Babe Ruth, these bushy-haired fellows are speculating deeply as to the steps in the development of China toward ultimate communism, arguing as to how best to reform the capitalistic tendency of Henry Ford — desiring and thinking out for themselves, within the limits of data at their command, a broad, idealistic view of life.

This seems strange until you remember that there have been other simple farmers to whom the theories of social justice were just as vital a workaday concern.

The communist principles that 'The happiness of some people be not based on the exploitation of others,' and that 'There be no compulsion except strongly developed social instincts,' appeal to the communist farmer's sense of justice much as appealed to the simple farmers of America the principles set forth in our own Declaration of Independence ——

We hold these truths to be self-evident, that all men are created equal, that they are endowed... with certain inalienable rights... among these... Life, Liberty and the pursuit of happiness... That whenever any Form of Government becomes destructive of these ends, it is the Right of the People to alter or abolish it, and to institute new Government.

I think all communists would endorse the substance of these principles, retaining, of course, their own passive definition of Liberty.

Subscribing to a doctrine in which the interests of individuals are subordinated to the interests of the mass, they apparently do not feel the absence of a Bill of Rights in their own Federal Constitution. Their Constitution does, however, subscribe to the principle of government with 'the consent of the governed,' for they safeguard against oppressive centralization by provisions such as that 'Each federated Republic has the right of freely withdrawing from the union.'

Of course, between the high principles of communism and some of the doings of communists, there lies an obvious gulf. But human principles and human performance are seldom bunkies for very long, and I should like to see George Washington's expression when perusing today's New York papers.

I'm glad I'm on a local train instead of the express, because, as it is, passengers are getting on and off all the time, and I meet new people every day, and learn more Russian. Now I know how to tell my whole story, always demanded by an endless series of questions and accusations, and I can understand, also, the stories of my scraped acquaintances.

We are always on very intimate terms, sitting and sleeping on each other's bunks, borrowing each other's teapots, and eating each other's food. We are getting to have teamwork in doing our errands in the small stations. One refills all the kettles, one rushes to the 'lavka' to buy bread for the bunch, one heads for the buffet for meat. These are some of the virtues of communism.

Here we are at the vast Lake Baikal — the lake a tremendous expanse of whiteness walled on the remote horizon by hazy, bluish cliffs of snow, and streaked ridges of black forest. Sometimes we can see, perhaps a mile or two out from shore, the speck of a lonely sleigher trekking homeward into the dreary distance.

All afternoon we nosed and tunneled our way among the crags and cliffs which dam the southern end of the great frozen sea, till at sundown we turned westward to follow a beautiful river valley toward Irkutsk. There were many snowy ridges about, and it looked very much like the Upper Yukon, except that the forest consisted more of birch than of evergreen trees. The snow was deep, and hewn into grotesque drifts by savage winds — and the air was cold as bloody hell!

Up till today I haven't noticed the cold particularly, although sometimes ten minutes in the kettle line tingled my ears a bit; but now — just stick your head out of the door for a second or two. Wow!

It feels as if the wind would rip your skin off. And if you touch your bare fingers to metal, they hold like glue, and it is painful as the devil to pull them off again. The tiny station-houses are fairly buried in the spume-swept dunes of snow, and our fuming engine is frosted even to the rods as it sizzles on before us in the night. At stations where we re-arrange our cars, the brakemen have to thaw the ice off the couplings with torches, so that they can unfold the links.

To the north, in the darkness, stretch pale fields of snow, and beyond, the ink of space, and the twinkling friendly Dipper balanced on its handle — looking just as it always did at home.

There's a very peculiar-looking man aboard now, with a head like a lampshade — absolutely smooth and round on top and with a lot of dangling tassels and stuff below. He hasn't a single blade of down on his whole upper hemi-sphere; but I never saw such a complicated outfit of whisk-ers in my life. It looks like the roots of a banyan tree.

A little while ago he called me over to his bench and se-cretly offered me a drink out of his bottle of vodka. He was obviously trying to keep anyone else from knowing he had the bottle. Drinking — though not illegal — is disapproved of by the communists, but knowing me to be from 'aristo-cratic America,' perhaps he figured I would appreciate it. I took a few swallows to please him, but vodka is really too powerful for me. It is practically pure alcohol and burns your throat.

February 5. There are some very pretty girls aboard now — but they are all busy taking care of their many toddling children.

Zmitrok Galun, a machinist with hair like steel wool, nose like a doorknob, leathery skin, and transparent eyes, bunks in a section near me with his pretty wife, or best girl, Irma Elimov. The distinction between wife and best girl is not always clear here, and matters very little. At any rate, Zmitrok has lived with Irma for three years and seems to love her very much.

I sat on his bunk talking with him this morning. I showed him my camera, which, of course, aroused his keen interest, resulting in his offering me twenty rubles for it. I wanted to take Irma's picture, as she is a typical peasant girl and quite charming—but Zmitrok grew jealous at the idea and would have none of it. He later consented, however, to let me take a picture of both Irma and himself together.

The Soviet marriage custom is very simple and seems to work well with these cool-blooded people. As neither puritanism nor chivalry has ever penetrated the vastness of Russia, the people have never had a sense of taboo or curiosity about sex. Instead, they have always been free and natural. It is an ancient custom for peasant boys to woo their girls by sleeping beside them in the hay.

This race has little of the Latin sensuousness in its blood. Here, the people's minds rule their hearts. Everything in Russia is more the product of mind than heart. This seems appropriate to a flat, dry, vast, cold country. It seems to go with communism, suppressed individuality, a race of chess-players, mental theorizers, and political dreamers.

I am getting off at Novosibirsk, our next stop, because I've heard that a farming-tool factory is being built there by American engineers, and that it is a progressive communist city — a boom town of which the population has increased thirty-eight per cent in three years.

Situated in the middle of this interminable, wavy plain, Novosibirsk is said to be about the coldest place in the world. The North Pole rarely gets more than fifty below zero, as the water under the ice, being at least thirty-two above, acts as a stove when brought in contact with things eighty degrees colder. But here in Novosibirsk the ocean is nearly three thousand miles away; the air is dry and very susceptible to changes in temperature. It sometimes reaches eighty below zero.

At one o'clock in the morning, we pulled into a big, dimly lighted station.

'Novo — sibeersk!' howled Vukol.

Across the icy platform stood a dozen little droshky sleighs, which, from the horses' appearance, might have been waiting there, frosted into immobility, all winter.

Gasping as the bitter air hit my lungs, I woke up one of the nebulously bundled drivers, and hopped into his droshky with Abu Kasparovitch, a Red soldier whom I had met on the train. He had generously offered to help me find a lodging.

With a jerk, the furry little horse lunged forward in the shafts...

It was snowing whizzing flakes that stung our faces, and the cold was terrible. The tiny sleigh offered no protection to our combined bulk and our bundles, which we clutched with freezing fingers. Five minutes in the wind made my ears feel as if they would drop off — but the snow whirled on, lights drifted by, and occasionally other sleighs — oh, for a warm room!

Finally we stopped before a wide low building with a lighted doorway. 'Hotel,' says Abu. We entered a low-ceilinged hall with no decoration other than a photograph of Lenin on the dusty wooden paneling, and an old man sitting dejectedly on the stairs. On consultation with this cheerless individual, Abu informs me that the place is filled up, and that all the other hotels in Novosibirsk are filled, too.

The prospect of camping out on such a night is not pleasant — we return to the droshky. 'Perhaps I know a place,' says Abu, and consults with the driver as the furry horse runs nimbly on through the flying snow. Neither Abu, the driver, nor the horse seems uncomfortable in this blizzard which makes my skin feel as if it were peeling off my bones.

I suddenly can understand why Russian sleigh-drivers take such good care of their whiskers.

At last we stop again. Down some steps to a dark little cellar door — heavy knocking, lengthy pleading with the frowsy proprietress who answers, and finally we are admitted into what is apparently a bunk-house, for the night. Through passageways we are led toward a room from whence comes the sound of revelry — clinking of glass and guttural guffaws. Entering, baggage in hand, we find ourselves in the midst of what appears to be a carousal in its late stages. A half-dozen men are lolling about in stocking feet, some seated on their plank cots, others leaning uncertainly against the table-load of bottles. Most of the cots, ranged around the sides of the room, are already occupied with soundly snoring comrades. Suddenly there is a terrific explosion over by the stove. One of the bleary brothers has tried out his shotgun against it, just to see if the trigger is in good order. Two of the sleepers sit up startled; the remaining snore steadfastly on.

Although a couple of the men make perfunctory signs of greeting to us, Abu and I go comparatively unnoticed to our cots and retire. Abu has soon dropped off — but I remain long awake, it being difficult for me to lose consciousness of such ribald companions.

In the morning, things seemed more cheerful, as they generally do when you arrive anywhere late at night. My comrades generously gave me of their breakfast, cheese and bread, and offered to escort me to the Workman's Palace, where I hoped to find out about the new tool factory. It was still snowing, but much warmer, almost up to ten below zero.

The streets are full of bundled forms moving along the sidewalks, and sleighs streaming along in an almost unbroken file with their cargoes of grain sacks, hay, and lumber from the country. Many of them are driverless, the little panting horses following each other mechanically, as from long training. Amid these hundreds of little droshky sleighs appears an automobile — property of the government — and occasionally a sleigh drawn by a camel, a great sauntering beast, very woolly, blowing dense clouds from his sagging, rubbery lips. These, I am told, come from Russian Turkestan, a few hundred miles southwest of here, where they are more numerous than horses.

The houses, mostly of wood, are never more than three or four stories high. New buildings are going up, wide and squatty like the rest.

A report that there are American engineers in Novosibirsk turns out to be a piece of that enterprising optimism that colors so much of communistic information. But at any rate, in the Workman's Palace I find a Russian engineer who tells me he is engaged in the construction of the huge new factory where modern farming machinery is to be manufactured. He says it is part of the 'five-year development program,' and one of several factories intended to facilitate the growth of state and collective farms, which the government is trying to encourage, in order to put all peasants on the same social and economic plane. Engineers and specialists are being offered huge salaries to come from America and other foreign countries, to ensure the highest standards of efficiency.

From feudalism the communists are trying to jump straight into large-scale production, following the example of Japan. Now receiving the first benefits of their division of labor, they talk excitedly about the amazing advance they have made within a dozen years; about the great progressiveness and efficiency of the U.S.S.R.; about how it will soon outstrip America and lead the world in production and system of every kind. Though it is quite true that their progress is remarkable, one must bear in mind that the great efficiency communists claim is efficiency *in comparison* to the way things were done in the Czar's days.

Where there was a small, isolated village, out of all communication with the world, now is a village with a post-office, a shack converted into a meeting-house for discussions, perhaps even a telegraph-office. Where the people used only wooden ploughs, now they use ploughs with metal tips, and perhaps have a tractor, which no one knows how to take care of or has spare parts for, to serve the entire village.

The Russian peasants are by heritage one of the most backward and inefficient people on earth. No wonder they are in difficulties when they try to surpass America in a couple of decades of effort. Of all the great wandering tribes that roamed across Central Asia, the ancestors of these people were the most easy-going, least-persevering, of all, for they were the tribes who straggled and got left behind; who were too listless to push forward and fight for a place in Europe.

They were content to stagnate on the fertile black earth of these plains and forest waterways, their minds becoming as dull as the easy, uneventful land around them, retaining all of the dark superstitions that Europe outgrew through her centuries of struggle. From the Orient, these people had received a patriarchal system which thwarted all invasion of new ideas.

Not until 1917, when at last came the great explosion of communism, was their stagnation shaken into life.

Now their archaic customs and beliefs are being wiped away. Tradition no longer guides these peasants, and so, being unable to think as individuals from lack of practice, they readily accept the doctrine of Communism with its release from exploitation. Like Orientals, for ages subservient to the rule of the local old man, they have not only no capacity, but also no desire, for individuality. They are entranced with the idea of remaining, all their lives, equal members of a society in which no individual may rise above the common level of prosperity and social standing.

This afternoon I went to the house of Mrs. Serbov, Bellia Korsakov's aunt, whose address Bellia had given me in Harbin.

It was an apartment house, more prosperous than the average in appearance. Having made sure I was not being followed, as I did not want to risk putting these people under suspicion, I entered and climbed the winding staircase to the third floor, where I saw the door number I was looking for.

In answer to my ring, a young girl, perhaps a maid, cautiously opened the door and peered suspiciously out at me. Then, nodding and murmuring the conventional 'Dobri dyen,' led me within — a long dark hall lined with rickety bookcases, old pieces of furniture, household supplies, and doors leading to rooms on either side — the smell of stew being prepared for lunch.

An old lady, probably Mrs. Serbov, rather gaunt and with white hair, but keen, intelligent eyes toddled toward me, wonderingly.

'Kak vui pazshivyiete?' I began, politely. 'I am a friend of Bellia Korsakov — your niece?'

'Oh, a friend of Bellia Korsakov? Sit down — you are in time for dinner.'

A pretty woman of about thirty-five, blonde, blue-eyed, pink-cheeked, well-rounded of form, appeared in a doorway. In her hand was a violin. Three neatly dressed children could be seen behind her, playing with blocks on the floor. The old lady ushered me within the room, introduced me to the young woman — Mrs. Barchevsky — and then toddled off to stir the stew and arrange dinner.

Mrs. Barchevsky very thoughtfully gave me a few biscuits, meanwhile telling me about her children. The oldest,

Francisk, about eight, was rather whimpering and depressed; I learned he had just been fed a spoonful of castor oil to cure his indigestion, and that he had put up considerable resistance.

Dinner ready, doors in the hall began to open and other members of this White Russian refuge ambled wearily into view — rickety old men, children, sisters-in-law, uncles — they all trudged into the dining-room and arranged themselves about the large round table for the meal. The old white-haired Mrs. Serbov presided, dishing out generous helpings of stew while a couple of children were sent on errands to the kitchen.

Among other things they brought out a box of butter upon which all eyes were fastened most reverently. The old lady buttered a few biscuits which she handed over to me. She offered none to anyone else and no one seemed to expect any.

I accepted these and, after unsuccessfully trying them on everybody else, ate them and found them delicious. She continued to prepare more for me, but her hospitality was somewhat diluted by her remark that this was the first time they had had butter for two weeks because of the terrific expense of this luxury. The others all joined her in a description of how terrible it was to be confined to a half-pound of butter a month. And then they offered me more butter, as if it meant nothing whatever to them, and were offended when I, of course, couldn't accept.

After the meal, I went into the room of one of the old men and talked with him for a while. His prize possession was an old flute which he manipulated gingerly, blowing intricate classical tunes with rather more alacrity than precision. He said he had never had a lesson — which I believed — and kept blowing tune after tune for me, becoming more and more pleased with himself with each successive puff.

Mrs. Serbov's son-in-law, Mr. Barchevsky, a tall, thin,

swarthy, aquiline man, is an administrative official for the
Soviet Government. Knowing how 'White' his true sympa-
thies are — as Mrs. Serbov cautiously confided to me — I
am amazed at the responsibility he accepts in a government of principles alien to his own, and how calmly he
performs the dangerous treason of wearing a Soviet uniform, for which he might easily be punished by death.
How many other Soviet officers are far from communistic
in their hearts the Lord only knows.

When I was about to leave, old Mrs. Serbov said, 'We
wish you would give a message from us to our relative in
Chicago, Klementi Ignatovsky.' She had already told me
about this brother whom she had not seen since before the
Revolution, and with whom she had not communicated for
some years. Her message, hardly calculated to bring back
tender memories of a long separated sister, reads:

Mr. K. Ignatovsky, 488 Melrose Street, Chicago. Send immediately:
5 kilograms of butter in tin box.
10 kilograms of pork.
2 cans of condensed milk.
And all other canned goods you can afford.
Your sister, Mrs. Serbov,
203 Malaya Nikitskaya, Novosibirsk.

When I got back to our dormitory, the evening's carousal
was already under way. There was almost continual rollick-
ing and laughter, gorging of cheese and bread, many vodka
bottles on the table, and heavy drinking 'to the Revolution.' The comrades taunted me with being from 'bourgeois America,' and insisted that I demonstrate my true
allegiance by drinking to the Revolution.

I tried hard to show them that the only revolution that
drinking would promote would be in my insides, and I
kidded them for out-dissipating the czars, but nothing could
stop their boozing. The only ones who abstained were two

soldiers, to whom liquor is forbidden. The rest gorged and imbibed boisterously far into the night.

When I lay down to sleep, they playfully poured water on my head, and got to be quite a nuisance. Finally all went to sleep except two, who remained sitting on their beds arguing noisily about a pencil factory, which they seemed to think should be built in Novosibirsk. They kept on for hours, rattling their bed planks and leaving the light burning so I couldn't get to sleep. Some of the others, however, their senses deadened by vodka, at length dropped off and commenced a truly communistic chorus of snoring...

Two hours passed, and still the light burned and the debate continued. I pleaded with them at least to turn the light off even if they wouldn't stop talking, but they were so engrossed that they paid no attention.

Another hour passed and still they continued with no sign of slackening. Once more I besought them to be reasonable, to no avail, and then, seeing that more forceful measures must be undertaken in order to be understood, I got up and turned out the light myself. They instantly made a howl about this and turned it on again.

As I didn't want to antagonize them, I promptly said, in my most convincing Russian, 'I am sorry to disturb you. I am trying to go to sleep.' But, like the Chinese, they seemed to regard an apology as an admission of fear, and, after a session of muffled growling between themselves, broke out in a loud verbal assault, hauled out their guns, and made it known that from then on they were my deadly enemies.

Furthermore, one produced papers proving he was a member of the 'Gay-Pay-Oo,' Secret Police, and, savagely denouncing me as an aristocrat and imperialist, said that in the morning he would have me arrested. I knew how sweeping are the G.P.U.'s powers of arrest, so I was somewhat perturbed by this announcement which was obviously made very much in earnest.

It was also very unpleasant to have two wild men pointing their guns at me, each working the other into more and more of a rage till the very house seemed to shake.

But I didn't let them know how I felt, and with as expressionless a face as possible, went quietly back to bed. They continued their diatribe for some time, however, and at last, villainously filling their magazines full of fresh cartridges, dragged their cots over in front of the door to prevent any possible escape and, with the light still on, went, muttering, to bed, automatics cocked and still in hand.

I slept rather lightly: it doesn't contribute to placid slumber to have two enraged and drunken communists waving automatics around in a casual way about ten feet from your pillow. But eventually their excitement died down from exhaustion and they drowsed off. All was still, save for the orchestral reverberations of sleeping throats and noses, which had accompanied the whole disturbance, no doubt immunized by a long experience of brawls in the past. I, however, took very little relaxation, for I had plenty to think over before morning. This was a situation which required careful figuring. I thought and thought. Escape out of the room was virtually impossible: the windows were double and both thicknesses tightly sealed, the door was locked and thoroughly guarded by my savage buddies, and it probably wouldn't do me any good to get out of the bunkhouse anyway, as it was more than thirty below outside, and there was no other place in town I could go except the railroad station. That could scarcely be called a hiding-place — as it would take half a dozen hours waiting in an open ticket-line, and many more waiting for the train, to get away. I must do something else. I must somehow get these people friendly again.

I knew by experience that Russian peasants are not very individual and are usually extremely sensitive to public opinion — so I decided the thing to do was, by some means or other, to get all those who had been asleep, easily the big majority, on my side. If I could do that, the two who were so mad would perhaps hesitate to go against me. At any rate, it would be worth trying. I planned carefully just how I was going to go about things, and then took a little sleep.

I woke in the morning early, before the others, and cautiously roused an old farmer, merely jiggling his bed gently so that he wouldn't think he had been waked. I jocosely told him the story of what had happened to me, making it as humorous as possible. While entertaining the old farmer, and taking care not to disturb the sleep of my two would-be captors, I succeeded in gently bringing to consciousness, one by one, all the other men.

Quite desperately amusing, I told my story to all, making up for my lack of fluency in Russian by vivid imitation of the facial expressions of my prospective 'executioners.' I was fortunate in soon getting everyone thoroughly diverted at this humorous aspect of their threats.

Then, judging the time to be ripe, I aroused said executioners, to confront them with the joke that was being made of their hostile intentions. It was an exciting moment for me. Would they accept this jocose rendering of their intentions or would they be further enraged at my impertinence?

They opened their eyes. Their first expression was clearly one of surprise that it should be I that was awakening them. Then, when they heard the ludicrous account of their last night's behavior, and were shown my drawings of the incident, they registered considerable annoyance, mixed with embarrassment. I saw instantly that they didn't have it in them to carry out their vengeful intentions in the face of this waggishness. They wouldn't risk being ridiculous. So my stratagem was going to work, after all. What relief! They looked at me rather awry, but, when they heard the laughs over their doings and facial expressions as depicted by me, they forced a smile.

As I hoped, they immediately pretended that they had been joking the whole time — making out that I was the butt of a pretended anger. It was the only thing they could do, I having thoroughly established as ridiculous any real antagonism they might show. As I knew they hadn't the slightest intention of joking with me this cold morning, I enjoyed seeing them smiling, though somewhat acidly, with the others.

Anyhow, the situation had been saved. It was a strange adventure, and revealing as to some of the dark corners of the Russian character.

In the afternoon, I set out to get a ticket to Moscow, and I was prepared for the worst. I brought my baggage along, so as to avoid having to go back to the bunk-house for it — though I knew it would be a handicap in the prospective scramble.

It was a tough outlook when I got to the station. The

ticket-office had closed for the day and wasn't to open till five in the morning — one hour before train-time. But already, here at six in the evening, there were hundreds in the waiting line. It was a tremendous station, yet packed so full of people and bundles that you could hardly move.

The ticket-line wound vaguely off into the distance till it was lost in the packed hordes at the far end of the great waiting-room. I didn't see how anybody could possibly find the end of it, if it had any end. It would be impossible to prove where its end was, anyway, because it became like the roots of a tree, branching into innumerable subdivisions till it was dissolved beyond recognition in the solid soil of the mob.

I won't again go into all the anxiety and grim waiting and ups and downs of despair inevitable to buying a railroad ticket in Russia. Suffice it to say that this night was worse than was the waiting in Habarovsk. And when dawn came, I was just as far from having a ticket as ever. I might just as well have remained in the bunk-house, instead of having to witness all the terrible hardships of these people, the whining of babies without enough blankets, the pathetic struggles of their mothers to keep them warm, the shivering and pacing up and down among clouds of breath rising from dazed, bundled forms heaped on the great floor, and the terrific icy wind that swept in through the busy doors, all but freezing those unfortunate enough to be camped near it.

It got colder and colder till, at half-past four in the morning, the thermometer outside the main door said forty-five below zero, Réaumur, which is sixty-nine below, Fahrenheit, and incidentally no temperature to sniff at.

I spent the night sitting on my sacks of baggage on which also sat an old peasant woman with a baby. We both leaned against a large bale of some sort of grain, beside which I had deposited my belongings. The lady, before long, also leaned on me, as did a couple of very ragged fellows who had pitched camp on the cold stone floor where my left foot would have been. I dozed a bit from time to time, but the poor lady had such trouble with her baby that I didn't have a very restful night.

As morning neared, it grew colder and colder. The baby began to cry. The small piece of fur with which the woman frantically tried to keep the baby covered was not enough, and as soon as she began to doze, it slipped off. I helped tie it in place around the baby and the mother was thankful, but the baby made further trouble and of varieties in which I could be of little assistance.

At dawn, instead of opening his window, the ticket-man announced that the train was twenty-one hours late, instead of only thirteen, as previously announced, and that tickets would not be sold until afternoon. Something like a deep sigh stirred through the big room, but no one moved; no one protested; all held solid. Mere time was no longer any hardship.

At about ten in the morning a girl with thick, dark, curly hair introduced herself and her five companions to me. All six, which included two other girls and three young men, were students, bound for a college in Moscow. Each man had his own girl and all were obviously very much in love. They seemed to be much thrilled at the idea of traveling, and asked me every conceivable question concerning my purpose and destination. They soon made me feel at home, and said that, through a porter, who had influence with the ticket-man, they could get tickets when the office opened without waiting in line, and would I, in the mean time, come to their house?

It sounded like the best news I'd heard in years, so away we went, off through the streets and the wind. That air was cold, I can tell you. It turned overcoats into mosquito netting, furs into cheesecloth. It made my bones ache, and my nose turned instantly red as a radish.

One of the girls, Najeda, wearing a red scarf, began to throw snowballs at me as we left the station. I think she has French or Italian blood in her because she is much more energetic and vivacious than most Russians. It being around fifty-five below zero at the time, I didn't fully appreciate the snowballs, but Najeda, warmly dressed and accustomed to this temperature, enjoyed herself to the full. Suddenly she picked up a handful of powdery snow and rushed at me, crying, 'Bellui! Bellui! Buistro!'

All I could think of was that 'bella' meant war in Latin, and then I remembered that 'bellui' was the Russian word for 'white.' Apparently my nose had suddenly turned white, and I must rub it with snow. It was freezing, swollen to twice its normal size, and had become hard as a rock, but so numb that I would never of myself have noticed its desperate situation.

We rubbed it with snow and took it into the nearest store until it got red again, and, on continuing on to Najeda's home, I kept the precious object wrapped up in a mitten. A nose, though its vicissitudes are always ridiculous, is something one hates to lose.

Najeda lives in a student dormitory, much like a barracks, in which about fifty cots are lined up in rows. The men sleep in one room, the women in another adjoining, and each have a small washroom. To eat, they go out to restaurants.

None of these students have any real family life. They seldom see their parents and brothers, as they travel about from place to place in the course of their education, and they do not seem to miss them. The government encourages youth to leave the home and to seek its particular place in the mass movement of communist progress. Its purpose is to rid the people of the constraint of patriarchism.

When we returned to the station, we learned that the train was now twenty-five hours late. As the reports of its progress were announced, it seemed as if the darned train must be going away instead of toward us. But there seemed to be absolutely no limit to the fatalistic endurance of these hordes of would-be passengers.

It is almost unbelievable that so many Russians want to travel. Where they are trying to go is a mystery. None of them are rich, and it is extremely difficult to get a railroad ticket anyway, yet here they are, sitting.

Najeda says: 'We earn more money than we need. We must buy something with it. There are no luxuries — no silks, no dress clothes, automobiles, jewelry, nor any other such diversion. So we travel. In this way we get our diversion, and learn about our country as well.'

Although this is one explanation of Russian vagrancy, I think another cause of these people's urge to travel is in their nomadic Tartar blood, handed down from the roving horsemen of the steppes.

But fatalism has its limits, and even when traveling in Russia, a human being has certain inalienable rights. All too evidently, the Russian word for 'toilet,' as given in my dictionary, means also 'barber shop.' With what delicacy I could command, and carefully consulting my dictionary, I asked Najeda to direct me. With discouraging monotony, again and again, she took me to the barber shop. At such times it is embarrassing to use sign-language.

Everyone with whom I became acquainted, during the dreary hours that we waited on that cold, dirty floor, said, 'Beware of pickpockets — they are here by the hundreds.'

It must be confessed that this doubt of the honesty of the Russian peasant is not unfounded. He has lied habitually to evade oppressive injustice and extortion. The habit inevitably extended into his family and business relations. From all accounts he was a pretty steady liar. Patriarchism deprived him of individual responsibility, and he knew no form of personal pride — such as patriotism in Japan, or 'face' as in China — to hold him above dishonesty.

One of the fundamental changes wrought by communism is in its effort to overcome this petty dishonesty in the peasant. It is instilling into him the pride of a ruler. Before him, as an ideal, is set Lenin, the pattern of integrity.

Still, however, I heeded the warning about pickpockets, for I noticed that I was never without a group of disciples who seemed especially intent on gazing steadfastly into space. Perhaps they were entirely innocent, but I gave them no opportunity to be otherwise, and at last — at last — came the train.

It took five more days to get to Moscow — days of the same rattling and swaying along across wavy plains, past forests of fir and birch, with always our shadow dancing on the snow to the north; days of monotony broken only by the rush for water and the coming and going of peasants, soldiers and workmen at station after station. I met many people, discussed the same questions, and found both the people and the answers almost all alike.

As we stop in a station to load fuel wood into the tender, my companions point with pride to the recent electrification of a part of the road. One, who bunks next to me, is a young farmer named Boris Nicholovitch. He has large wide-open blue eyes, intelligent red face, straight hair, brushed pompadour, and a genuine smile — in the moments when he is not serious. Though not a party member, he is enthusiastic for communism, and feels great pride in the achievements of the Soviet régime. Ever since Novosibirsk he has taken pains to show me each little bit of modern machinery or construction we encounter in this long journey. He is thrilled by them.

In the details of his own personal appearance he also has unusual pride and is very dressy. He even has some spats, to put on for special occasions, and he is so fond of his necktie that he wears it outside his collar instead of underneath.

The generator in our car is out of commission, so at night we use candles. The whole train is in a pretty dilapidated condition. We must stop often to give our engine a rest — it was built in 1910 and is now getting a bit tottery.

It acts very much like an old horse, except that, instead of hay, it is fed birch logs, which are loaded into the tender at every station while we wait in line for bread and water. And between stations, especially now when we are bucking a head wind, the old engine frequently has to stop to get its breath. The puffing of steam seems to give it a sore throat, and it is getting hoarser all the time. I only hope it doesn't finally turn up its toes far from the nearest town. My companions tell me that this happens sometimes — and everybody has to get out and walk.

Najeda and her five companions are riding five cars back of me. There is no such thing as a chaperon in Russia, and, as they have never heard of puritanism, these people no doubt enjoy themselves to the full. When I asked her whether or not she is married, Najeda, who knows a few words of English, replied, laughing, 'No, no — I am still girl.'

Boris usually comes back to get me when I stay more than a few minutes with this erotic gang. I don't know his purpose in so doing, but he just waits around without speaking to any of them, until, not wishing to detain him longer, I comply with his wishes and return home to car four.

I don't believe many of the women in this train waste much time in making themselves up. There is nothing veiled or subtle in their efforts to be attractive. They rely entirely on their natural ruddy complexions and vigorous health. Not only is this type of beauty idealized by communist leaders, but, in this land of no chivalry, no puritanism, no sex taboos, it is the most popular and successful type of beauty — and very satisfactory to the men. There is, however, a Western influence creeping in, and which, I am told, is spreading more and more rapidly. Every now and then I see evidences of lipstick.

Western ideas, of course, lead to the spread of individualism — the antithesis of communism. The communists naturally make every effort to control this influence — through bans on imports, etc.; but it seeps in more and more, and is slowly, steadily making headway. I am told that, a few years ago, wearing a white collar was a sign of being bourgeois, and that no one wore white collars for this reason. But now, white collars may be seen frequently, even among the staunchest communists, and a few women have somehow smuggled themselves clothes which savor suspiciously of Paris.

The communist leaders at first disregarded this individualism, but as it awakened more and more in spite of their suppressive measures, they have had to consider it — and seriously. By 1921, the peasants had not coöperated as part of the communistic mass, and Lenin then made the first great concession to individualism. He said, 'I regret it, because our experience, which is not very long, proves to us that our conception was wrong.' And he adopted the 'New Economic Policy' which allowed the peasants some individual profit in marketing their produce.

At present, in the 'collective farm' campaign, the failure of coercive methods has necessitated an appeal to the individual's desire for self-advancement. Through free moving-picture shows, circulating from village to village, the government represents the collectivist peasant prospering with his tractors and modern farm machines, with his reduced taxes, his scientific management, his coöperative marketing system. This is the only method of enrollment that works. The peasants, taken in by the personal advantages in collectivism, readily accept the new system.

Until recently, the government prohibited the private saving of funds, but it has now abandoned this inhuman idea, and actually encourages saving by paying out eight per cent interest on personal investments.

Where all workmen were formerly treated indiscriminately as members of a common proletariat, they are now classified as 'skilled' and 'unskilled,' and the privileges of the skilled workman over his unskilled brother are increasing day by day. He gets higher pay, larger living quarters, and better clothes.

In numerous ways the government is rewarding individual effort, for it has learned that the Golden Rule is like the Volstead Law. Some people may obey it — others may not. But it cannot be enforced.

Of course, in spite of this gradually awakening individualism, Russians are still, in the main, an Oriental, patriarchal people. They still call relief from private enterprise 'liberty.' They still consider themselves 'free' because they have removed the possibility of any man's rising appreciably above his neighbors in wealth or social status.

At night, by our blinking candle light, I play chess with the soldiers, and learn more Russian, and make more friends. Chess, by the way, seems to be a universal game. On every ship I've been on, I have found at least one chess-player in the crew. In its almost purely mental diversion, it seems to appeal to a certain type of mind all over the world, and, among this mental race of Russians, it has reached a high state of development. If, in a car full of illiterate peasants, anyone pulls out a chess-board, he is immediately swamped by challenging opponents.

It may seem inconsistent that these people are so inefficient and at the same time such ardent students of chess. Their minds, however, as I analyze them, are restless, brilliant, and theoretical rather than methodical or exact. They are not a naturally dynamic people, in spite of the fact that the recent upheaval and a few brilliant leaders have succeeded in temporarily stimulating them into action. They are excitable, but about ideas, not about action.

My young farmer friend with the pompadour, Boris, has taken me very much under his wing. Today we were talking about his hopes and plans for his farm in the Ural Mountains. It appears that he has received instruction in the latest farming methods at the farmers' instruction center in Moscow, and is looking forward with enthusiasm to putting into practice what he has learned, to the benefit of his beloved acres.

'First,' he says, 'I must go to Odessa. It is in Odessa,' he adds solemnly, 'that my mother is now living — my mother.' I was suitably impressed with the privilege accorded Odessa. 'But,' he continued, 'I must first stop for a few weeks in Moscow.' He gazed at me with the now familiar bulge of the eyes which accompanies communist mention of that city. 'Moscow! A city so great — so full of interest! You must see everything in Moscow!'

'I intend to see everything I can,' I said. 'I'm going there for that purpose.'

Boris became very thoughtful. Suddenly he leaned forward.

'Listen —' he said. 'It is I who will show you Moscow!

Why not — you are my friend. I am a farmer and I can get permission for you to stay as a guest at the Farmers' Home — where I stay — where all the farmers from all over Russia live while they learn the new farming. You will stay there with me — with me will you see Moscow — and all that Moscow is to the world — I insist!'

'You are very good,' I said.

'I am your friend,' said Boris. And so it was arranged.

We have passed great rivers — the Amur, the Lena, the Yenisei, the Ob—which are slowly winding ever north-ward across this vast bleakness, on and on into the mighty forests of the North, and, a thousand miles beyond, still on and on, even into the endless whiteness of the Arctic.

Now the towns are getting closer together. No longer are the great plains and forest patches absolutely devoid of civilization. We are approaching Moscow.

Now, as we rumble along with that frenzied acceleration of trains about to arrive at a terminal, we can see crowded suburbs, rows of brick houses, streets, loaded sleighs, trolley cars. The passengers are all on their feet, putting away their loaves of bread, tying up their bundles of blankets and food, in preparation to leave the train. We are all lined up in the passageway — waiting, waiting. Boris says, 'Moskva — bolshoi gorod — big city — three million people ——'

A long platform. A big station. Having arrived, the first thing to do was to get permission to stay in Moscow. It was accomplished after a half-hour's hunting, and a wait in line at the office of an administrative station official. Then, at last, with our baggage, Boris and I boarded a tiny sleigh and swished off through the winding streets.

Long rows of low, warped buildings of old brick drift past on either side, clinging desperately together at the corners. The street-paving is of solid ice sculped into insidious troughs and ribs in the general form of an arch, so that the droshkies are continually sliding sideways down off the road, pulling around the rear end of the exasperated horse, who has to struggle along in the gutter until a tree or lamppost bats the droshky out to the center of the street again, to be caromed off other loaded sleighs.

All of this, of course, makes the riding quite exciting, as you frequently come near being catapulted out of the vehicle — especially when you have a high center of gravity as did I with all my earthly possessions in my lap, plus Boris and his possessions.

At length, with raw hands and red faces, we arrived at a huge wide yellowish building, known as 'Doma Krestyanena' — the Farmers' Home — where we were to stay. We left our baggage there, and after a two-mile walk and a long wait in line in the Soviet Administration Building to get permission to stay in Doma Krestyanena, we returned and entered the old lodging.

The thick double doors of the building are very hard to open. Sometimes you see a man struggle with the knobs for three full minutes before catching just the right twist and jerk that will combine to undo the latch, and yet no one ever thinks of stopping to fix the lock. The doors will likely remain unrepaired until they fall apart of their own accord.

Inside, one confronts a wide staircase, with peasants standing about chatting or sitting on the steps fingering their whiskers and wondering if they will ever feel at ease again after this invasion of tractors and harvesting machines. In a side room — a man with white rubbery lips and gaunt face assigns beds to the inmates, and collects lodging fares. On the other side — a large hall in which farmers sleep by the hundred. Upstairs — more dormitories, some for men, some for women. Down the corridor — common rooms supplied with radio, piano, and magazines, and in which groups of peasants discuss their problems; a restaurant room; library; a museum, full of pictures and models of new farming machines, samples of farm products, and other educational material; a store; and even an auditorium where nightly movies are shown and speeches delivered.

The exquisite cornices and chandeliers of this building are left over from the pre-revolutionary days when it was one of Moscow's most aristocratic restaurants.

It is very interesting to see the farmers having their discussions in the common room. Everyone takes part, the women being fully as active and interested as the men. They are all politicians at heart, really, and are familiar with many details of the processes of government. It is no wonder, when almost every magazine or paper they ever get their hands on is full of the stuff.

They are friendly and pleasant in debate, and always address one another as 'tovarish' — comrade. It is beautiful to hear a discussion carried on in that spirit. They are, at the same time, barbarically unreserved, and apparently cover a great deal of argumentative ground.

When Boris introduces me into one of these gatherings, I am first greeted by a phalanx of stares — some curious, some sympathetic, some suspicious, some resentful. Having viewed my friendly countenance, the comrades ask me a few questions to feel their way into this mysterious American; then, becoming bolder, they cordially launch an abusive harangue against all capitalistic institutions, which they assume I have come here to escape.

Reciting wild statistics about the American press, the government, the church in America, and many other things of which they know nothing, they indulge themselves in a feast of communistic gloatings. They then return to the burning question of tractors.

One of the principles of the Soviet legislative system is that every political problem be talked over in meetings by the people, until public opinion is formed and defined, so that, when a proposed solution of the problem comes up to the Central Congress, as a bill, the ensuing legislative action may conform to and represent the will of the people.

Describing this system, one authority of Russia states that, 'finding a strong minority opposition, the framers of a bill withdraw it and send it "to the country" in factory and village meetings. This discussion will pass no majority votes and call no rolls; it will merely keep on discussing till the matter becomes so clear that a new bill can be drawn which will meet with practically no opposition. This form of law-making is something new in the history of governments, and illustrates the soviet theory of its own government, as not a "parliament" or debating organization, but an "executive committee" carrying out the joint and common will of the toiling masses, which is assumed to be, after education and discussion, reasonably unanimous.'

The communist leaders are very shrewd in adopting this policy, for, as Lenin once said: 'Among the masses of the people, we communists are but drops in the ocean, and we cannot rule unless we give accurate expression to the folk-consciousness. Otherwise the Communist Party will not be able to lead the proletariat, the proletariat will not be able to lead the masses, and the whole machine will fall to pieces.'

It may be added that, to avoid its falling to pieces, the leaders of the above machine take darn good care of the above folk-consciousness. The power of the press here is almost unbelievable. The communist press is teacher and leader, unchallenged, of the people, who read with absolute credulity. They have nothing to read that duplicates the purposeless diversion of our detective story, true story, or romance magazines. Everything they get is flavored with politics. Much of their information comes from two papers called, respectively, the 'Truth,' and the 'News.' The White Russians have, with what justification I know not, a saying that 'there is no news in the "Truth" and no truth in the "News!"'

My Russian, undependable though it be for the higher flights of bunk-house eloquence, is quite sufficient to take me around when, daily, I escape from Boris and his whisker-laden friends, and prowl about in this magnificent city, built of despotism and cruelty — and staging now such an epic incident in man's struggle.

To find your way through these streets is a topographical nightmare. Moscow is laid out like a spider web. The Kremlin is in the middle. Out from it stretch streets in every direction, and hopelessly irregular. Circular streets surround the center of the web in circles getting larger and larger as they are farther from the Kremlin. If you follow one of these streets long enough, you will find yourself back where you started, and if you go off on the haphazard side streets which connect the circles, you will never be heard of again.

But Moscow is a thrilling city to be in — beautiful — tragic. Everywhere are Greek church domes, looking like clusters of inverted turnips, and many exquisitely designed buildings, remnants of the Czar's magnificence, now used as administration halls, meeting-houses, hospitals, barracks, or schools. The church domes stand against the clear blue of the sky with faded gilt, and the remains of pre-war scarlets, yellows, and purples.

Between puffs of the horses' breath I can see the bundled pedestrians trudging along irregular sidewalks, with perhaps a round loaf of black bread or a package of tea under the arm. All are warmly clad, in black or other drab colors, with scarfs around their necks, wool caps, and shawls on the women. Some walk in twos and threes talking seriously together; some trudge alone in an attitude of deep reflection. Some few are gay, but their smiles seem masks to hide the somber souls that wear them.

The Kremlin at night is one of the most beautiful sights on earth. I saw it last night during my evening's exploration. Tremendous walls about one hundred feet high and five hundred years old — great turrets and towers and moats and gateways, and over all flying the Red flag, streaming out to its full length among the whizzing snow-flakes in the icy night wind. And, near by, the huddled spires of great cathedrals ——

It seems strongly inconsistent with the communists' relentless opposition to czarism and religion, that, at the highest point on the capitol of communism, on the tower of the Kremlin, even above the Red flag, still soars the double eagle of the Czar and the cross of the Greek Church. The vast inertia of Holy Russia cannot be ignored, and this blatant inconsistency typifies the patient tolerance of the Soviet leaders in their indomitable program of revolution.

Though many of the churches have been transformed into clubs and schools, these monuments to God still exist, and a few continue their daily services, witness to the communists' aim to reform, as far as they think possible, by education rather than by force.

There is still solace for a few sad old men and women in the dim and empty churches — still, for broken and bewildered age, a beatitude in the ikons above their flickering lamps. But I never hear of any young people going to church — they all want to get rid of 'religion.'

Just as the communist's idea of a capitalist nation is based on his memory of Russia under the Czar, so the communist's conception of religion is based on the Greek Orthodox Church, the only religion with which he has ever come in contact.

He has denounced religion along with capitalism. He has abolished gods of all descriptions. But it must be remembered that he knows but one meaning of these things. He knows only that they were all part of czarism, and that everything connected with czarism is an evil to be ruthlessly exterminated.

It is inconceivable that a thing so vital as religion could be taken from these peasants and nothing put in its place. Something had to take its place — something vital — and, in order to take its place, the new thing had to be a religion itself, in the broader meaning of the word. That religion is Communism.

Though the communists understand by the word 'religion' a superstitious worship of a god who is represented by temple bells, ikons, candles, and old priests in fancy robes — all of which they denounce — they do recognize the larger meaning of religion — a superhuman, guiding, vital force. This force, they call 'naouka,' which means 'science' or 'nature.' They believe that naouka is the great force behind communism, which makes communism not only possible but inevitable.

The Soviet leaders, having learned the folly in being only *de*structive about religion, are turned *con*structive. Science they set up in its stead. Faith in God is being changed to faith in science. They realize also the appeal of beauty, and they set before the people the beautiful ideal that 'no man shall exploit another.' They recognize the power of personality — and they distribute pictures of Lenin, the great scientist, who gave his life to lead the world to a truer scientific development — toward coöperation, harmony, communism. His picture hangs in every communist home, in every public gathering-place, the symbol, the personality from whom the people receive their inspiration of morality.

I know a communist girl here whose grandmother still attends church regularly. The old lady has followed the Greek Orthodox creed all her life and, like the few other aged people who still hold true to their old faith, she can find no solace in atheism. The girl's mother, on the other hand, though she admits there may be something of value in the Church, has long since given up attendance. While the girl herself, an outright atheist, agrees neither with her mother nor with her grandmother, but gallantly defends the theory that science alone can explain the mysteries of life.

This shifting of spiritual allegiance is very common in Russia, and seems but an extreme example of the drift of youth away from the Church all over the world. The young people here are taught that the old idea, that the gold ikon holds all the secrets of creation, is a superstition. They are getting rid of ikons, and as the ikons go, so does the Church.

'Why,' I asked an old lady, 'can't they still use some of the cathedrals which are now schools during weekdays, for Sunday services, as before?'

'Oh, impossible,' she replied. 'They have taken away all the ikons.'

The vital importance of these graven images is part of the evidence of benighted superstition and fathomless ignorance which convicts this Church of unworthiness. No wonder the young communists, beginning to think for themselves, are glad to get rid of it. The churches here are empty, not because young people aren't allowed to go to worship — but because they don't want to.

But, while they have no Church, these young people have a religion. I know, from what I have seen here in Russia, that Communism has as much inspiring force as any religion, and that its essential principles are fully as high. In principle it is remarkably similar to Christianity — as Christianity was in its pristine simplicity. And there is the same gulf between the principles and their application that there is between the teachings of Christ and the enforcement by the Church of its interpretation of those teachings.

Communist missionaries go out, inspired by their ideal and give their whole energy and risk their lives to spread their doctrine. Communists raise money and bring relief to needy workmen and to the oppressed all over the world. Sometimes, in performing what they consider a service to humanity, they are doing great harm: as has often been the case with Christians and others.

When they believe that nine tenths of the people of a great nation like the United States are workmen 'in a condition bordering on starvation' and oppressed by an imperialistic class of capitalists who take all the money for themselves, it is a natural impulse to communists to try to free these masses from the class that is their oppressor.

If harm is done by communist interference based on their false assumptions, the evil of their action is due to misinformation and misinterpretation rather than to any fundamental immorality. In time they are almost certain to see the error in their assumptions, and then the great force of their faith may be turned to a useful end, so that the astounding sacrifices in its behalf may not be made in vain.

Boris is active in his rôle of mentor. It is he who translates for me the endless argufying that goes on here in the common room and at meals, who takes me sight-seeing, who explains the confluent interests and excitements of this vast city. Without him I would miss much of what I now see and hear.

I can't make out why Boris is taking so much trouble about me. He may be actuated by a desire to impress me, as a foreigner, with the glories of communism, or he may be just a friendly soul who likes me and wants to be kind. With the barrier of language between us — I have about fifty words of Russian to every million square miles of its territory, of which there are eight — it isn't easy for me to define his motives.

One thing about him is certain — and that is his well-developed acquisitive faculty. Today, in a letter, I received a dollar bill. The usual crowd of peasants quickly gathered to see this piece of real capitalist money.

'Will you give it to me?' questioned Boris expectantly.

'To you? What good would it be to you?' I ask.

on the envelopes. Stamp collecting seems to be the rage in Russia.

There is likewise great enthusiasm among my comrades in regard to my camera. Boris, particularly, admires it. His acquisitive tendency seems stimulated by its novel appearance. Also he has tried to make me give him my shaving outfit.

It was at the Moscow race-track this afternoon that I saw a man working out a race-horse, a stallion and pure white. He was galloping just as tight as he could go. It was thrilling to see his great muscles bulging, his snowy mane flying, his beautiful head outstretched, sensitive and keen — and to hear those sledgehammering hoofs go thundering into the distance, every ounce of energy in his superb body and spirit bent to that single purpose — speed.

In a large pre-revolutionary building back of the grand-stand, in the trophy-room, full of cups, blue ribbons, photographs, and other horsey souvenirs, I met the high-class Soviet sportsmen. These smooth boys of the race-track were dressed in anything but proletarian attire, and swaggered about like race-track fans in any other country.

There are thirty million horses in this great land, and the competitive element in racing is utilized in the communist eugenic campaign to improve the Russian horse. This track is run in connection with a large breeding farm, but the appearance of these sporty race-track boys does not impress me with their solemn interest in eugenics.

Apply communism, if you like, to every other human interest, but sport will remain — of its very nature — a glittering denial of communist principles. Here is something that is based on individual competition; in which inherited attributes make rigid class distinctions; and in which the strong survives and eliminates the weak without mercy. Communistic sport is a contradiction in terms — and the Moscow race-track shows it up.

Never before have I seen such crowded trolley cars. There are over three thousand of them in the city, but every one is so overloaded that it is almost impossible to get aboard. Perhaps, it occurs to me, they have a trolley system such as this as part of their effort to keep all the people in one class. Everybody must fight to get a ride. The weak ones have to walk, and thus get exercise until they are strong enough to beat those who have been weakened by excessive riding. And so, by a circulation, all are kept at the same average strength, Q.E.D.

There are thousands of soldiers here, just as everywhere else in Russia. They seem to do very little drilling, but a lot

of studying, which is a good thing for them. All young men, unless they have some special exemption, must join the Red Army for two years or so, and thus illiteracy is being done away with. I see them when they aren't at their books, out for skiing practice. Skiing is not a sport here — there are practically no hills in this part of the country — but is just a means of getting over the ground.

Sometimes I go around to see spinning mills and other factories. They are going busily all the time, day and night and Sundays. It is the Soviet method of increasing production and decreasing unemployment. Each man takes one day off in five, but not the same day as his fellow workmen. There are always four fifths of the total number on the job. And I visited a prison the other day, an old one which has been modernized. Most of the 'criminals' were kulaks — prosperous and recalcitrant peasants — and private landowners who had resisted the communist taxation system. They seemed very well cared for — but, judging by the stories of Ratovsky and others, I suspect that all Russian prisons are not as nice.

These communists are not totally unaware of the difficulties they are up against in their campaign to overthrow all capitalistic governments in the world. They have some conception of the immense wealth and strength of these capitalistic powers, but they expect, with time, to attain even greater strength themselves, when they will be in a position to serve the united 'workers of the world' in completing the inevitable world revolution.

Realizing the odds against them, they have adopted the policy in regard to treason, that it is better to convict several innocent men than to risk letting a single traitor go free. The vital cause of the Revolution demands this extreme policy, the communists believe.

Some of the girls in this town are of unsurpassed beauty.

The best, I think, are the Georgians. They have skin as smooth as a plum, and their eyes glow with a deep, rich brown. Their features are perfect.

Personally, I have had no hand-to-hand encounters with them as yet. But according to my farmer friends, they are seldom as good as they look and the warmth and softness of their appearance is not borne out by their behavior. A fellow I talked with in the prison even said that he was glad to be where he was, to get away from them.

At night I return to Doma Krestyanena and sit around on the beds to talk with the farmers about their problems. In such an atmosphere, anyone who is the least bit alive ought not to remain long ignorant as to the affairs of the country. And we always have a teapot, so things are very sociable. One night we even had some Russian applesauce. It has prunes in it, among other things, and is good, but not in the class of United States applesauce.

At last when the men begin to doze off to sleep, the dormitory becomes a horror such as one could not possibly imagine till he had lived under its spell as I have. The snoring is perfectly astounding, not only in volume, but also in quality.

There are one hundred and eighty farmers in our room, sleeping in beds lined up side by side — I have bed number one hundred and seventy-six — and I don't think there is a single man here who fails to join in the mighty chorus. It sounds like ten riveting machines and twenty-five roaring lions accompanied by a trombone quartet and five hundred woodpeckers. There is an unearthly rattling reverberation in the sound which nearly drives me wild, accustomed as I am to public snoring.

Most of the men keep all their possessions under their pillows — that being considered the safest place — and consequently, since one needs a considerable number of possessions in this cold climate, many have their pillows raised so high by what is underneath that their necks are about twisted off. And, of course, having beards and whiskers, said whiskers are very apt, under these circumstances, to get tangled up in their mouths and noses, and add a certain weirdness to the deep trills emitting therefrom. The Russian peasantry have not yet lost any of their tonsils or adenoids, which, being in full bloom, lend a spirited woodwind development to the nightly theme.

The general tone in this institution makes me think that this may be where the expression 'sound sleeping' originated.

Boris is very mysterious about his start for Odessa. He has postponed it several times, and is hanging around in a sort of aimless condition, saying that he must do some errands in Moscow for his mother. He is very solemn about that mother. But he doesn't do any errands, and I can't imagine what he is waiting around for.

Tonight, after supper of tea and a ham sandwich, as Boris and I were waiting in the auditorium for the evening's moving pictures to begin, we met a young girl named Vera, a chubby, buxom, red-cheeked little thing who was very cheerful and bright. She sells magazines in Doma Krestya-nena and she seems to enjoy her job, which, I must say, is soft and also provides much social contact.

'Ha-ha,' she says to me in Russian. 'You must go back to America. That is too bad. You have very hard times in America. You have five million unemployed there, yes?'

'You would be surprised how well off we are in America,' I reply. 'Workmen go to work in automobiles there. We have twenty-five million automobiles in America. They are not a luxury. Every family has one, just as you have horses in Russia.'

'Ah, no, my friend,' says she with a tolerant smile, 'you are mistaken. Your newspapers lie to you in America. They are not free like ours. Here, anyone can write and publish what he pleases. You can see that the papers are full of criticism and suggestions for improvement of Soviet methods. There is freedom of the press in the U.S.S.R. But in America everybody is trying to get money. The editors want money. They will write what pays them the best — they will write lies to advertise for people who pay them much money. They are very prejudiced politically and will give only one side of a question. They are deeply involved in lobbyism, graft, and bribery of every kind.

'Here,' she went on, beaming with enthusiasm, 'the editor gets practically no more pay than the reporters, and the success of the paper or the effect of what he puts into it has no influence whatever on the editor's salary. He writes all the news and everything anybody will say — with, of course, the one exception that he cannot put in capitalistic, imperialistic propaganda, for that is dangerous, and we have all proved to ourselves that communism is right and capitalism wrong.'

February 20. One of the first things I noticed this morning, on waking up in the great room of frowsy, sprawled sons of the soil, was that my camera had disappeared. I had carefully concealed it under the casual heap of my clothes which lay between my bunk and bunk number one hundred and seventy-five, occupied by Boris. He alone knew where I had hidden it. The clothes remained as before, but no camera. Boris had arisen before me and had gone out, ostensibly for breakfast.

Returning soon, he seemed greatly disturbed to learn of my camera's disappearance. He hunted around and tried to console me about my loss. Seeing that I looked at him a little distrustfully, he said, with an offended air, 'You do not suspect *me?*'

'No, Boris,' said I, thinking how loyal he had always been.

But my camera was never found.

At lunch-time Boris informed me of his intention to depart for his home in Odessa. He expressed regret that he had to leave, and gave me a photograph of himself in order that I should better remember him. Thereupon, looking at me hopefully, he again told me how well my dollar bill would fit into his collection.

I could not refuse him this time, and handed it over. He thanked me, we shook hands good-bye, and he left for his train.

In getting a fresh shirt out of my suitcase, which still remained in the checkroom, I noticed a slight disarrangement of its contents. Investigating, I found that my film package had been opened and that all the films I had exposed since Seishin, Korea, were gone.

Though temporarily overwhelmed by this irreplaceable loss of many rare, and perhaps valuable, pictures, which I had taken with great pains, I did what I could to discover the identity of the thief. It was likely that the same person who had stolen my camera had taken the films, as that instrument would be valueless without films, and vice versa.

After considering all available clues, the circumstantial evidence pointed very definitely to Boris as the guilty party. Boris had often expressed a great longing for my camera, which he considered would be of much greater value to him than it was to me, who, he reasoned, could soon replace it in America. He evidently concluded that the camera was but a fair reward for his generous services in ushering me through Soviet officialdom. Through the checks left in his care, he had easy access to my baggage, in which he evidently mistook my exposed films for unused ones. The poor fellow will ruin all his own pictures as well as mine, through double exposure.

I went, last night, to the big theater, and saw a very extraordinary pantomime which depicted the epic of the Red Revolution. Tickets were very expensive, and, after the customary tribulation in getting one, I found my way up to a balcony full of bloused and keen-eyed workmen, peasants, and soldiers. Some were with their girls, some with their workshop buddies — all evidently very thrilled by the performance, which was executed with extraordinary grace and feeling.

All these humble workmen were spending many days' pay and a long evening to witness a thing they love — an expression of emotion in art. They love it — without a trace of affectation, with a spontaneous enthusiasm that is touching. To enjoy it, they have sacrificed material things that they need — but not more than they need this.

Since Boris's departure, my status as a guest in Doma Krestyanena has been less secure. Several times lately they have refused to issue me my ticket for the bunkroom. On these occasions I have slept just as soundly in my usual place without one, as there was no check as to whether I had a ticket or not.

But last night, the Soviet officer in charge tried to kick me out. I don't know what his grounds were, exactly. When the Russian language begins to boil with passion, a good deal of it goes over my head. As far as I could make out, it was because the Gay-Pay-Oo had informed him that signs of bourgeois influence had been detected in my mail, and he had decided that Doma Krestyanena, at fifty kopeks a day, was no place for a capitalist.

'Why don't you stay at the Grand Hotel?' he said.

I remembered that, there being no waste-baskets about, I had merely torn some of my letters across once, and thrown them into a corner. These, apparently, had been salvaged and read, and had provided evidence of capitalistic influence in my past.

Some of my bewhiskered farmer friends came to my rescue. There ensued a hot debate with the official — a strange, gaunt creature, with skin like a white rubber sheet stretched tight over his bones, and drooping, watery eyelids. But he was immovable. It looked bad for me.

I finally got them to call in another, and luckily a higher, official whom I had seen about, and who had authority over the white rubber man. I pressed him with my credentials.

I gave him a lot of discharges, and certificates proving I had worked in various places and ways as a rabochi — workingman — and which proved that I really belong to the proletariat. He surveyed them thoughtfully.

On the chance that he couldn't read English, I handed him a gaudy, pink, San Francisco cafeteria card. He regarded it solemnly. So I gave him everything I possessed — all sorts of Japanese tea advertisements, Filipino baggage checks, various calling cards, some laundry tickets, and a pass to the Hollis Street Theater, Boston. He was tremendously impressed.

He gazed at me with renewed respect — obviously a man so extensively documented was not to be precipitately given the gate. The day was saved — or the night, rather — and I stayed unmolested among the snoring farmers.

It is a terrible job to get out of this country. I am not allowed to stay after April 5, but it appears next to impossible to get the necessary visa before that date. I've been waiting in line for hours every day now, fighting through a dense jungle of red tape — but I haven't yet a visa. I'm therefore in the awkward position of being forbidden to stay in a country which I cannot get permission to leave. I think this standing in line, which has become almost a profession with me, is a vital indication of the psychology, not only of these people, but of communism itself.

The people spend a large part of each day, month after month, in these long lines of dreary waiting, which reduce a man's personal initiative and ambition and energy to the dead level of impersonal routine. No matter how quick a thinker he may be, or how expeditious in his own habits, a man standing in line can accomplish his objective only at the rate and in the manner of all the other men standing with him. The energetic fellow chafing at delay can get up to the window no faster than the lazy dullard leaning against the wall next to him in line.

This, to the mass of these people, is communism. They stand in line to get what they want. By so standing they are assured of getting it — in turn, and in exactly the amount and quality apportioned. By no individual effort or ability can they get it any sooner or in any more desirable form or quantity.

Think of the abusive impatience that would attend an hour of such tedium in an American crowd. If you can analyze the psychology of the long lines of patient Russians that stretch across the days and nights through Soviet Russia, you can understand why Russia is communistic and why America is not.

There is no parallel on earth to Russia today. But no less true is it that Russia, before the Revolution, was just as unique among nations in circumstance, heritage, and psychology as she is now. What has happened to her could only happen to Russia.

Her exploited masses of ignorance lay fallow to any liberating idea that Fate might bring. Enormous, submissive, ignorant, she lay virgin to hope. What she is now is built on what she was. And what she will be, no man can say.

She is both East and West as is no other country. What their marriage will bring forth under communism is unpredictable. Standing in line in Soviet Russia, shuffling along foot by foot and hour by hour, I pondered on the matters of heredity and environment, and thought now and then of the corner of Fifth Avenue and Forty-Second Street, of the survival of the fittest, of the Golden Rule, and of my aching feet.

Here is a list of the lines in which I have stood in Moscow. This compilation includes only lines of over five minutes' wait, and does not take into consideration all the 'Red' tape involved.

1. Line in station to get permission to stay in Moscow — stood twenty minutes.
2. Line in Administration Building to get permission to stay in Farmers' Home — stood one hour, fifteen minutes.
3. Line in Farmers' Home to get bed assignment — stood from ten to thirty minutes each day.
4. Lines to get meals in restaurants — stood five to thirty minutes, twice a day.
5. Line to get ticket into the opera house — stood thirty minutes.
6. Line to get mail in the post-office — stood fifteen minutes.

7. Line to get pails in public bath — stood twenty minutes.
8. Line to get shower in public bath — stood thirty-five minutes.
9. Line to get permission to leave Russia — stood thirty hours, spread over four days.
10. Line to get Polish visa — stood two hours, thirty minutes.
11. Line to get German visa — stood twenty-five minutes.
12. Line to get railroad tickets out of Russia — stood one hour, ten minutes.

Total: fifty hours, forty minutes — a new world's non-refueling standing-in-line record.

I am now on the train heading into Poland. Around me lies snoozing a mixed assortment of Europeans, mostly Germans. In the dim light, curtains and coats swing in unison with the lurching car. Far ahead, the engine squeals as we tear across the switch-points.

With every clack of the wheels I am drawing nearer to the life I know, and farther and farther back into memory is sinking this past year of wandering, with its pageant of lands and seas, its heat and cold, its suns and storms.

I was a poor man when I set out, and I am returning rich in things I can never lose.

Never shall I forget the smell of morning bacon on a Yukon sand-bar. Nothing can ever erase the awe I felt before the disciplined fury of a three-hundred-foot propeller shaft, its hideous power driven true to a thousandth of an inch. Never shall I entirely lose the sense of immemorial peace that lives under the trees of Japanese temple gardens.

These things are wealth, and, with a thousand others like them, will live for always in my memory. But, in something nearer to my heart than memory, will live, for me, my friends of this long journey — they whose warm human flesh and blood was, by a whimsy of their Maker, encased sometimes in yellow skin, or brown, or black, or white.

We have eaten and slept, sweated and shivered, hungered

and angered and laughed — together. And I am bringing home with me, from forty thousand miles of men, the sure knowledge that under their skins — be they yellow, brown, black, or white — they are prisoners, just as I am, of their lives and heritage, of hopes and lusts, of fears and loves and dreams, like mine. They are different — on the skin — but, beneath, there is no alien mystery in any race of man.

Though eyes be slant, they crinkle with fun, and change when they look at children; they cloud with pain, and shift with fear, just as do eyes set straight. The sweat that streams out of a brown skin is salt like mine.

And I know that, in the shared orange held out to my hunger by a dirty yellow hand in a Chinese way-train, is the world's hope.

New York — standing like a roaring dream out of the fog of a cold morning, as we come slowly up the bay.

Beside me, later, in the steerage gangway, stands a bewildered little Hindu, clutching his pasteboard suitcase, and gazing with terror down into the cavernous gloom of the wharf shed, with its bustling officialdom and its piles of waiting freight.

Busy with the deck-lashings of the gangplank is a huge young sailor, whistling through his teeth as he makes it fast and shipshape.

'Hey, there,' I say to him, indicating my petrified Hindu associate, 'do you know of any good boarding house where this guy can get a bed?'

Out of the corner of his eye he takes in the Hindu and is evidently not interested.

'Shure, Sout' Street's full of 'em,' he says, still coiling down the line.

'He's sort of up against it,' I continue. 'He's got to get to Chicago, where his wife is sick. He doesn't speak much English, and I think he's pretty near broke.'

At that he straightens, and regards the Hindu from his six feet of healthy brawn.

'The hell you say!' he observes. 'Well, now, that's a tough break. Why, shure I kin fix him up in me time off — I know just the place ——'

Together we three move down the slanting gangplank. The Hindu fairly shudders as he finds himself upon the dock.

'This man,' I say to him carefully — 'this man will show you place to sleep — place to eat ——'

He glances up fearfully at the giant beside him.

'Shure,' says the big sailor. 'There's a good place just acrost th' street from here, an' I know th' ol' woman w'ot runs it. Here, you — le' me give yer a hand on that bag, an' watch yer step — come on, buddy.'

THE END

DATE DUE

DEMCO 38-297

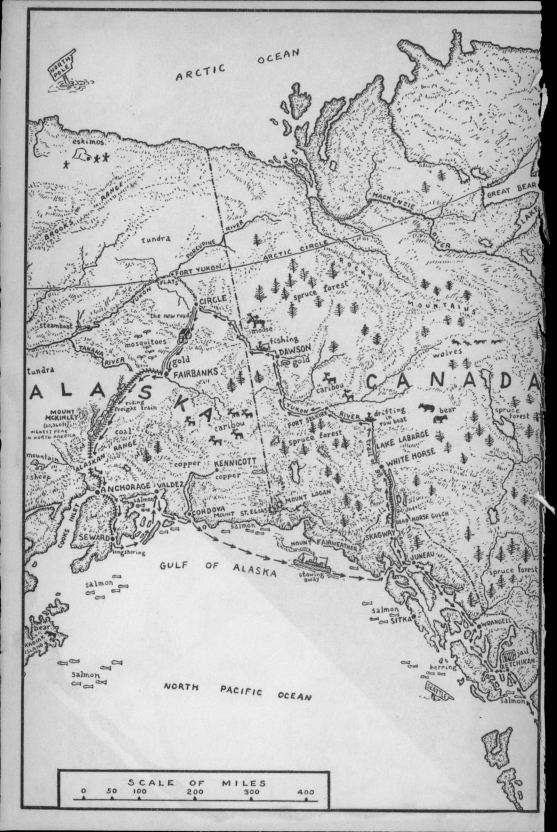